PRAISE FOR *WHAT A UNICORN KNOWS*

"While anyone running a company knows that valuations like the unicorn stage are just a step in a journey, if you want to move faster on the road to building a great business, this book is for you."

—Nick Mehta, CEO, Gainsight and Bestselling Author of *Customer Success*

"*What a Unicorn Knows* gives readers an essential how-to guide on five powerful yet timeless principles that will help young companies mature, and mature companies stay young."

—Reshma Saujani, Founder and CEO, Girls Who Code and Marshall Plan for Moms, New York Times Bestselling Author of *Girls Who Code* and *Pay Up*

"We experienced firsthand the power of putting into practice the principles in *What a Unicorn Knows*. Our sales and post-sales teams literally doubled their performance by taking a lean process approach. If you're looking for effective, proven methodologies to accelerate your growth efficiently, look no further."

—Ashvin Vaidyanathan, Chief Customer Officer, LinkedIn and Bestselling Author of *The Customer Success Professional's Handbook*

"The journey of scaling up a high-growth technology company is enormously difficult. This book delivers a solid model for easing the load, speeding the trip, and lighting the way for leaders looking to join the unicorn club."

—Sue Barsamian, Board of Directors, Box, NortonLifeLock, Xactly, Gainsight, Five9

"*What a Unicorn Knows* wowed me with the S.C.A.L.E. framework, and the oh-so-useful, punchy, and entertaining guidance that fills every page of this gem. Whether you are the founder of a young startup or a leader in a big company, Matt and Pablo's lessons on strategic speed, experimentation, esprit de corps, and much more will surprise you, spark your imagination, and help you grow your company."

—Robert I. Sutton, Organizational Psychologist, Stanford Professor, and New York Times Bestselling Author of seven books, including *Good Boss, Bad Boss* and (with Huggy Rao) *Scaling Up Excellence*

"If you're looking for an essential operator's guide to achieving efficient growth, this book should be your go-to source. Leaders will learn how to scale companies and achieve their growth potential. It's a lofty goal that this guide delivers."

—Hilary Gosher, Managing Director, Insight Partners

"I can't imagine a business leader who won't benefit from *What a Unicorn Knows.* It's a rare book that adeptly blends conceptual grounding with ample step-by-step advice for practical application. This is a book that could only have been written by highly experienced practitioners who are themselves highly read. And it is a book that will benefit both new founders and seasoned veterans."

—John Shook, former CEO, The Lean Enterprise Institute and
Author of *Learning to See* and *Managing to Learn*

"Finally, an actionable framework based on proven methodologies, *What A Unicorn Knows* is a must-read, filled with lean principles, fresh insights, and essential templates to efficiently scale companies of all sizes. May and Dominguez will unleash the velocity of growth in your company."

—Wayne McCulloch, Chief Customer Officer, WalkMe and
Bestselling Author of *The 7 Pillars of Customer Success*

"Like the magic healing properties of the unicorn's horn, this book is the timely medicine to heal your business' ailing growth ambitions. Taking lessons from entrepreneurs who have achieved unusual customer-savvy momentum using lean principles, the authors have crafted the S.C.A.L.E. framework as the reliable antidote to 'big-company syndrome' and many other corporate indispositions."

—John Maeda, Chief Technology Officer, Everbridge and Author
of *How to Speak Machine* and *The Laws of Simplicity*

"In *What a Unicorn Knows,* Matt and Pablo show us how to grow up without slowing down. Whether you are leading a startup or an emerging line of business at a large enterprise, this book will show you how to approach your first growth inflection point and keep the upward momentum going."

—Philip Potloff, GM, AWS Marketplace, Amazon Web Services

"*In What a Unicorn Knows,* Matthew May and Pablo Dominguez provide a brilliant summary of the principles that bind together all successful growth ventures. Combining storytelling with easy-to-follow, practical guidance, this book should be required reading for anybody who leads, works in, or advises early-stage businesses."

—**Matthew Dixon, Coauthor of** *The Challenger Sale* **and** *The JOLT Effect*

"The S.C.A.L.E. framework that May and Dominguez have developed is applicable for both early-stage companies that are beginning their journey to scale and more mature companies that are yearning to maintain their innovative roots."

—**Deven Parekh, Managing Director, Insight Partners**

"*What a Unicorn Knows* is a fascinating and thought-provoking read. Irrespective of your current level of success, any enterprise, leader, or individual who is tired of optimizing the status quo will definitely feel a renewed sense of purpose to take a hard look at their organization. May and Dominguez offer a comprehensive yet remarkably simple playbook on how to scale and sustain a culture of innovation, strategy, and execution."

—**Ken Krivanec, Division President, Tri Pointe Homes**

"By applying the principles in *What a Unicorn Knows*, we improved our sales process efficiency and effectiveness by nearly 30 percent. No matter where you are in your growth journey, the S.C.A.L.E. model the authors put forth will help you optimize your operation."

—**Hendrik Isebaert, CEO, Showpad**

"This insightful read will help you unlock scale through the magic of subtraction. The S.C.A.L.E. framework contained in this book will give you an actionable way to avoid the pitfalls, find the leverage points, and complete your journey from startup to unicorn. This compelling framework will give you a foundation to build the type of culture that moves quickly, avoids waste, and, most importantly, operates from a customer value perspective."

—**Tim Sanders, VP Client Strategy, Upwork and New York Times Bestselling Author of** *Love Is the Killer App* **and** *Dealstorming*

"*What a Unicorn Knows* delivers an intuitive, powerful playbook for scaling up new business ventures in today's disruptive world. The book's five lean ScaleUp principles combine proven approaches that will take any new business to the next level."

—**Soren Kaplan, Cofounder, Praxie and Author of** *Experiential Intelligence*

"A unique and powerful framework to apply lean principles to accelerate value and effectively transition from startup to ScaleUp."
    —Kevin Meyer, Cofounder, Gemba Academy and Author of *The Simple Leader*

"We all face a common challenge: how to stand out, stay relevant, and sustain growth in a world of massive disruption and distraction. The five principles in *What a Unicorn Knows* provide leaders at every level a means to find the focus they need to tackle that challenge."
    —Nir Eyal, Author of *Hooked* and *Indistractable*

"A must-read book for explosive, yet sustainable growth. May and Dominguez have distilled the best practices from countless organizations that scaled up and stayed up . . . and they reveal how you can do the same."
    —David Burkus, Author of *Leading From Anywhere*

"The authors bring an unparalleled understanding of 'lean' and reveal a heretofore unexplored dimension: its ability to drive growth. This book brings fresh insight and discipline to strategic leadership."
    —Michael Bungay Stanier, Author of *The Coaching Habit*

"Fascinating insights for anyone interested in innovating at scale."
    —Tomas Chamorro-Premuzic, Chief Innovation Officer, Manpower Group
    and Professor of Business Psychology at Columbia University and UCL

"Think of *What a Unicorn Knows* as your guide to achieving the extraordinary. Skillfully weaving together stories and practical applications, the authors show you how to apply operating principles central to 'unicornship and beyond.' And for me, what's at the heart of this type of growth is the profound role of people and culture. Grab a highlighter. You'll need it."
    —Shawn Murphy, Author of *The Optimistic Workplace* and *Work Tribes*

WHAT A
UNICORN
KNOWS

ALSO BY MATTHEW E. MAY

Winning the Brain Game:
Fixing the 7 Fatal Flaws of Thinking

The Laws of Subtraction:
6 Simple Rules for Winning in the Age of Excess Everything

The Shibumi Strategy:
A Powerful Way to Create Meaningful Change

In Pursuit of Elegance:
Why the Best Ideas Have Something Missing

The Elegant Solution:
Toyota's Formula for Mastering Innovation

WHAT A UNICORN KNOWS

How Leading Entrepreneurs Use Lean Principles to Drive Sustainable Growth

MATTHEW E. MAY
PABLO DOMINGUEZ

Matt Holt Books
An Imprint of BenBella Books, Inc.
Dallas, TX

Matt Holt is an imprint of BenBella Books, Inc.
10440 N. Central Expressway
Suite 800
Dallas, TX 75231
benbellabooks.com
Send feedback to feedback@benbellabooks.com

BenBella and *Matt Holt* are federally registered trademarks.

Printed in the United States of America
10 9 8 7 6 5 4 3 2 1

Library of Congress Control Number: 2022033460
ISBN (hardcover) 9781637742815
ISBN (electronic) 9781637742822

Copyediting by Rebecca Taff
Proofreading by W. Brock Foreman and Christine Florie
Indexing by WordCo Indexing Services, Inc.
Text design and composition by Aaron Edmiston
Cover design by Brigid Pearson
Cover image © Shutterstock / Svetlana Ivanova (unicorn); gd_project (dollar); Filippo Carlot (euro); Vladirina32 (shekel); helloRuby (renminbi)
Printed by Lake Book Manufacturing

Special discounts for bulk sales are available.
Please contact bulkorders@benbellabooks.com.

Matt
To my family, friends, colleagues, and clients.

Pablo
To my family for all their support and patience:
Maritza, Nicolas, Lukas, Austin, and Marty.
Hook 'em.

CONTENTS

FOREWORD

The first time I met Matt May in person, I walked into a workshop where he was having all of my top executives play with toy cars. Immediately, I knew I'd love this guy!

Pablo Dominguez and I had been friends and partners for years, most recently with Insight Partners as an investor in my company, Gainsight. I knew there was no one savvier about scaling go-to-market functions than Pablo. So when he introduced me to Matt, I was excited to dig in. A couple days of offsite work learning how lean continuous process optimization works—plus several bungled toy car manufacturing facilities later—we walked away with four solid experiments that began our transformation.

At Gainsight, we have seen the S.C.A.L.E. framework that Pablo and Matt created up close. Indeed, that framework has helped us reaccelerate our company growth over the last three years.

Strategic Speed was the only way we could work, so our culture fit well with the framework. Constant Experimentation allowed us to get out of meeting analysis paralysis and start trying some things. Accelerated Value tied so closely to the DNA of our company, which is all about Customer Success. Lean Process was new to us, but fit perfectly with our goal of helping our clients accelerate Time-to-Value, which is a critical measure for every software-as-a-service company. And Esprit de Corps was music to our ears, since we are a very values-driven company.

A year after that first toy car workshop, we had increased our sales growth rate while reducing Time-to-Value for our clients by 66 percent. While anyone running a company knows that valuations like the "unicorn stage" are just a step in a journey, if you want to move faster on the road to building a great business, this book is for you.

Nick Mehta
CEO
Gainsight

INTRODUCTION

Now I will believe that there are unicorns.
—William Shakespeare

D uring a senior leadership team meeting at the Palo Alto headquarters of venture-backed subscription software company Gainsight in late autumn of 2019, CEO Nick Mehta and then-chief customer officer Ashvin Vaidyanathan set two strategic goals for the coming year.

First, they wanted to cut in half the business-to-business sales cycle—from initial customer quote to contract close—from eighty days to just forty. Second, they wanted to reduce the time it took for a newly signed customer to be onboarded and achieve a desired business outcome—a critical measure called "time-to-value" in the software-as-a-service (SaaS) world—with the Gainsight product going from thirteen weeks to just five.

The big question was, of course, *how?* Internal capabilities and operating methods were simply not up to the task, at least not yet. Truth be told, the company was growing at such a furious pace that operational controls and disciplines had struggled to keep up. But some key customers weren't so happy, and for a company that was in the business of customer success, that wasn't ideal. The irony of the situation wasn't lost on senior leaders.

Launched ten years earlier to help enterprise software companies better manage their customer relationships, Gainsight was well known for its customer success platform. Both Mehta and Vaidyanathan had authored popular books on how to leverage customer intelligence and build internal capability to improve client retention, reduce account churn, and identify new and more profitable revenue growth opportunities. Gainsight was approaching the $100 million mark in annual recurring revenue and was poised to take growth to the next level.

Mehta and Vaidyanathan sought the outside counsel of equity investor Insight Partners —where we sit as operating specialists in the Sales & Customer Success Center of Excellence within the Insight Onsite advisory unit—on possible ways to approach their objectives. We suggested a process optimization methodology based on Toyota Production System's "lean" principles. We were confident that our approach would work because we had developed a solid track record of accomplishing daunting goals (like those of Gainsight) in a manner faster, better, smarter, and cheaper than more traditional approaches to performance improvement with software technology companies.

After a few short logistical meetings, we arrived at a challenging statement of work:

1. Select two dozen professionals from across the Gainsight organization with integral frontline experience with the sales and customer onboarding processes. Train them on a powerful methodology for operational improvement, and also point that methodology toward dramatically shrinking the sales cycle and time-to-value.
2. Emerge with a portfolio of well-thought-through concepts, complete with experimental plans for proving them quickly without disrupting ongoing operations, and do so without any additional capital expense or new personnel.
3. Do all of that in less than two days.

Given that one of Gainsight's stated core values is *shoshin* (roughly translated from Japanese as "beginner's mind"), the Gainsight team was game for trying a new approach.

Following a half-day immersive training exercise devoted to an experiential simulation enabling both the leaders and the selected teams to create some esprit de corps and gain an intrinsic understanding of a lean system in action—namely the vaunted Toyota Production System—the real work began. We formed four teams: two focused on the sales process, two on the post-sale process. Over the course of six intense hours the following day, we guided the teams through our lean framework, arriving at unique experiments the teams believed would yield proof of concept for their proposed solutions. Each team pitched their concept in a short, Shark Tank–like presentation to a board of senior Gainsight leaders, including Mehta and Vaidyanathan.

The sales process optimization countermeasures focused on improving mechanisms to better understand and align with customers on their desired business outcomes much earlier in the sales motion. This would eventually lead to more standardized offerings and reduced waste associated with unnecessary customization. Post-sale improvements included templated configuration wizards and phased implementations (involving a series of "soft" launches and go-live rollouts, versus one "big bang"), resulting in earlier value delivery.

Because the proposed solutions were universally perceived as having real impact, and since we had delivered on the statement of work, the senior leadership board granted approval to proceed with the experiments.

Fast and frugal proof of concept tests were successfully carried out during the first quarter of 2020, with both targets being exceeded, followed by a companywide rollout that set new sales cycle and onboarding records.

In November 2020, just shy of one year from the initial gathering of Gainsight teams to learn and implement our lean-based methodology, Gainsight was acquired for a reported $1.1 billion, and so became a card-carrying member of the business club known as "unicorns."

RISE OF THE UNICORN CLASS

On the morning of Saturday November 2, 2013, Cowboy Ventures founder Aileen Lee posted an article on Techcrunch.com entitled "Welcome to the Unicorn Club: Learning from Billion-Dollar Startups." Most people recognize a unicorn as the magical horned horse popularized in European folklore, fabled to be rare but real, and never seen. But Lee coined a new meaning of the word *unicorn*, and that meaning stuck.

"Many entrepreneurs, and the venture investors who back them, seek to build billion-dollar companies," she wrote. "So, we wondered . . . how likely is it for a startup to achieve a billion-dollar valuation?" She defined unicorns as "U.S.–based software companies started since 2003 and valued at over $1 billion by public or private market investors."

At the time, unicorns by this definition were indeed as rare and magical as their mythical namesake: less than forty in existence, yielding an average of only four per year and representing less than 1 percent of startups.

Much has changed in the decade since Aileen Lee's article. We have become a subscription-based, technology-as-a-service economy, with dozens more unicorns born each year. In a COVID-influenced technology startup feeding frenzy among leading investors, 2021 saw nearly six hundred new unicorns crowned, bringing the atmospheric total to well over one thousand by year-end. The side effects of global geopolitical conflict emerged early in 2022, eventually contributing to a more modest birthrate for new unicorns. Still, it's safe to say that unicorns are no longer as rare and mythical as they were in 2003. In fact, it may not be too long before we will be talking about the Unicorn 500 in the same breath as the Fortune 500.

Rapidly growing startups that have found what is commonly referred to as "product/market fit" and a viable business model now find themselves facing an inflection point that signals an even more daunting stage of maturity: that of "ScaleUp."

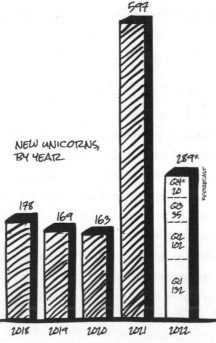

Source: Crunchbase Unicorn Board

A ScaleUp is a more mature yet still adolescent company generally characterized by rapid annual growth of over 20 percent for at least three years.[1] ScaleUps, and those that invest in them, face the next-level challenge of growing revenue at scale; that is, exponentially relative to expenditures in capital, people, and technology. Where startups search for product/market fit and consistency in customer retention, ScaleUps search for *scalable* product/market fit, or go-to-market fit.

Many business leaders believe ScaleUp to be the most difficult phase of a company's lifecycle, requiring the most help, support, and guidance on the development of specific disciplines to ensure that the business does not crumble under its own weight. And it is precisely this stage in which many ScaleUps giddy from growth get ahead of themselves, stumble, and fail.

Jeff Horing, cofounder and managing director of private equity and venture capital firm Insight Partners, believes that the task of scaling up a rapidly growing technology company is so difficult and complex that it may require two CEOs.[2]

According to a recent report published by Wakefield Research, "Startups need to graduate to ScaleUp. To enter this phase, companies must demonstrate that they are robust, with the ability to survive unique challenges not faced by startups or mature legacy companies. Specialized resources and education are needed to address these impediments and ensure that ScaleUps are empowered throughout their journey."[3]

Sharing some of those specialized resources and education are the focus of this book. Our aim is to help answer the central question: *Why do some young companies become unicorns, while others don't?*

The Wakefield Research quote above gives a hint. It's not the technology; it's the impediments, the obstacles, and the forces of resistance all working against them as they attempt to scale, grow, and build a sustainable, competitive position.

This book is meant to help you minimize those opposing forces by drawing on a framework of battle-tested, lean-based, tool-supported operating principles. Employing these principles and practices will help startups become ScaleUps, ScaleUps become unicorns, unicorns become grownups ($1 billion+ in revenue, 1,000+ employees), and grownups recapture the spirit and growth curve of a unicorn.

THE PHYSICS OF
SUSTAINABLE GROWTH

If a picture is worth a thousand words, then a metaphor is worth a thousand pictures. We like to think of a company in the throes of scaling up as a vehicle for rapid yet sustainable growth whose movement is like that of a Formula 1 race car. Both have amazingly advanced technology. Both need speed, acceleration, aerodynamic efficiency, and maneuverability to succeed. Competition aside, both face opposing physical forces that must be overcome to win. These naturally occurring forces have business corollaries that can determine whether or not a company realizes its long-term potential.

Four primary forces work against any object in motion, including a rapidly growing company: *drag, inertia, friction*, and *waste*.

DRAG

Drag is the resistance of air against a moving object. Drag in the business context often manifests itself at the strategic level and can be experienced by such adverse indicators as sluggish market moves, inability to change direction with agility, and companywide misalignment of strategies and objectives.

Companies vulnerable to drag lack clarity on exactly where and how to dominate specific spaces and segments to grow beyond their initial product/market success. And even in companies that do not lack this clarity, there is a general lack of alignment down and across all operations and functions. Many don't have a sound method to synchronize strategies, initiatives, and objectives, which in turn makes it nearly impossible for supporting levels of the company to know precisely what matters most or where to focus. In these conditions, everything slows down, not the least of which is decision-making.

INERTIA

Inertia is the resistance to any change in the current state of motion. The now common metaphor of a flywheel is often used to illustrate the power of inertia in business. Inertia gets the blame for waning product performance and competitiveness, feature fatigue, and poor innovation pipeline throughput. But it is also inertia that can keep the flywheel of growth spinning.

Inertial slowing sets in when headcount grows, approval layers increase, and functional silos crop up. Without an effective system for consistently guiding new ideas from inception to launch, it's difficult to have a winning product development pipeline. As growth ramps up, it becomes increasingly difficult to keep or rekindle the entrepreneurial ethos of rapid-cycle experimentation that was undoubtedly what allowed the company to find their product/market fit in the first place.

FRICTION

Friction occurs when moving parts rub against each other. It's a common cause of slow adoption speed, poor customer experience, retention/renewal difficulty (aka "churn"), and undelivered customer outcomes. Of course, not all friction is bad. Without the friction between the tires and the tarmac, a Formula 1 race car would be uncontrollable. The goal in business is to discover an optimal level of friction that produces a distinctive customer experience at a profit.

The function of "customer success," a post-sale concept attributed to SaaS pioneer Salesforce and introduced to tech companies over a decade ago, was developed to help reduce friction between a software company's products and the customer experience. If customers cannot pull value from your products quickly and effortlessly, friction will remain a difficult challenge. For friction to be minimized, you must understand the jobs your customers are trying to do and align the delivery of your products and services to their desired outcomes, supported by a clear roadmap to continually improve the customer/user experience.

WASTE

Waste is performing work that not only adds no value, but detracts from it. It is perhaps the most prevalent impediment to value, not because the work being performed is inefficient, but rather because it is *ineffective*, defined as doing the wrong work. As Peter Drucker once rightly noted, "There is surely nothing quite so useless as doing with great efficiency what should not be done at all."[4]

ScaleUps seem especially vulnerable to waste, often exhibiting all the usual symptoms, including: key customer value-adding activities that are not linked to optimize quality, cost, speed, and experience; critical information that fails to move effectively between functions and process users; key process performance indicators that are opaque and out-of-date; lack of a companywide continuous process improvement capability; and senior leaders who are not actively involved in identifying, championing, and participating in process optimization.

The effects of these forces are anything but metaphorical. Those who have ever struggled to understand their company strategy, been frustrated by their inability to implement new ideas, scratched their heads wondering why things are done the way they are, or had a bad experience as a customer, has felt the impact of these forces. They are real. They are the archenemies of efficient scale and sustainable growth. But they are manageable.

Our work together centers on helping companies eliminate these kinds of organizational impediments. Matt is fortunate to have spent nearly a decade inside the Toyota organization, learning to master continuous process improvement and the Toyota Production System, known for its ability to achieve the maximum effect through minimum means, the underpinnings of which have become synonymous with "lean" thinking. Pablo has helped dozens of companies, including many well-known unicorns, build their revenue-generating machinery. Our partnership began over ten years ago, and in nearly all the time since, we have focused on what some may consider a rather unconventional application of lean-based principles to the technology space; most recently, to the go-to-market operations of subscription software ScaleUps. That work has produced new insights and opened new pathways to performance that have universal relevance.

FIVE LEAN SCALEUP PRINCIPLES

John Krafcik, the recently retired CEO of Google's Waymo division, first coined the term "lean" in a 1988 *MIT Sloan Management Review* article culminating from his work as a researcher on an MIT-led global manufacturing study team. Krafcik had been the first manufacturing engineer hired at the joint Toyota-General Motors assembly plant in Fremont, California, called New United Motor Manufacturing INC (NUMMI). "Lean" was his term to express what he believed to be the essence of the game-changing Toyota Production System: a lack of waste in the system.

The term came into management vogue with the 1996 bestseller *Lean Thinking* by James Womack and Daniel Jones, who led the MIT study during the previous decade. Lean has moved beyond the production environment to become an organizing principle that engages people in adding the highest possible value for customers across all operations. What makes lean compelling and different as a management philosophy, however, is *how* that value is created: the process is essentially one of addition by subtraction, reducing or removing anything that unnecessarily impedes the free flow of customer-defined value. Amazon founder Jeff Bezos, a student and fan of the Toyota Production System, called it "working backwards," and the concept is now one of Amazon's leadership principles.

While lean methods are the benchmark in manufacturing settings and have been applied with a modicum of success to entrepreneurial startups, broad application of lean methods specifically to software ScaleUps remains limited. Our aspiration is to change that reality, because we have discovered that applying a broader interpretation of lean—one of *balanced optimization*—can be a powerful way to battle the momentum-stealing effects of drag, inertia, friction, and waste.

By keeping a goal of balanced optimization front and center in our efforts to help tech firms scale for growth, we began to see certain themes repeat. Those patterns evolved into a set of five guiding principles that, when adopted, made ScaleUp success much more likely. These principles form a framework for using lean-based operating principles that enable any company to effectively accelerate its scaling and growth. The model sits at the heart of our Lean ScaleUp program at Insight Partners. We've been trained as visual thinkers, so we like drawing models. The original sketch for what we affectionately refer to as The Unicorn Model appears on page 10.

And because five of anything is hard to remember, even if you do repeat it seven times, S.C.A.L.E. offers a quick mnemonic:

Strategic Speed
Constant Experimentation
Accelerated Value
Lean Process
Esprit de Corps

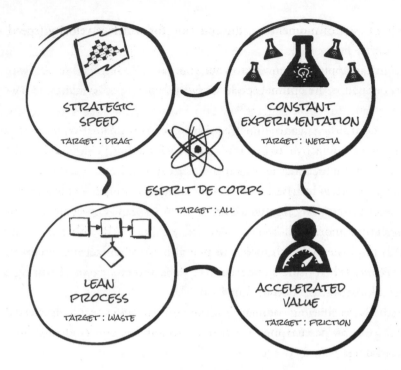

A cursory glance at each of the individual principles in the S.C.A.L.E. framework might lead you to ask whether there is anything new here. That's a fair question. After all, there are no scholarly constructions, no sophisticated terminology.

What is unique is the lean interpretation of the principle: well-worn terms like "strategy" and "value" and "experimentation" take on new meanings when viewed through the lens of lean. The synergy created from integrating any one of the individual principles with the other four and using the collective model to scale efficiently and achieve sustainable growth by leveraging a lean mindset is unique.

We have organized this book around the S.C.A.L.E. framework.

PRINCIPLE 1: STRATEGIC SPEED

Fighter pilots, professional cyclists, and race car drivers know what geese flying in a V formation know: you can travel faster and farther with half the effort by "drafting" in the slipstreams created by those in front of you. The faster you go, the more energy you save. It's a virtuous cycle. And the more people in alignment, the bigger the slipstream, so you can go even faster. This is the simple physics of momentum, the equation for which is velocity (speed with direction) × mass.

You can apply the concept to your company's strategies. We call it *strategic speed*, defined as the optimal speed for swift strategy deployment and decision-making.

To create the organizational equivalent of slipstreams requires strategies, priorities, and objectives to be simultaneously linked vertically and horizontally. While every ScaleUp has an enterprise strategy and initial product/market fit, the unicorns seem to have discovered the power of companywide alignment.

Mechanisms like Japan's *hoshin kanri* ("strategy deployment") and the younger but more well-known Western cousin, OKRs (objectives and key results) implemented with tools and practices like the lean alignment practice of *catchball*—the business equivalent of the children's game of tossing a ball back and forth—help boost strategic speed.

ScaleUps achieving company-wide alignment can expect to accelerate their growth over 30 percent more than those feeling the effects of misalignment-induced drag.

PRINCIPLE 2: CONSTANT EXPERIMENTATION

Continuous innovation is a survival need and competitive must. Without innovation, inertia will govern speed. But innovation cannot be relegated to departments, or reserved for the next-level killer app that may never materialize. It is tempting to put the responsibility on others, but instead one must make simple, fast, frugal, and scalable experimentation an operating norm. As Netflix's cofounder and first CEO Marc Randolph wrote in his 2019 book, *That Will Never Work*, "The key to being successful is not how good your ideas are, it's how good you are at being able to find quick, cheap, and easy ways to try your ideas."

One of the big misperceptions about lean is that it's all about quality and cost. Those who have spent time embedded in the Toyota culture will delight in correcting you, letting you in on the fact that the Toyota Production System was developed as a way to shorten the time from order to delivery and create a "dash to cash" without requiring the deep resources of the big U.S. automotive companies. The entire system evolved through a series of desperate experiments to scale up and grow revenue faster with less. Today, Toyota runs over one million experiments a year at all levels of the company. Some scholars maintain that continuous learning through rapid experimentation is the company's sole source of competitive advantage. Toyota was named the Number 1 Most Admired Auto Company by *Fortune* in 2020 for the sixth consecutive year and held the highest market share globally at 8.5 percent that same year.

For high-velocity ScaleUps, creating a steady stream of innovative new product and process concepts that consistently make it to market requires an equally fast, lightweight, high-impact method for constant experimentation, one that is unfortunately missing in most cases.

PRINCIPLE 3: ACCELERATED VALUE

According to Matt Garman, senior vice president of Amazon Web Services, the single biggest obstacle to growth is a failure to understand and align with customers on their desired business outcomes. If left uncorrected, this failure can generate enough downstream friction to produce what every recurring revenue business dreads: customer attrition, a.k.a. *churn*.

The tendency is to equate the concept of a customer or buyer journey with a sales funnel or consumption model coupled with a monolithic view of the customer, which is wrong. In other words, thinking "customer equals account" can lead to head-scratching when seemingly satisfied customers churn.

At the root of the issue is the difficulty of thinking and operating horizontally in a vertical world. Customers are organized vertically, as are most company support functions, but the customer experience is horizontal. Rather than think like an NFL coach sending plays in from the sideline to the quarterback, who then gives the command to execute (vertical), think like a Formula 1 pit crew, a team of over twenty with specific roles so tightly synchronized that they can mobilize on demand, stabilize the car, change the tires, make adjustments to the aerodynamics, and safely release the car to get back in the race in under two seconds.

Enabling customers to realize value quickly promotes product adoption and positively impacts community spread and customer retention, renewal, and expansion. Ensuring that everyone in your company is aware of how to enable that value quickly, in a unified fashion, helps to accelerate your growth. According to a benchmarking study of over 1,350 companies in eighty countries by Qualtrics, over 80 percent cited customer experience as a competitive advantage, with benefits including increased customer loyalty and uplift in revenue.[5]

PRINCIPLE 4: LEAN PROCESS

Lean as a concept encourages simplicity as the path to speed. It holds that less is best, to make more room for what truly matters, and to eliminate what doesn't. It's a subtractive approach to continuously improving and simplifying even the most complicated workflows. It starts with clearly defined value, then systematically removing everything blocking the path to delivering it. It's a relentless endeavor, a different way of thinking, and it requires a mind shift. As *The Little Prince* author Antoine de Saint-Exupery once noted, "Perfection is achieved not when there is nothing more to add, but when there is nothing left to take away." When juxtaposed with the endless nature of continuous improvement, this means that perfection is not a goal, but a vector.

Companies in the ScaleUp stage are often fraught with waste simply because growth has outpaced development of standardized operational processes needed to sustain the business. Our work with dozens of ScaleUps reveals that waste most often takes the form of performing work that no one, especially a customer, is asking for or needs.

Targeting waste involves using a methodology over eighty years old developed by the U.S. War Department in 1940, who coined the term *continuous improvement*. The aim was to convert the American manufacturing base to the war effort. Nearly two million personnel were trained during the five-year period 1940–1945. It was then utilized to stabilize war-torn Japan under the leadership of General Douglas MacArthur during the seven-year U.S. occupation. Japan, having scarce resources other than human creative capital, termed it *kaizen*, meaning "change for better."

With fast-moving tech ScaleUps, an adapted method of traditional continuous improvement we call a *lean kaizen sprint* works best. Our lean kaizen sprints, conducted both in person as well as remotely, produce an average improvement in quality, cost, speed, and customer experience of roughly 25 percent.

PRINCIPLE 5: ESPRIT DE CORPS

You can't build a Formula 1 car by yourself, nor a company, especially not a unicorn. It takes an experienced team and leaders to create the kind of environment that enables the first four operating principles to come to life.

Enter the notion of esprit de corps. French for "team spirit" and the last of Henri Fayol's fourteen principles of management, esprit de corps figures centrally in military and paramilitary organizations, which are notorious for being results-oriented when it comes to leadership. "Mission first, people always" is the mantra. But a peek at how military organizations actually build leadership skills reveals that establishing a culture of esprit de corps is by taking a "people first, mission always" approach.

Research by UCLA social psychologist Matthew Lieberman supports this view. In a study examining social skills and leadership behaviors, those viewed as having a predominant results focus have only a one in seven chance of being viewed as great leaders, while those viewed as having a predominant social or empathic focus have about the same or slightly less chance. But for those strong in *both* results and social skills, the likelihood of being seen as a great leader is five times greater.[6]

This is consistent with what NASA's Jet Propulsion Lab leader Brian Muirhead refers to as a "grease and glue" model of leadership. Muirhead's team built and landed the *Pathfinder* rover on Mars more quickly and for less than it cost Hollywood to produce the blockbuster movie *Titanic*. Grease and glue leaders understand that establishing a people/culture fit is every bit as important as a product/market fit when it comes to scaling for growth. Your star product requires a team of star players to advance it to market and capture maximum value . . . so much so that Netflix is happy to advertise to all jobseekers that they will pay an ill-fitting employee an industry-leading severance of four months' pay while they search for a star replacement.[7]

Like any set of traits purporting to describe the differentiating attributes of star players—athletes, artists, unicorns—one does not need all of them in equal measure, nor can having all of them guarantee ultimate success. But we believe that having some degree of each trait, tailored to your specific situation, can certainly help your odds. Just how to find the right mix is what a unicorn knows.

Our great hope is that *What a Unicorn Knows* delivers a useful and applicable blend of insight, inspiration, and implementation that enables you to chart your company's path to unicornship and beyond.

Principle 1

STRATEGIC SPEED

Speed is the ultimate weapon in business. All else being equal,
the fastest company in any market will win.
—Dave Girouard, Founder & CEO, Upstart

In the final four laps of the fifty-five-lap 2021 Formula 1 Russian Grand Prix, the McLaren team's twenty-one-year-old Lando Norris could taste his very first victory. He had secured the pole position in qualifying the day before against the best of the best, including the greatest of all time, Lewis Hamilton of Mercedes. Race day looked like a repeat performance. Hamilton was mere seconds behind Norris, but conditions were changing rapidly. Clouds that had been threatening rain all day moved in from the Black Sea and a light drizzle began to fall on parts of the track. Wasting no time, Mercedes' race director immediately ordered Hamilton to "box," meaning take a pit stop for intermediate rain tires. The choice was a calculated risk: if the rain stopped, Norris was a lock to win. If it continued, any drivers running dry tires became vulnerable, a danger to themselves.

With uncertainty looming large, the McLaren race strategy was under pressure. The choices they had to make, while no different from the choices involved in any other race strategy, now became overwhelming with a win on the line: *Can we hold the lead with the tires we have? Do we risk our lead by taking a thirty-second pit stop with so few laps to go? We have two rain tire compounds: Which is best? Will rain tires drag too much on the dry parts of the track?*

Norris and McLaren waited. The rain continued, Lando's car looked like Bambi on ice, and Lewis Hamilton won his history-making 100th Grand Prix. Norris finished a distant seventh.

When it comes to strategy, it turns out that speed matters.

SPEED MATTERS

A company looking to efficiently scale for sustainable growth must treat speed as the dominant priority: speed to market, speed *in* market, speed to value, and, if backed by private investment, speed to exit. ScaleUps are unique from younger startups and more mature grownups in this regard.

Newer startups are generally fast by nature because they have little to bog them down: investors, employees, bureaucracy, facilities, processes. An overwhelming sense of uncertainty and of risk feeds a fear of failure that fuels startups to move fast to find a product/market fit and viable business model.

More mature grownups on the other end of the spectrum are more focused on deliberate, measured, predictable growth that yields healthy profits and pleases shareholders. Having much to lose feeds an altogether different kind of fear, one that produces drag and slows the company down.

ScaleUps occupy the challenging middle ground, which often results in a sort of bipolar organizational tension where half the company is still in run-and-gun startup mode while the other half, usually hired-in senior executives from larger established firms, operates in a more slow-and-steady grownup mode.

Speed is the essence of Peter Drucker's first of four entrepreneurial strategies outlined in his now classic (and still relevant) book, *Innovation and Entrepreneurship:* "Fustest with the Mostest." Drucker attributed the wording to a Civil War general describing his secret to success.

Dave Girouard, best known for building Google's enterprise apps division into a $1 billion-plus global business, concurs. Now the CEO of a fintech ScaleUp, Upstart, Girouard firmly believes that "this is the age of billion-dollar startups, where the best and brightest companies compete at a breakneck speed. Today, the fastest win, as long as the organization keeps speed, efficiency, and innovation as a core foundation. Organization speed defines the company's ability to seize opportunities, act against external threats, innovate, expand to new markets, learn quickly, and hire and retain talented people that thrive in a fast-paced environment."[1]

Speed is indeed a key determinant of success, yet it is certainly not without risk, as Drucker pointed out: "Being 'Fustest with the Mostest' is very much like a moon shot," he wrote. "A deviation of a fraction of a minute from the arc and the missile disappears into outer space."[2] In other words, the margin of error isn't very wide.

Be that as it may, every downhill mountain biker knows that speed is your friend when attempting to conquer a difficult descent. As unnatural and counterintuitive as it seems, carrying speed is the only way to maintain control, increase stability, and minimize risk of injury from a fall. Losing momentum by going too slowly or overbreaking is a surefire way to lose your balance, fall over, or go over the handlebars, just as going too fast for your skill and capability is.

And to carry the Formula 1 analogy a bit further, consider for a moment an entire F1 organization in which speed is the de facto currency. The whole enterprise is aligned around speed, from the huge investments by corporate sponsors to the executive boardroom to the enormously sophisticated technology of the car to the race strategy and control team to the driver and all the way down to the pit crew who perform their work in under three seconds. Cars travel at average speeds greater than the takeoff velocity of an aircraft, often exceeding two hundred miles an hour in certain zones. Yet it can literally all go up in smoke on the track in the blink of an eye. And has.

Enter the need for finding your *strategic speed*, defined as the optimal executional velocity achieved through company-wide alignment of strategies and objectives that reduces drag as well as risk. In nearly every business activity imaginable, your strategic speed will depend on how well difficult strategic decisions and critical choices are made and acted upon.

The late colonel John Boyd, a United States Air Force fighter pilot and renowned military strategist, codified this concept in what he termed an OODA loop: *Observe-Orient-Decide-Act*. Not coincidentally, Boyd was also a student of the Toyota Production System, which incorporates a similar loop for carrying out continuous improvement, known as the Shewhart or PDCA cycle: *Plan-Do-Check-Act*.

While the terms in an OODA loop are simple enough, the context in which they are implemented is most relevant. In an aerial dogfight, the pilot who executes this rapid, iterative cycle fastest wins, because he is operating inside the opponent's own OODA loop. This disorients and confuses adversaries, which puts them at a significant disadvantage. The OODA loop concept has been broadly applied not only to tactical combat situations, but to military campaign operations and processes in general, as well as to legal litigation, law enforcement, firefighting, other types of rapid response operations, and, of course, business strategy.[3]

The concept of strategic speed in the context of an entrepreneurial company —leveraging lean simplicity to generate, and go to market with, a winning strategy—captures the spirit of rapid iteration represented by the OODA loop. While strategy and speed have traditionally been somewhat at odds with each other, the goal of strategic speed is to rethink and resolve problems with that relationship.

Rather than offer a comprehensive treatise on strategy, we offer insight into how strategy viewed in a leaner, simpler light can help your company boost its velocity (as Dave Girouard referred to it) by reducing the forces of drag. Drag is nearly always related to a lack of alignment among the various entities involved in strategy- and decision-making.

A LEANER VIEW OF STRATEGY

Strategy means different things to different people. There are probably as many definitions of strategy as there are those claiming to be strategists. It's surprising how many companies will trounce out something other than a true strategy when asked to provide theirs, producing instead a wide variety of materials masquerading as strategy: mission/vision/values documents, financial plans and forecasts, customer segmentations and personas, marketing plans, and collections of borrowed best practices.

Some executives seem to think that their company is too small to have to worry about strategy, mistaken in the belief that strategy is somehow a function of size, not discipline. There are even those (never market leaders, mind you) who believe that strategy is a waste of time because defensible, competitive advantage is fleeting and unsustainable, especially in times of great uncertainty and rapid change.

Another common lament heard among senior executives is that strategy is necessary and important, but it's complicated, takes too long, and all too often yields mixed results. These executives would rather ride the wave of rapid growth as long as they can, forgetting that all waves crest. As a result, they tend to default to actions centered on simply exploiting and optimizing what brought them initial success in terms of their product/market fit and business model. That may be fine for some, but it isn't strategy, and it seldom if ever leads to the kind of market dominance worthy of a unicorn.

OLD-SCHOOL STRATEGY

The fact that strategy alienates and confounds many leaders is entirely understandable. What's surprising is how many senior executives still labor under an outdated, linear, calendar-based, and situationally irrelevant paradigm of strategy undoubtedly learned years ago in business school, which goes something like this: Analyze, Plan, Execute. Rinse and repeat every January.

JANUARY 1 ————— JANUARY 1 ————— JANUARY 1
ANALYZE-PLAN-EXECUTE   ANALYZE-PLAN-EXECUTE   ANALYZE-PLAN-EXECUTE

Here's how it generally works.

Somewhere around the calendar year transition, a need for "strategy" magically appears on the company agenda, irrespective of whether a new strategy is actually needed. Someone higher up in the company assigns this year's strategy to someone (or someones) usually much lower down in the organization, often a young MBA, or a team of them.

Step one is to conduct an analysis, the most common form of which was taught to our young MBAs while in business school is SWOT: strengths, weaknesses, opportunities, and threats. SWOT remains the dominant way to begin strategy efforts. And it all sounds so legit. "I'm on the SWOT team." It's a great acronym, it sounds like SWAT (special weapons and tactics), which is sticky. Curiously, no one knows who actually came up with SWOT.

To unpack SWOT, you start with the S, for strengths, a concept loaded with silent pretext. All strengths are relative, meaning no single strength remains a strength in all contexts. A strength in one situation can be a weakness in another context. The same holds true for the other elements of SWOT: there is no such thing as a universal weakness, opportunity, or threat.

Therefore, our gallant MBAs must make some situational assumptions in order to know what to pay attention to and what to ignore, because one cannot perform a SWOT analysis of everything . . . it would take a century and a few million pages. To make the job manageable and easier, our SWOTers generally just adopt the assumptions under which the old strategy was formed, which explains why most new strategies end up looking a lot like the old ones, albeit with some new numbers, dates, and names. But hey, step one is done.

ZenDesk's chief technology officer Adrian McDermott shared the ZenDesk version of this situation on The SaaStr Official Podcast:

> *[In] 2015, we have an edict from on high that we're going to be a billion dollar business by 2020, we're looking at the plans of our actual book of business, we're preparing for an all-company event, most of the company is going to Whistler in Canada, for a sales kickoff which is a company kickoff we're launching, it's a big deal, we're already a public company at this point, so we're living our lives in public. We have an upmarket business, we have a repeatable transaction business in SMB [small business] . . . and we look at the actual book of business, and we look at the emerging products that we have, and some, ya know, strategy guy, newly minted MBA from Harvard Business School comes in . . . he runs a Monte Carlo analysis, a thousand scenarios and figures out what are the most likely ways that we get to a billion. And the clear conclusion is that we need to keep launching products and we need some of those products to grow, add on, expand the TAM, increase ACV with customers . . . all the things you would expect us to do, right? What's interesting as I look back at this analysis is that it was complete bollocks. It was actually wildly wrong and incorrect.*[4]

The second step is the plan. Now, the word *strategy* is often used in adjective form with *planning*, that is, *strategic planning*, a phrase that has unfortunately and incorrectly become synonymous with strategy, calling to mind a process that is perceived by many as that rather laborious annual chore to produce a thick and weighty multiyear document that captures all the amazing things you're going to do in the coming months or years, along with budgets, assignments, and timetables. Executing the plan is, of course, the last step.

But as Michael Porter told us thirty years ago in his definitive book *Competitive Strategy*, in order to prevail against others in a given space, you must consciously choose to *do* some things and *not do* others.

Having a plan is all well and good, and can certainly be complementary to strategy, but it isn't the *point* of strategy. The reason strategy even matters at all is that resources are quite simply finite, and we can't possibly do everything we might like to do. The intent behind strategy is to force often difficult choices and make very clear, specific statements about what you are and, perhaps more importantly, aren't going to do, and why or why not, in order to maximize the use of those finite resources and increase the odds of success. While one might reasonably argue that a plan does this, the reality is that although they may imply some of those choices, most strategic plans are not explicit about them. This explains why most plans get such mixed results and why some senior leaders often take a rather dim view of strategy.

NEW-SCHOOL STRATEGY

A more useful (and indeed scalable) definition of strategy is the one offered by former Procter & Gamble CEO A. G. Lafley and Michael Porter's close colleague Roger Martin, former managing director of Porter's Monitor Group and one of the world's foremost thinkers on strategy, in their bestselling book *Playing to Win—How Strategy Really Works*.

> *Strategy is an integrated cascade of choices that uniquely positions a player in its market to create sustainable advantage and superior value relative to the competition.*

Thinking about strategy as integrated choice-making rather than comprehensive plan-making is an important distinction, because irrespective of size or scale, a company that doesn't decisively focus resources on doing some things and not others will not succeed. Also, a mental model of strategy focused on making choices rather than producing plans lends itself nicely to the emphasis on speed at the heart of Boyd's OODA loop.

This definition of strategy raises several important questions, however. First, if strategy is about making integrated choices, what are they? Lafley and Martin argue that a strategy is best thought of as a set of five tightly integrated choices: winning aspiration, where to play, how to win, critical capabilities, and management systems.[5]

PLAYING TO WIN FRAMEWORK

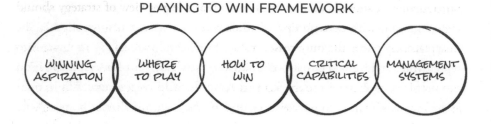

WINNING ASPIRATION   WHERE TO PLAY   HOW TO WIN   CRITICAL CAPABILITIES   MANAGEMENT SYSTEMS

It is the tightly integrated nature that makes these seemingly simple choices at all difficult; they must logically fit together and reinforce each other as a cohesive whole. As such, they cannot be made in a linear, planning-like fashion. Over a decade of experience in working through this framework with executive teams proves the point: the strategy-development motion is much more like putting a jigsaw puzzle together than anything resembling planning: iteratively choosing and deciding in real time, continually toggling back and forth, never locking and loading on any single choice until just the right fit comes together. It's not much different from what a startup does when searching for a product/market fit and viable business model. In fact, generating a strategy in this view is more like rapid iterative prototyping, which is by design faster, leaner, and more agile than perfecting and manufacturing a final product.

Second, what prompts the need to initiate strategic choice-making, and where does one start? Certainly the calendar becomes wholly irrelevant given the new strategy definition by virtue of the fact that no temporal element is included and is, in fact, conspicuous in its absence. Finally, what does the end-to-end strategy formulation process look like and how does it differ from the conventional analyze-plan-execute linearity?

The model pictured here provides a visual reference to the integrated, iterative, and continuous nature of lean strategy design and deployment.

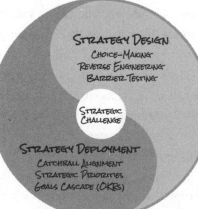

STRATEGY DESIGN
CHOICE-MAKING
REVERSE ENGINEERING
BARRIER TESTING

STRATEGIC CHALLENGE

STRATEGY DEPLOYMENT
CATCHBALL ALIGNMENT
STRATEGIC PRIORITIES
GOALS CASCADE (OKRs)

New strategy construction centers on, and begins with, the identification of a **Strategic Challenge**. Given the definition of waste offered in the introduction, it should come as no surprise that a leaner view of strategy should logically begin with determining whether you even need a new strategy in the first place, as that is the only reason to craft one! Are you seeking to move into new markets? Have you developed a new product? Has your leadership position slipped? Is your share of the market shrinking? Is the product/market fit as tight as it once was? Have competitors crept into the mix with superior products? Is growth not happening as fast as you'd like? Are your capabilities becoming increasingly irrelevant to customers?

Once a Strategic Challenge becomes clear, it is not immediately analyzed in a typical problem-solving effort, but rather reframed into at least two opposing high-level possibilities. There is always more than one way to skin the strategic cat, so to speak. Imagine a future in which the strategic issue you're facing no longer exists. What is the short happy story that tells how it was resolved? "We moved down market," for example, or "We decentralized."

The Strategic Challenge step starts the Strategy Design cycle and drives the need to quickly develop the Lafley/Martin integrated set of five choices for each of those possibilities. In practice this **Choice-Making** step is a fluid and dynamic method of strategy formulation blending logic and creativity in an effort to produce an intelligent hypothesis about the future. And, because it is focused on the future, which is by definition uncertain and unknown, any strategy is just a set of best guesses laced with leaps of faith that if not made explicit may become a risky blind spot that can render strategy formulation an engaging but ultimately academic exercise.

Choice-Making drives the need for immediate **Reverse Engineering** of the logic behind your choices. If you ignore this step, it will be done for you by customers and competitors once you go to market with your shiny but untested new strategy, which in all probability may result in experiencing what Mike Tyson was referring to when he said, "Everyone's got a plan, until they get punched in the mouth."

A simple but powerful technique exists for effectively surfacing worrisome risks during this step, namely asking what Lafley/Martin maintain is the most important question in strategy: *What Must Be True?*

Asking What Must Be True about your choices allows you to tease out the preconditions for success. It's important to note that the question is not concerned with what *is* true, or what *could be* true, but rather what would *have to be* true for the strategy to work as you envision it. Additionally, your What Must Be True? list then becomes a strategic dashboard that you must continually monitor to gauge whether a new or different strategy might be needed: when a critical What Must Be True? is no longer true, it may constitute a new Strategic Challenge, which would restart the Strategy Design effort. It cannot be emphasized enough: new strategies are to be developed *only when the current strategy is no longer working*, when the items on your list of What Must Be True? are no longer true, NOT when January rolls around!

If you're worried that a specific condition necessary for success may not be true, it becomes a potential barrier to eventual success, and **Barrier Testing** must be conducted to determine validity and provide a level of confidence to the company. This effectively flips conventional practice on its head, because the lengthy and usually time-wasting analysis comprising the first step of the old school method has been replaced by a highly specific, contextualized, and therefore swift analysis that comes *after* strategic choice-making in the evaluation of tests meant to validate any underlying assumptions.

The entire strategy design process and output are now significantly faster and lighter; multiple strategy prototypes ready for testing can be formulated in one day with multiteam strategy sprints, rather than weeks or months under the conventional model.

It is important, however, that you view your strategy at this point as just that: a prototype with solid validity. Completion of Barrier Testing initiates the **Strategy Deployment** effort, beginning with an internal process that was affectionately referred to as *catchball* during Matt's time in the Toyota world and is fairly commonplace in Western lean-oriented organizations. Originally used to streamline the cross-functional decision-making process, the concept is literally based on child's play: a simple game of passing a ball to each other.[6] In the context of business, the "ball" is an idea, concept, or, in this case, a strategy.

The goal of the **Catchball Alignment** step is to achieve company-wide alignment behind your top-level strategy by developing and synchronizing nested strategies both down as well as across the organization, effectively creating a whole-company slipstream that reduces decision-making drag and optimizes strategic speed.

Furthering the effort to deploy all developed strategies requires the identification and selection of **Strategic Priorities**, defined as the most important high-level guiding goals. These are then broken down into nearer-term targets that are set and aligned using the Catchball process and supported by tried-and-true mechanisms for creating a **Goals Cascade**. Two such mechanisms are the Japanese method known as *hoshin kanri* and the Western equivalent, known in tech circles as Objectives and Key Results (OKRs).

Let's unpack the entire strategy motion further.

UNPACKING STRATEGY DESIGN

To help unpack strategy design, we will interweave the example of the secret luxury vehicle project launched by Toyota in the mid-1980s. Codenamed F1—for "flagship one"—the example is a master class in strategy design for several reasons. First, it is a story of phenomenal scale and growth for a company known as the birthplace of lean. Second, it is a story of how a large, very mature, grownup, non-digitally native product company can find a way to win in a saturated, highly structured market and be every bit as entrepreneurial as any modern high-flying tech firm. Third, it is a story of an audacious play by an organization that most analysts performing a deep due diligence would say had no business even attempting to do what the company aspired to do, much less succeed at it, and exhibit the kind of disruption and domination any would-be unicorn would envy.

Finally, it is a demonstration of how strategic speed really works in a most complex situation.

STRATEGIC CHALLENGE

As mentioned previously, new strategy construction begins with settling on the most pressing and troublesome strategic challenge you're facing. As with any problem solving, you have to grasp the current situation and identify the strategic issues that make you think you need a new strategy in the first place. If you're not sure where to start, consider the most pressing current challenges in your chosen segments, your channel partners, your customers, and your capabilities and costs in comparison to your competitors. Most senior executives know what's keeping them up at night; they just need to frame it properly. Language is important here, as you want to state the challenge in a way that keeps your mind wide open to *possibilities*, which should always be considered before *options*.

The preferred phrasing of a strategic challenge uses the language "How might we . . ." The word *might* is superior to *can* or *should*, both of which are limiting constructs. *Can* implies a capability, which at this point is irrelevant, because capabilities can always be acquired. *Should* implies a judgment, which is also irrelevant at this point because it adds an unnecessary mental constraint.

For Toyota, the Strategic Challenge was rather daunting. Toyota leadership in 1984 wasn't too keen on the fact that as Toyota customers were growing in wealth and success, they were choosing to purchase more upmarket, luxury brands: Mercedes, BMW, Jaguar, and the like. Toyota was vulnerable to *churn*, in today's vernacular. The desire, of course, was to keep those customers in the Toyota family. Unfortunately, the company did not have a product suitable for the luxury market. Thus, the Strategic Challenge was framed as "How might we avoid losing increasingly affluent Toyota customers to more upscale brands?"

Once the challenge is framed, it must be reframed. Here's where strategy development differs from typical problem-solving. It is tempting to begin analyzing a well-framed problem. Don't, for all the reasons mentioned earlier in our discussion of SWOT. Instead, reframe the problem as at least two opposing (and thus mutually exclusive) possible approaches to the problem.

For example, if your problem is one of having inferior capabilities compared to your key competitors, the choices could be between building new capability, buying an entity with that specific expertise, partnering, or outsourcing. At the most generic level, the choice is always going to be between broadening and narrowing. The goal with this "framestorming" step is to lay the groundwork for the Choice-Making phase.

Toyota considered a few different possibilities in reframing the problem. They could extend their existing top-level model by providing a new trim level offering a "makeover": a facelift with luxury appointments. At the end of the day, though, a Camry is still a Camry. They could focus on the youth market, choosing to attract newly minted drivers and concentrate on keeping them in the Toyota family for the next twenty-five years. Unfortunately, it would be another fifteen years before the total addressable market would make that possibility attractive. They could partner with a European automaker known for luxury and performance and explore a rebranding and rebadging relationship. Toyota's joint manufacturing partnership with General Motors, known as New United Motor Manufacturing Inc. (NUMMI) had just lifted off and was beginning to show real success. But to make a joint effort viable, there needs to be something to gain for both parties, and Toyota had nothing of interest to offer the BMWs and Mercedes of the world . . . such a play would only dilute that brand's existing share. Finally, they could start from scratch to build the world's best car, under a different brand name, and win the full share of their customers' garage. Luxury and performance weren't completely uncharted territory for the company. Toyota built limousines for executives and dignitaries. Some of Toyota's senior engineers early in their careers had worked on Zeros, Japan's World War II fighter jets. And by 1984, Toyota had competed in motorsports for over a quarter century.

This was the chosen possibility, as highly speculative and resource-intensive as it was.

CHOICE-MAKING

Winning Aspiration

A Winning Aspiration is a future-oriented, externally focused statement that spells out what winning means in concrete, specific, and ambitious language. It describes in measurable ways both who you're winning *for* and who you're winning *against*. It also captures a measurable strategic ambition that guides and helps to align the other choices. It's not a modest statement, and downgraded statements describing playing to play or playing to avoid loss won't work.

Gravitas around winning is absolutely critical and non-negotiable, because while no space is entirely safe in business, the safest spot is on the podium (notwithstanding Ricky Bobby's assertion that "if you ain't first, you're last"[7]). If you're not winning or aiming to win, you will likely not focus your resources in a manner needed to do so. As a result, you will be far more vulnerable to those who *are* winning in your space and who will use the greater resources that accrue to winners to beat you up in the market.

When thinking about a Winning Aspiration, having external focus is critical. This is a key difference between a Winning Aspiration and vision, mission, and purpose statements, all of which are predominantly internally or organizationally focused. Also, many purported Winning Aspirations aren't true Winning Aspirations, although they sound like they are.

For example, "Double our unit sales" certainly sounds ambitious and measurable, but it is not necessarily a Winning Aspiration in the context of strategy formulation, for a few reasons. Not only is the concept of "doubling" a completely internal orientation and rather meaningless without a measurable starting point, but without an external focus there is no way to realistically gauge your competitive position—doubling your sales may only get you from tenth place to ninth.

The sine qua non of strategy is having a true Winning Aspiration with the right leadership measure. Without it, you won't be able to determine whether you are *actually* winning, and you won't do what you must to win.

Toyota's Winning Aspiration was twofold:

- Become the number one U.S. luxury import brand, displacing Mercedes and BMW
- Become the number one U.S. luxury import brand overall by various business measures, including share of market, share of garage, and third-party rankings and reviews in magazines such as *Car & Driver* and *Motor Trend*, as well as J.D. Power & Associates' Initial Quality Survey and Customer Satisfaction Survey

Nicknamed the "Beat Mercedes" strategy by Toyota rank and file, this winning aspiration was felt to be a true moonshot, especially by the 1,400 designers and 3,700 engineers who shook their heads in disbelief when Toyota president Eiji Toyoda announced to the world in 1984 that Toyota would beat both Mercedes' and BMW's flagship models across the board in every attribute typically measured by automotive reviewers.

Where to Play

Choosing Where to Play requires you to map out the specific spaces where you will and will not focus your resources to compete. At the corporate level, playing spaces generally include customer segments, distribution channels, product/service categories, and geographies. While the tendency is always to play "everywhere customers need us," it's best to limit yourself to spaces in which you believe you can, in the reasonably foreseeable future, achieve a "podium" position—1, 2, or 3. This goes for function-level and internal strategies as well, because while it seems as though these groups may not have an external direct competitor, there is always a competing alternative. It is better to think about where to *win*, versus where to play.

Being explicit about spaces in which you will not play, or will stop playing, is critical but can be surprisingly difficult. As Jim Collins wrote so eloquently two decades ago, "It is the discipline to discard what does not fit—to cut out what might have already cost days or even years of effort—that distinguishes the truly exceptional artist and marks the ideal piece of work."[8]

Steve Jobs shared a similar perspective. In his award-winning biography of Jobs, Walter Isaacson wrote that, "One of Jobs' great strengths was knowing how to focus. 'Deciding what not to do is as important as deciding what to do,' he said. 'That's true for companies, and it's true for products.'"

Upon his return to Apple in the late 1990s after being ousted over a decade earlier, Jobs slashed 70 percent of Apple's product line, as well as exiting other businesses such as printers and servers. As Isaacsen retells the now-legendary story, Jobs went to a whiteboard in a product strategy session, drew a quadrant, labeled the columns "Consumer" and "Pro," then labeled the rows "Desktop" and "Portable." The Where to Play product choices were made that simply . . . one product for each quadrant. "The room was in dumb silence," writes Isaacsen.

Consistent with these examples is a core element of the Netflix operating culture called the "Canada Principle," a reference to the company's early decision not to enter the Canadian market to capture what seemed to be an easy extra 10 percent in revenue. As cofounder Marc Randolph tells it in his 2019 book *That Will Never Work*, a quiver of small but complicated details like currency and dual language requirements would have resulted in the move becoming mostly a distraction. Choosing to avoid that early entry in favor of focusing the same amount of effort on the core U.S. market brought a revenue bump double that of Canada's potential. The Canada Principle is behind other difficult strategic choices, such as scrapping DVD sales in favor of rental income and never advertising on the site. Randolph argues that whenever you discuss what you are going to do next, you must also be prepared to discuss what you are going to stop doing, urging entrepreneurs to be conscious of feature creep in their business by "scraping the barnacles off the hull."[9] Meaning that improving your strategic speed avoids the seemingly easy but ultimately distracting additions.

While ScaleUps in general have found a great initial Where to Play—that is, their product/market fit—moving beyond that first position in order to grow often presents a challenge, and it is quite common not to give enough thought to the question of Where to Play. Equally common is adopting a stationary stance, acting as if current spaces are somehow inert, a la: "This is where we play, it's where we've always played, and it's where we should always play." That kind of stay-in-your-lane thinking is behind the disruption and demise of many giant companies and household name brands. Imagine if the FAANG group (Facebook, Amazon, Apple, Netflix, Google) played that way.

Your Where to Play should never be considered set in stone. It should *always* be adjusted to accommodate the realities of a constantly changing marketplace. You might be focusing on a ground game today, but tomorrow may demand an air attack. Some will argue that this is tactics, not strategy, but with the lightning speed of change today it's a meaningless distinction. You should continually experiment with the Where to Play choices so that you can win in new and different (i.e., innovative) ways. It's a discipline many companies struggle with.

Toyota chose to play *only* in the U.S. luxury performance sedan market, and *only* target affluent consumers aged forty-five to sixty. The choice of geography not only reinforced their Winning Aspiration, but also made it clear that competing with a Mercedes or BMW in Europe would be a fool's errand, as would selling into the comparatively lower income and far less ostentatious Asian market. The choice of market and consumer segment also removed high-end sports car and ultra-luxury brands from the competitive set.

How to Win

Choosing a How to Win in each chosen space is an exercise in pinpointing *why* you will win over all competing alternatives in that space, and spells out the specific manner by which you will dominate that space. It is perhaps the most difficult question in strategy.

There is only one way to consistently win in business: provide better value than every other player in the space. The customer is the final arbiter of that value equation, which of course is the real challenge. Creating a strong How to Win means giving customers clear and specific reasons to choose your offering over others competing for their business.

A strong How to Win is differentiated and defensible over the long term, and so it becomes your competitive moat. A differentiated and defensible advantage is defined as one that can't be copied—built, bought, or borrowed—easily or inexpensively. Often the two characteristics go hand-in-hand, because highly differentiating choices are naturally more bold, thus risky. And since no one truly likes risk, a defensible moat is built into effective strategy.

There is a tendency to consider ways to win in the abstract, which can result in weak choices, or even non-choices. The first clue that what you think are your competitive advantages are in fact not *actual* advantages is when everyone else in that space seems to claim those advantages, too. Your choices are generic, and thus non-differentiating. They're the vanilla choices of strategy.

Take, for example, the oft-listed yet supremely vanilla How to Win of "great customer experience." While it may sound good on a website or in collateral material, it inevitably leads a company into believing they have an advantage when they really don't, and believing they're making a strong choice when they aren't making a choice at all. What company wouldn't seek to offer a great customer experience? More to the point, can you imagine any company taking a significantly different or even opposite approach, ala "terrible customer experience"? It sounds silly. That's why *Saturday Night Live*'s "Samurai Deli," *Seinfeld*'s "Soup Nazi," and NBC's *The Office* are so hilarious. In other words, great customer experience is the ante to the game, not a choice.

Finally, when considering your How to Win choices, avoid anything reminiscent of yesteryear advantages that have seen their better day: customer focus, customer service, feature X, more and better features, better data/SEO/social media, contracts/patents, intellectual property, lower price, and first mover advantage. It isn't that any of these aren't advantages in the right context, it's just that their importance is short-lived in today's whirlwind business climate. Features are only an advantage until someone copies them. So-called better data/SEO is short-lived. Contract, patents, and other intellectual property rights that once offered almost guaranteed protection rarely stave off competitors in today's open world of advanced technology. Lowering your prices lasts only until a competitor lowers theirs. Being first to market is not a sustainable advantage; in fact, without a strong complementary value proposition— "the mostest" as Peter Drucker would say—fast followers often beat the first movers by offering a better value equation.

While there is no such thing as a universal advantage, a few categories are worth pursuing, including:

- Exclusive partnerships (e.g., "powered by")
- Strategic acquisitions/mergers (e.g., Salesforce + Slack)
- Brand dominance (e.g., Microsoft Office)
- Market aggregation (e.g., Uber, Airbnb, Amazon Merchant Services)
- Massive scale (e.g., Amazon.com)
- Network effects (e.g., LinkedIn)
- Deep expertise/knowledge (e.g., Gartner, Forrester)
- Special authority/designation (e.g., "Board Certified")
- High switching costs (e.g., SAP)
- Obsession with a signature experience or element (e.g., Apple design)
- Fierce customer loyalty (e.g., WhatsApp)

All of these are very difficult, time-consuming, and/or costly to acquire.

Yet none can be considered a realistic How to Win without the context of a suitable Where to Play. In fact, locking down what seems like a great Where to Play choice without considering a matching How to Win is the most common (but correctable) pitfall when designing a new strategy. Because although How to Win and Where to Play form the heart of any winning strategy, one without the other leaves you with little.

Without Steve Jobs' focus on key playing spaces, for example, Apple would never have become one of the most valuable companies in the world. Also, they possessed the How to Win of seamless "it just works" hardware/software integration and instantly recognizable design aesthetics. As another example, upon her arrival as CEO of Burberry in 2006, Angela Ahrendts would not have been able to transform the brand into the fourth fastest-growing global brand (behind Apple, Google, and Amazon) by moving downmarket to capture the millennial buyer without being the first fully digital luxury goods maker and completely social enterprise. Her way to win caught the eye of Apple, who brought her in to run their retail division. Salesforce realized early on that hitting their best strategic speed in expanding and quickly capturing complementary spaces adjacent to their core CRM platform required a How to Win that might be best thought of as "winning with winners," the acquisition of leading providers in those spaces (the most recent and notable example of which is the nearly $28 billion purchase of Slack completed in 2021).

Returning to our story, Toyota had a clear How to Win that they believed would offer superior value:

- Offer the very best comfort, styling, performance, handling, noise reduction, aerodynamics, curb weight, and fuel efficiency in the luxury performance sedan segment, as measured by external reviewers.
- Offer a retail price $30,000 less than top-of-the-line BMW and Mercedes vehicles without sacrificing quality.
- Provide an upscale image and retail experience commensurate with the vehicle, modeled after Nordstrom's philosophy. The Toyota brand image would not suffice; neither would the traditional car dealer experience, which the majority of Americans ranked below a visit to the dentist.

Producing and delivering this level of value to the market would require a game-changing operating model: critical capabilities and management systems the likes of which had yet to be seen in the U.S. automotive market.

Critical Capabilities

Like the Where to Play/How to Win duality, the choices of Critical Capabilities and Management Systems comprise the essence of your operating model and are equally inseparable.

Critical capabilities bring your Where to Play and How to Win choices to life. They are the specific current and future practices, skills, and activities that must be performed at the highest level to help you win in the spaces and ways you've chosen.

A few key points are worth making.

First, *capabilities* are not to be confused with *competencies*. Competencies are just things you're currently good at, and there's a dangerous tendency to simply list your strengths as the capabilities you need. The problem with that approach is that your strengths may or may not yield unique value or be relevant to customers.

For example, Southwest Airlines would never consider pilot quality as a critical capability, because their pilots don't need to be any better at flying planes than any other airline, and passengers do not make their travel plans based on an airline's pilots. It's an assumed competency, not a strategic capability. However, they would consider skill in activities like route planning, fast gate turnaround, high aircraft utilization, and fleet standardization as critical capabilities. Why? Because to realize their winning aspiration of leading the airline industry in profitability by capturing the short-haul segment as the low-cost provider demands passengers in seats and planes in the air. Southwest also uses the economy of maintaining a single type of aircraft.

Second, whether the needed capabilities are currently in place when formulating a strategy is irrelevant; in fact, for many new strategies, the capabilities needed to produce altogether new value may have yet to be built, borrowed, or bought. This is where planning comes into play and complements strategy formulation. You need an investment of X to build, borrow, or buy certain critical capabilities, so you need a concrete plan of action that details the who, what, and when.

Without Jony Ive's extraordinarily elegant design and human factors sensibilities, Apple's chosen How to Win of integration and clean design would not have been realized. Likewise, without recruiting and retaining designer Christopher Bailey to find and harness the creative skills of great young designers to produce fresh, relevant fashion design, Angela Ahrendts' How to Win might have remained a distant dream.

In the case of Toyota, they had to master three critical capabilities to produce their How to Win. Most were not in place, and all needed significant development:

- **Deep understanding of the American luxury consumer.** Japan's is a very humble culture, with ostentatious wealth and luxury anathema to the Japanese existence.
- **Radical innovation in design and engineering.** Toyota engineers needed to redefine the luxury performance sedan, because the value elements were in conflict. For example, greater speed and acceleration conflicted directly with fuel efficiency, noise, and weight, because higher speed and acceleration required a more powerful engine, which is usually bigger, heavier, makes more noise, and consumes more

fuel. These conflicts drove a creative tension that, when combined with a "no compromise" mantra, produced many automotive firsts, including door handles built into the door frame, an internal trunk spoiler for aerodynamic efficiency, an all-aluminum engine block, and recording studio–level soundproofing coupled with a one-piece drive shaft for a nearly silent cabin.

- **Brand building supported by riveting advertising.** Typical automotive marketing would not distinguish the car. No brand extensions would be allowed. A new name, a new brand image, and head-turning messaging had to be in place at launch. After a global search for a new identity, the name *Lexus* was chosen, complete with a top-shelf logo design introduced to the world through stunning imagery and a distinguished spokesperson adorned in elegant formal attire touting, "*The Relentless Pursuit of Perfection.*"

Management Systems

Management Systems refer to processes, structures, standards, rules, and metrics that reinforce, support, and sustain your Critical Capabilities. Including Management Systems as a key component of strategy may seem curious to some, primarily because a Winning Aspiration and a Management System appear to be so far apart in terms of their level of abstraction. But they are both part of having an integrated strategy that works.

For Toyota, that meant leveraging their vaunted Toyota Production System (TPS), designed to produce the highest quality at the lowest cost with the shortest lead time in an effort to outsell the competition. In other words, they decided that a Lexus would be assembled using the same production system as a Camry or Corolla.

But while TPS was necessary, it was not sufficient. Toyota needed to separate the Lexus division, select the highest potential American managers to lead it, and employ a stringent retail dealer selection process supported by a new and fully enforceable franchise agreement to ensure a consistent upscale experience. Only 81 of the best dealers in the nation were selected out of 1,600 possible candidates, each of whom were required to build an entirely new facility, adhere to strict brand identity standards, and go through exhaustive product, sales, service, parts, and customer relations training.

Voice of the Operator

INTERVIEW WITH MICHELLE COLLIGNON[10]

Michelle Collignon leads Global Strategic Partnerships for OwnBackup, a top-ranked backup and data recovery SaaS solution on the Salesforce.com AppExchange and a Gartner "Cool Vendor" in Business Continuity and IT Disaster Recovery.

How did you come to adopt the Playing to Win framework for strategy formulation?

Both my undergraduate and graduate degrees are in business, and in my first job out of college with Deloitte consulting as an analyst in the strategy and operations practice, I got my first taste. But it wasn't until I went back for my MBA at the University of Chicago that I began to get a good grasp of strategy. I had a b-school professor who talked about the key questions that you need to ask to formulate a strategy. In retrospect those questions were like Playing to Win, but not exactly the same. I went back to Deloitte after my MBA, and in my work with clients I kept applying that approach to strategy, of asking questions to drive focus.

Then, right around when Deloitte acquired Monitor, I was working with one of the other partners on a particularly difficult and diverse client, and we needed a quick and accessible way to help them get their arms around their strategy. We wanted the latest thinking on strategy, so I went to *Harvard Business Review*, and stumbled onto Playing to Win. It took everything my professor talked about and put it in an easy framework that allowed us to walk the client through strategy in a workshop format. It allowed the client's executive team to have a focused conversation, with less debate and conflict, and they collaboratively came to agreement on key strategic decisions and choices relatively quickly.

That sounds like a great start. How did you leverage it beyond that point?

It worked so well, we agreed that we needed to be using the framework on all of our strategy projects. We began implementing it across the board at Deloitte in our strategy and operations practice. That was very much how we leveraged it. When I came to OwnBackup, I was given the charge of developing the systems integrator partner motion. What was nice about that is that it's like your book of business, and you can set your business strategy. Naturally I decided to use what had worked so well with my clients all along, the Playing to Win framework, to craft my ultimate strategy for how we would go about managing the business. Part of that strategy is building out my team and educating them on the framework.

How are you going about doing that?

Mostly by example, very grassroots. When I got here I began asking my peers and sales leaders where they saw opportunity for growth, where they thought a partnership motion should focus, and what our unique value proposition might be. Basically, we were asking the Playing to Win questions sort of informally, then using that feedback to build out the framework. Then they see how I've incorporated their feedback into an easy framework. And honestly, as many of them are former athletes, the whole notion of seeing the playing field, the market, and focusing on certain parts of the field and coming up with the plays to win in those spaces, resonated well enough that our head of alliances said we should think about our entire business that way. When you're coming up with strategic plays and tactical actions that you can take, it becomes a much more positive experience, people's brains switch on, and they begin to think "this is doable," and the whole big scary idea of strategy becomes less so.

What is your philosophy on strategy deployment?

For me it's really about dissecting the broader aim and focus into solid plays, then breaking those plays down into manageable shorter-term objectives. I come from consulting, so analytics is part of my DNA. If you say "We want this big number X," then my response is "Let's break that down and line it up with our strategic plays and priorities, then we can set team goals to get to the big number."

As I mentioned, our teams are business athletes, so the idea of having a playbook and following the playbook—the right play at the right time—feels more natural and intuitive. The Playing to Win framework gives them clear guidance on what they need to do daily. As I manage my week against my strategy, I advise my teams on what I call strategic next actions, the priorities to ensure you're advancing the strategy each week. Having OKRs and the Quarterly Business Review cadence in place to measure your progress against is very helpful. What you measure is also what drives the behavior and it's how you get the results.

What advice or pro tips would you give for those considering adopting the Playing to Win framework to speed up strategic decision-making?

The framework allows you to anchor back to decisions that have been made. There's a tendency to react quickly to an emerging situation, but without the anchor you may take action or make a decision that doesn't sync with the strategy—and could possibly work against it. Or you have these endless discussions on what to do. Being able to say "Look, this is what we agreed would be our Where to Play and How to Win" eliminates so much swirl and that management-by-consensus spiral that can drag on. It allows you to point back to how the decision we need to make right now answers some part of the framework, how it's going to help you make a certain play. So strategic decision-making momentum is faster, because you can get the answer in the room in the moment . . .

it sort of refocuses the brain. It's like, "We can solve this right now because, look, we've already agreed this was the strategy, this is where we're headed, and this is the play." It's all about alignment, and no one should question that decision. It increases speed to market and speed in market.

The other thing is this: When I have gotten teams to align around a play or set of plays, I always encourage them to try it and figure out relatively quickly if it's not working . . . fail fast and learn. And then you can shift to maybe one of the other plays and put more attention there. Having a strategy doesn't mean you always have all the right answers. When you're coming up with your plays, you're testing them out and doing some research, you're setting them in motion. But I've always held that we should have enough of them that we can skin the cat, so to speak, a few different ways. We can hit our number, hit our objectives in our OKRs by hitting two of the three or two of the four. By being able to assess and figure out whether one of them isn't working or not cutting it, you can move to or get more out of one of your other plays quickly.

REVERSE ENGINEERING

Once the five integrated choices are made, the first step in strategy development is complete. The choice cascade is now ready for **Reverse Engineering** and **Barrier Testing**. These two steps represent a significant challenge for most strategy-making teams, who, in their enthusiasm over what appears to be a winning play, immediately begin marching out their master stroke to the market. They tend to forget that any strategy, no matter how good it looks on paper, is simply a string of beliefs and hypotheses—guesses, really—about what they want to happen in the future. And most of us learned in seventh-grade science that a hypothesis must be tested to confirm its validity.

The reverse engineering method of asking What Must Be True for a given set of choices sprang from a disappointing consulting engagement in which the client went against Roger Martin's advice, with disastrous results. It was enough to make Roger reflect on his consulting approach.

Then, during a subsequent engagement in which he had a strong view of what the best strategic option was, he suddenly realized that it didn't matter at all what he thought. He realized that what mattered most was what his *client* thought, since they were the ones who were going to have to take action one way or the other, not Roger. As Roger tells it:

> *At an impasse, an idea popped into my head. Rather than have them talk about what they thought was true about the various options, I would ask them to specify what would have to be true for the option on the table to be a fantastic choice. The result was magical. Clashing views turned into collaboration to really understand the logic of the options. Rather than having people attempt to convince others of the merits of options, the options themselves did the convincing (or failed to do so). In this moment, the best role of the consultant became clear to me: Don't attempt to convince clients which choice is best; run a process that enables them to convince themselves.*[11]

In practice, that process runs by considering What Must Be True across the key dimensions of your strategic choices as well as the potential competitive market reaction. More specifically, it entails asking four What Must Be True questions:

1. What must be true about the openness, structure, and dynamics of our chosen spaces?
2. What must be true about what our company, channels, and customers value?
3. What must be true about our critical capabilities and relative costs?
4. What must be true about how our competitors might react to our strategy?

Answering these questions should result in multiple assumptions and preconditions for success. The most uncertain of these—those that are most worrisome—may in fact be giant leaps of faith, critical risks and potential obstacles that must be tested and validated to the level of collective confidence that produces a belief that the What Must Be True is actually true.

For Toyota, the first listed Critical Capability became a clear What Must Be True condition that put the Lexus strategy at great risk: the ability to understand what affluent Americans truly value. Toyota designers needed to get inside the hearts and minds of American luxury buyers, to learn the ways of the wealthy, to understand their wants, needs, and requirements.

BARRIER TESTING

A newly developed strategy is no different from any other conceptual prototype in that it must be tested. Although the whole reason for Reverse Engineering and Barrier Testing is to increase the likelihood of success, this step is the most difficult and uncomfortable for many people, perhaps because experimentation does not exist in old-school strategy methods. It's an underdeveloped muscle in many companies, which is why Constant Experimentation is one of the key principles in our model.

The aim of Barrier Testing is not validating that your choices are good, but rather that they aren't bad. There is no such thing as a perfect strategy; the best you can hope for is to shorten your odds. Therefore, the wisest and most expeditious move in the name of strategic speed is to perform an "acid" test of the What Must Be True condition that would prevent a good night's sleep if it weren't actually true. While optimism and enthusiasm usually run high when a team develops a new strategy, there is usually at least one individual who adopts the role of barometer for the team and naturally loses more sleep than the rest: a skeptic, a devil's advocate. Use them! Involve them in the test design. If skeptics aren't confident in a strategic choice, it'll be tough to move forward. Experience shows that skeptics tend to naturally design something that builds their confidence.

Toyota had learned the hard way about going to market without testing, having suffered a Mike Tyson–worthy knockout punch on American soil nearly thirty years before the Lexus strategy was developed. When Toyota entered the U.S. passenger car market in 1957, they quickly realized that their cars were too small for the average American and significantly underpowered for the high-speed U.S. freeways, requiring several years of redesign and reengineering. If the company is good at anything, though, it is good at learning from experience, if not experimentation. They could ill afford another such misstep.

To address what nearly all of the engineers and designers viewed as a blind leap into a bottomless chasm, Toyota chose to run a fairly intense and expensive experiment, sending the senior design team to Southern California with the instructions to not just observe, but *live* the lifestyle of the rich and famous. They leased a multimillion-dollar beachfront house in Laguna Beach for several months, shopped at designer boutiques, ate in five-star restaurants, played golf at exclusive country clubs, night clubbed at trendy hotspots, and leased Mercedes, BMWs, and Jaguars. They interviewed valets, caddies, chauffeurs, housekeepers, concierges, and caterers to find out the druthers of the wealthy.

Following the Southern California stint, they took similar tours of San Francisco, Miami, New York City, Houston, Denver, and Chicago. The luxury scene was a whole new world for the team, but the experience armed them with a deep and empathic understanding of their target customer. The Toyota designers felt confident in the Lexus strategy. The venture took nearly half a decade of radical innovation involving 900 engine prototypes, 450 test models, and nearly two million test miles.

When the first Lexus made its debut in 1989, it stunned the automotive world and set a new luxury standard, indeed beating the top-of-the-line Mercedes 420SEL and BMW 735i. Within six months, Lexus hit the billion-dollar sales mark with the $35,000 LS400. It took just two years for Lexus to displace market leaders Mercedes-Benz and BMW, which had been entrenched for decades, as the top-selling luxury import nameplate in America. It took another eight years to become the overall luxury performance brand in America, a leadership position Lexus held for well over a decade. Today, the podium positions are shared by Lexus, Mercedes, BMW, and now Tesla, who take turns in the top spot each year in a tightly contested competition.

Done right, you can fit an entire Strategy Design on a single page, using a template like the one shown here. Your strategy is now as lightweight, aerodynamic, and drag-resistant as a Formula 1 car prototype. In practice, it works best to follow the one-pager with a page devoted to each of the five key choices, explaining it in narrative form. Your entire strategy is then six pages. Even Jeff Bezos would approve.[12]

The Lexus strategy remains a study in strategic speed. Rare is the company in any space, in any industry, at any time that can boast of $1 billion in sales within six months of launch, irrespective of ramp-up time or resourcing.

Below is an at-a-glance look at what the Lexus strategy design might look like using the Strategy Design Framework template, as well as the structure of a strategy design session (see Toolkit: The One-Day Strategy Sprint). Having an entire strategy captured in such a brief and portable format greatly improves the speed of deployment, which is our next topic.

TOOLKIT: STRATEGY DESIGN FRAMEWORK

STRATEGIC CHALLENGE	1. WINNING ASPIRATION
What key issue are we solving for? ("How might we _____?")	What is our bold ambition? What measureable outcomes define winning?

2. WHERE TO PLAY	3. HOW TO WIN
In what spaces or segments can we consistently sustain a podium position (1, 2, 3)? Where must we not play, or stop playing?	On what basis will we capture chosen spaces? What superior and defensible value will make us unique? Why will customers choose us over competing options?

4. CRITICAL CAPABILITIES	5. MANAGEMENT SYSTEMS
What key skills or activities must be in place to produce our competitive advantage?	How will we support, standardize, and sustain our critical capabilities?

WHAT MUST BE TRUE	BARRIER TESTING
What must be true for our choices to succeed: about our chosen spaces, about what customers truly value, about our capabilities, and about how competitors might react?	What condition concerns us the most? What test would give us confidence?

THE LEXUS STRATEGY

STRATEGIC CHALLENGE	WINNING ASPIRATION
• How might we avoid losing increasingly affluent Toyota customers to upscale brands?	• #1 U.S. luxury import brand, displacing Mercedes and BMW • #1 U.S. luxury import brand overall

WHERE TO PLAY	HOW TO WIN
• United States • Luxury performance sedans (Mercedes, BMW) • Affluent consumers aged 45–60	• Beat Mercedes 420SEL and BMW 735i: comfort, styling, performance, handling, noise, aerodynamics, curb weight, fuel efficiency • Lower price point by USD $30,000 • New upscale image and luxury retail experience commensurate with product (e.g., Nordstrom)

CORE CAPABILITIES	MANAGEMENT SYSTEMS
• Deep consumer understanding • Innovation in design and engineering • Brand building supported by riveting advertising	• Toyota Production System • U.S.-lead business division • Exclusive retail dealer selection • Enforceable dealer franchise agreement with strict standards

WHAT MUST BE TRUE	BARRIER TESTING
• We can understand what affluent 45–60 year old Americans truly value	• Experiment: Live the American upscale lifestyle for six months; effectively become the U.S. luxury performance buyer in order to better understand them.

TOOLKIT: THE ONE-DAY STRATEGY SPRINT

Forget your detailed analyses and planning. Construct multiple winning strategies in a single day with the Playing to Win Canvas.

Rapidly scaling companies don't have time for the single-perfect-plan approach to constructing winning strategies. Markets and customers move too quickly. By adopting the Playing to Win strategic choice–making framework, you can design not just one, but several strategies inside a normal working day's time by running a Strategy Sprint and using the Playing to Win canvas (see page 47, and we have provided a link to download a digital copy in the Toolkit Resources section at the end of the book). If conducting the sprint in person, multiple teams can work at once in the same room. If conducting the sprint remotely, either use features like breakout rooms, or take it one team, one strategy at a time. Here's the time blocking.

AGENDA ITEM	TIMING	DESCRIPTION
Strategic Challenge	30 minutes	Identify the strategic issue, using the "How Might We" framing. *Examples: How might we enter the enterprise market?*
Reframe the Challenge	30 minutes	Identify at least two different high-level possibilities that would solve the issue. Example: *1. Extend the product line. 2. Develop new product.*
Winning Aspiration	30 minutes	Define your measurable strategic ambition. Don't be modest; don't play to play. Who are you winning for and against?
Where to Play + How to Win	90 minutes	In what spaces or segments can you consistently sustain a podium position (1, 2, 3)? Consider all relevant resource focal points. Be explicit about where NOT to play or to stop playing. What superior value will make you truly unique in each space? What will be your defensible advantage (your "moat")? Be very specific about value elements (quality, cost, speed, experience, etc.).

Critical Capabilities	45 minutes	What key skills and activities will produce your How to Win?
Management Systems	45 minutes	How will you support, standardize, and sustain your critical capabilities?
Reverse Engineering (What Must Be True?)	45 minutes	What must be true about the openness, structure, and dynamics of your spaces? What must be true about what your company, channels, and customers truly value? What must be true about your critical capabilities and relative costs? What must be true about how your competitors might react to your strategy?
Barrier Testing	45 minutes	What condition concerns you most? What do you need to confirm? What test would give you confidence? What will be your measure of success?

UNPACKING STRATEGY DEPLOYMENT

Designing a winning strategy for your company is one thing. Getting it to permeate and drive the entire organization is another challenge entirely. Successful deployment rests on the ability to achieve cross-company alignment. To ensure you're ready for deployment, use the following checklist.

Deployment Readiness Checklist

- Your team is aligned on what it means to win with and for customers.
- Your team is aligned on what it means to win against competitors.
- Your strategic ambition includes clear and meaningful success metrics (internal and external).
- Your team is aligned on your key playing spaces (regions, segments, channels, product/service, etc.).

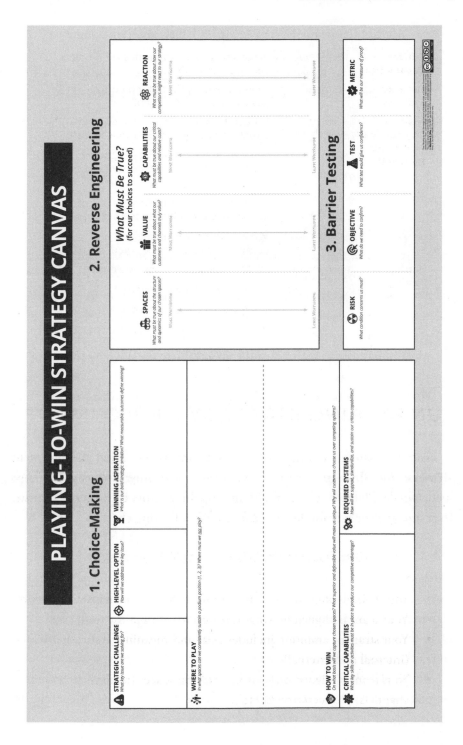

PLAYING-TO-WIN STRATEGY CANVAS

1. Choice-Making

STRATEGIC CHALLENGE
What key issue are we solving for?

HIGH-LEVEL OPTION
How will we address the key issue?

WINNING ASPIRATION
What is our bold strategic ambition? What measurable outcomes define winning?

WHERE TO PLAY
In what spaces can we consistently sustain a podium position (1, 2, 3)? Where must we too play?

HOW TO WIN
On what basis will we capture chosen spaces? What superior and defensible value will make us unique? Why will customers choose us over competing options?

CRITICAL CAPABILITIES
What key skills or activities must be in place to produce our competitive advantage?

REQUIRED SYSTEMS
How will we support, standardize, and sustain our critical capabilities?

2. Reverse Engineering

What Must Be True?
(for our choices to succeed)

SPACES
What must be true about the structure and dynamics of our chosen spaces?

Most Worrisome

VALUE
What must be true about what our customers and channels truly value?

Most Worrisome

CAPABILITIES
What must be true about our critical capabilities and relative costs?

Most Worrisome

REACTION
What must be true about how our competitors might react to our strategy?

Most Worrisome

Least Worrisome

Least Worrisome

Least Worrisome

Least Worrisome

3. Barrier Testing

RISK
What condition concerns us most?

OBJECTIVE
What do we need to confirm?

TEST
What test would give us confidence?

METRIC
What will be our measure of proof?

- You have chosen only those spaces in which you can maintain a "podium" position (1, 2, or 3).
- Your team is aligned on what your winningest offerings are.
- You have a specific and unique value proposition in each of your chosen spaces.
- You know exactly why customers choose you over competing alternatives.
- Your competitive advantage in each space is defensible (hard or costly to copy).
- You clearly understand the key strengths and activities that produce your competitive advantage.
- You know the specific performance levels required to maintain your competitive advantage.
- You know which of your capabilities are most relevant to customers.
- You have systems in place to support and sustain your critical capabilities.
- You have a method to measure and evaluate the ongoing success of your strategy.
- You clearly understand and monitor the conditions that might present barriers to success.

In the remainder of this section we will first share the preferred deployment mechanism for getting strategies and goals for deploying them to sync across the company, then discuss how best to shape them. As W. Edwards Deming once said, "A goal without a method is cruel."

CATCHBALL ALIGNMENT

Catchball is a lean-based, multidirectional alignment mechanism that moves down, then across, then back up the organization. It is a method that works very well in culturally collaborative organizations. It does not work well, or at all, in strict chain-of-command organizations, such as military and paramilitary units, where orders are non-negotiable and flow only one way: down.

The term itself comes from the Japanese management concept of *nemawashi*, the practice of which is related to the art of bonsai and means "preparing the roots for transplanting." Catchball is basically a socialization technique. Here's how it works.

The high-level company Strategy Design (the "ball") is first "tossed" by the C-suite to the next level down—for example, all business unit leaders—who then design strategies that support and align with the integrated choices communicated in the upper-level strategy. Those strategies are shared horizontally among the business unit leaders to ensure alignment. Adjustments are made, then shared back up to ensure alignment with the company strategy. The process then trickles down to functional, departmental, team, workstream, and even individual levels.

Ideally, a business unit's Winning Aspiration is linked to and supports the company's Winning Aspiration. The Winning Aspirations of functions such as Marketing, Sales, Research, etc. are linked to and support the business unit's Winning Aspiration, and so forth. The same is true for where to play, how to win, critical capabilities, and management systems choices.

Having the entire organization conceptually aligned to key choices is a powerful step toward being synchronized for speed. Done right, Catchball produces the business equivalent of the well-known V-formation of migratory birds, high-performance fighter jet units like the Blue Angels, and professional cycling pelotons, all of which travel faster and further with less effort due to

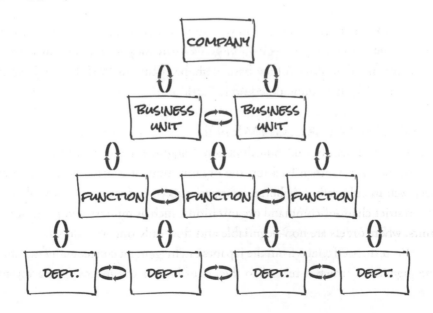

dramatically reduced drag. It also works to align and balance the wheels on our Formula 1 car.

The diagram on the previous page illustrates how Catchball is carried out.

Catchball Benefits

The Catchball process flips the typical strategy buy-in process on its head every bit as much as the Playing to Win framework in the Strategy Design phase does. Recall our strategic planning team from our earlier discussion who have spent weeks analyzing everything under the sun, then a few more weeks crafting the perfect plan containing the one right way forward and strong arguments for their case. Practicality, conformity, and financial certainty preside over creative but logically valid choice-making. They must now sell that document to key management to get their buy-in as the precursor to senior leadership approval and eventual execution. Bone-picking and deep dives into the numbers begin, as do tedious and often heated arguments over what is true or could be true, versus what would *have* to be true. Those arguments are inevitably followed by long and laborious negotiations and compromises on certain actions deemed risky, aggressive, or bureaucratically challenged, or all three. Difficult choices are diluted or ignored in favor of consensus. At the end of all that, senior leadership finally takes the marginalized plan, and after a cursory review sans insight and input, grants approval, and the mandate for execution is given. The process is quite literally a drag.

Catchball removes the time, pain, costliness, politicking, and lack of creativity. And instead of one lone strategy, there are many well-aligned supporting strategies, all with integrated choices. Buy-in is built in, not bolted on. Catchball produces a greater understanding of the capabilities critical to marketplace success of the company strategy. Strategic priorities are translated and integrated into the daily operations, processes, and workstreams.

In the end, Catchball significantly boosts strategic speed by reducing the drag. That is why it is used to cascade strategies as well as goals.

STRATEGIC PRIORITIES

With strategies in place at multiple levels, the question remains of what to work on. Most people struggle to translate a set of choices into daily action. We know we do. Neuroscience tells us that the average person can only focus on or remember seven things, plus or minus a couple. The challenge is that the collective number of goals required for any team to translate any given strategy into organized operations effectively is far greater than that. That's where Strategic Priorities come in: broad target categories and thematic goals sitting between a Winning Aspiration and shorter-term (and often temporary) objectives that guide coordination and delegation of the work to come. Having such a mental frame helps you segment goals, initiatives, and workstreams. Strategic Priorities provide a constant guiding beacon, helping you steer the ship in even the most violent of storms, when North Stars can't be seen and the path to true north runs through the rocky coastline.

For example, Toyota's Lexus strategy had several Strategic Priorities for the Engineering unit: Performance, Handling, Aerodynamics, Curb Weight, Noise, and Fuel Efficiency. Design had Comfort and Styling as their Strategic Priorities. Retail Operations had Dealer Selection, Dealer Standards, and Facilities. All of these had "World Class" as a defining vector.

Amazon Web Services in its early days might have had Strategic Priorities of Computing, Storage, and Database. Similarly, Uber's initial strategy for scaling up San Francisco might have had the three Strategic Priorities of Driver Team, Geographic Coverage, and Driver Satisfaction. A fintech ScaleUp we worked with that was looking to deploy a new strategy to move upmarket had Product Development, Inbound Marketing, Outbound Marketing, Business Development, and Customer Experience as their Strategic Priorities. The Operations business unit of a biotech firm Matt worked with had Strategic Priorities of Reliability, Efficiency, Agility, and Differentiation.

This is by no means a difficult or complicated step, yet it is often bypassed or forgotten. All too often, companies are so excited by their shiny new strategy and so eager to get going that they immediately dive into initiatives, workstreams, and projects. The original strategic focus becomes diluted by the shotgun approach to deployment. That presents a real problem and leaves leaders scratching their heads wondering what went wrong.

GOALS CASCADE

Finally, we come to the basic yet critical step of setting goals that provide measurable milestones and deliver concrete results that enable a team to know whether and to what degree their strategy is on course and working. These goals should cascade in the same way as the strategies they support, using the same Catchball process. Two mechanisms are designed specifically to enable well-aligned strategies to be synced to an equally well-aligned supporting deployment.

Hoshin kanri was first popularized in post-war Japan during the early 1950s and is attributed to Professor Yoji Akao, who taught that an organization's overarching strategic goals should guide action at every level of a business. The goal is to get everybody pointed in (and working toward) the same direction. *Hoshin* roughly translates to "compass needle" or "direction," while *kanri* roughly translates to "management" or "control." Over time the two terms have come to mean strategy deployment. Hoshin kanri is a staple of lean-oriented companies.

The younger, Western-born equivalent is widely practiced and well-known in tech circles as Objectives and Key Results, or OKRs. OKRs evolved from Peter Drucker's "management by objectives" (MBO), introduced in his classic 1954 book *The Practice of Management*. OKR was coined in the mid-1970s by Intel's legendary CEO Andy Grove, in his efforts to create a means to propel execution in his role as a senior engineering manager. Grove took Drucker's original concept of MBO, which had fallen out of favor as a mainstream practice, and improved it, making it more user-friendly, transparent, and engaging. While staying true to Drucker's core concept of using measurable objectives to manage a business, OKRs were everything MBO wasn't.

Instead of top-down edicts, OKRs were partially bottom-up, which in Grove's view promoted employee ownership and creativity. Instead of functionally siloed and opaque, OKRs were meant to be transparent and openly shared. Instead of an annual "set and forget" activity, OKRs were to be quarterly and flexible to accommodate shifting strategies and priorities. Instead of being tied to employee performance reviews and compensation, OKRs were not allowed to be used for those purposes. Instead of a long list of to-do items, OKRs were limited to a handful that were linked to strategic aspirations, and were thus intentionally audacious goals requiring innovative thinking to achieve versus a "business as usual" mindset. Instead of acting as key performance indicators (KPIs) on the business dashboard, OKRs were navigational in nature. Instead of a fuzzy wish list, OKRs were easily measurable. Instead of a spray-and-pray approach, OKRs were to be stewarded by designated or self-appointed "Sherpas," who worked with teams and individuals to develop their OKRs and ensure that they were structurally sound and linked appropriately across the company.

Grove was Intel's master Sherpa; he taught OKRs to all those in his charge, among them a young engineer named John Doerr, who after five years with Intel would go on to join Kleiner Perkins, a Silicon Valley venture firm he now chairs. Doerr actively encouraged Kleiner Perkins portfolio companies like Google to adopt OKRs. And we all know how that worked out.

Hoshin kanri and OKRs work the same way, and since OKRs are far more prevalent in the tech space, I'll use OKRs to talk about the Goals Cascade from here on.

In his 2018 book *Measure What Matters*, Doerr writes that Grove explained his simple but effective perspective on Management by Objectives this way: "Now, the two key phrases . . . are objectives and the key result. And they match the two purposes. The objective is the direction . . . the key result has to be measurable. But at the end you can look, and without any arguments: 'Did I do that, or did I not do it?' Yes. No. Simple. No judgments in it."

In practice, OKRs should be organized under Lighthouse Priorities and tied to annual goals, but are set, monitored, and reviewed quarterly, as originally conceived by Andy Grove. As former Google Ventures operating partner Rick Klau maintains, "OKRs tell you and your team clearly what exactly you are working on this quarter and, more importantly, what you are NOT."

The structure of OKRs is simple: three to five Objectives, each with three to five Key Results. The cascading mechanism is equally simple: a higher-level's Key Results become the basis for the Objectives of the next level down. That

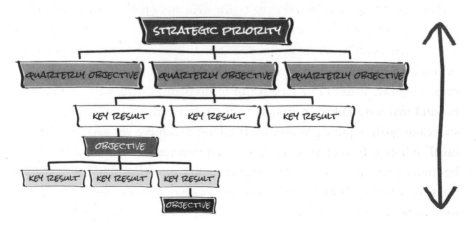

level then sets their Key Results, which become the Objectives of the next level down, and so on. The Catchball process is used throughout to ensure that the Goal Cascade is bidirectional.

Like any good framework, OKRs are accessible and allow for input and interpretation from all parts of the organization, including lower levels and outer edges. Team workshops are a fast and effective means to develop OKRs. To make things work smoothly, it helps to use a large canvas such as the one shown here that allows teams to focus on developing OKRs while simultaneously promoting transparency, engagement, and collaboration. (We have provided a link to download a digital copy in the Toolkit Resources section.) The vertical orientation helps show dependencies better than the horizontal orientation of most other tools. The canvas is easy to reproduce and tailor to your needs. Remote sessions using a digital version with online collaboration tools are just as effective as in-person workshops.

STRATEGIC PRIORITY			STRATEGIC PRIORITY			STRATEGIC PRIORITY		
	OBJECTIVE (Directional. "We will_____")			OBJECTIVE (Directional. "We will_____")			OBJECTIVE (Directional. "We will_____")	
KEY RESULT ("...as measured by _____.")	KEY RESULT ("...as measured by _____.")	KEY RESULT ("...as measured by _____.")	KEY RESULT ("...as measured by _____.")	KEY RESULT ("...as measured by _____.")	KEY RESULT ("...as measured by _____.")	KEY RESULT ("...as measured by _____.")	KEY RESULT ("...as measured by _____.")	KEY RESULT ("...as measured by _____.")
	OBJECTIVE (Directional. "We will_____")			OBJECTIVE (Directional. "We will_____")			OBJECTIVE (Directional. "We will_____")	
KEY RESULT ("...as measured by _____.")	KEY RESULT ("...as measured by _____.")	KEY RESULT ("...as measured by _____.")	KEY RESULT ("...as measured by _____.")	KEY RESULT ("...as measured by _____.")	KEY RESULT ("...as measured by _____.")	KEY RESULT ("...as measured by _____.")	KEY RESULT ("...as measured by _____.")	KEY RESULT ("...as measured by _____.")
	OBJECTIVE (Directional. "We will_____")			OBJECTIVE (Directional. "We will_____")			OBJECTIVE (Directional. "We will_____")	
KEY RESULT ("...as measured by _____.")	KEY RESULT ("...as measured by _____.")	KEY RESULT ("...as measured by _____.")	KEY RESULT ("...as measured by _____.")	KEY RESULT ("...as measured by _____.")	KEY RESULT ("...as measured by _____.")	KEY RESULT ("...as measured by _____.")	KEY RESULT ("...as measured by _____.")	KEY RESULT ("...as measured by _____.")

Ideally, the outcome of an OKR session should be shared openly, adjusted based on feedback, and fed into an easy-to-use system to track and communicate progress toward completion visually. Such a system does not need to be super-sophisticated, or even digital; however, for larger companies, software does help scale the management of OKRs, and thus facilitates Strategy Deployment. A word to the wise, however: do not let the tool become the purpose, lest you wish your OKR effort to go the way of the Time Management fad of the 1990s, which flamed out due to the entire concept of productivity being displaced by the activity of filling up day planners with endless and ultimately unproductive lists.

STRATEGIC SPEED RECAP

The principle of Strategic Speed is focused on the driveability of, in this case, a high-growth ScaleUp. It defines and provides context for the company's optimal strategic decision-making speed. Optimizing your Strategic Speed arms you to battle the evil forces of drag. Achieving Strategic Speed begins with replacing the conventional analyze-plan-execute model with one that frames strategy as a set of integrated choices. Those choices must permeate throughout the company using the collaborative Catchball process, a method used to create the organizational equivalent of slipstreams in the inverted "V" formation of cascading strategies and goals that sync up, down, and across the company, allowing teams to effectively draft off of each other.

CHECKPOINTS

☐ Does your company have clarity on Where to Play and How to Win?

☐ Do all business operations and functions have supporting strategies aligned to these choices?

☐ Does your company have clearly defined and relevant strategic priorities?

☐ Do all business operations and functions have contributing metrics?

☐ Are cascading goals in place to deploy strategies and achieve metrics?

Principle 2

CONSTANT EXPERIMENTATION

I've realized that the key to being successful is not how good your ideas are, it's how good you are at being able to find quick, cheap, and easy ways to try your ideas.
—**Marc Randolph, Cofounder and First CEO, Netflix**

A very successful young founder once told us about a nightmare she had: She arrives at her office on a typical Monday morning, but something seems off. In fact, everything feels very wrong. The buzz of growth, the energy, the engagement, the excitement of having just secured a generous Series C investment . . . all gone. The vibrant entrepreneurial spirit that defined her company as one to watch, a potential unicorn, has evaporated. Absent is the sense of urgency, that oh-so-productive fear of failure that actually spurred her team forward faster to prove the product viable and valuable, test after test. Everyone is in slow motion, going *through* the motions. Every discussion seems to revolve around asking her for more money, more people, and more space. Her people are consumed with promotions and bonuses, and every idea entails a costly program. Absent is the obsession with creating value for customers, and the only purpose she can detect is securing a budget. Expenses are outpacing sales, and her senior managers spend hours in endless cost-cutting meetings. Product adoption is waning, churn is rising, but new features just keep piling on. The lab-like curiosity that once coursed through the culture has been replaced by a defensive posture aimed at avoiding risk and protecting the status quo. Her once high-speed, free-spinning flywheel of growth has ground down, and sedentary inertia has set in.

Except . . . it's not a dream. It happens all the time.

THE ENTREPRENEUR'S NIGHTMARE

Without *it*, Facebook might have been just a campus photo directory, Amazon just another online retailer, and Google just another search engine. Without *it*, Netflix might have disappeared with the DVD, Apple might have faded away beside Nokia, and Toyota might have filed for bankruptcy like General Motors. The *it* is Constant Experimentation, the lifeblood of innovation, without which the sleep-stealing threat of stagnation and eventual irrelevance looms large.

The loss of constant experimentation as the primary lever of innovation is a loss at the most basic human level: learning. Learning and innovation go hand in hand, but learning comes first. For the record, we are not referring to formal education, which is primarily about transfer of existing knowledge. Rather, we are referring to the instinctive manner in which all humans create new knowledge through a discovery process that produces new insights. Learning is the sole goal of experimentation.

Learning is innate. Just watch children in high chairs experiment with how to put their food on the floor, using a variety of flicking and flinging. No need for training, coaching, or special systems and tools. In this kind of learning, the test comes *before* the lesson. There is no sense of failure, so the experimenters are free from fear. For the better part of five years, that kind of experimentation is repeated. As children learn to talk, they accumulate more data for themselves, augmenting and informing their experimentation with a single question that always sparks great learning: *Why?*

Everything changes once children enter the classroom, however. Fearless learning through testing is replaced by a different kind of learning. Teachers now ask the questions, and students must answer correctly. The need to be certain and correct grows. In a complete reversal of their early learning, a new kind of test happens, one that comes *after* the lesson. There is a right answer involved and a grade "F" for failure. Along comes a fear of the dreaded F. As the demands of homework assignments, quizzes, and tests grow, so does the need to plan time to prepare to avoid failure. It's not long before all of us know and understand the difference between tests and experiments: experiments are reserved for science class. Tests determine whether we advance or not.

That mindset travels with us throughout our formal education and follows us into our chosen careers. Instead of trying to please a teacher, we try to please the boss by giving the "right" answer." It should not come as a big surprise that experimentation is difficult and feels so foreign in many companies. It also helps explain why the Amazons, Googles, Netflixes, and Toyotas of the world remain long-lived market leaders: they hold constant experimentation as the *de facto* way to not only innovate, but to do better work. It *is* the work.

INNOVATION ANEMIA

Constant experimentation is the vehicle to rapidly move ideas into action. This is where Isaac Newton's first law comes in, suggesting that "a body at rest tends to stay at rest; a body in motion tends to stay in motion." In other words, there is a natural resistance to any change in your current state.

Inertia is the principle behind the "Flywheel Effect" metaphor for business success introduced by Jim Collins over two decades ago in his 2001 book *Good to Great*. A flywheel (like the one in your car, for example) is an energy-storing disk requiring significant energy to move it from rest, overcome the "moment of inertia," and make it start to spin. As the flywheel spins ever faster, it stores energy, enabling it to generate its own momentum, requiring less external input to maintain rapid spin. Collins argued that this is the moment in which companies go from good to great. His point was that no single act or special event is responsible for that moment, but that it is the culmination of a series of constant, self-reinforcing inputs that drives a virtuous cycle and powers the business long term.

Unfortunately, the concept was often misinterpreted to mean that once the flywheel is spinning fast enough, you can sort of kick back, relax, and just let it spin. The problem is that no flywheel, physical or metaphorical, can spin indefinitely on its own momentum, because the other physical forces—drag and friction—slow it down. In other words, if you stop feeding the flywheel, stop doing the things that allowed you to spin it up in the first place, the flywheel eventually returns to its initial state of rest, requiring that same enormous first effort to overcome the inertia. When you turn off your car's ignition, for example, your flywheel spins down. All that stored energy is wasted, dissipated in the form of heat. Business inertia works in much the same way, except that the spin-down can be a nightmare.

Constant experimentation is one of the most critical inputs required to initiate as well as sustain a flywheel for both rapid growth and long-term success.

Sadly, it is also among the first activities to be abandoned once performance is humming along or begins to slow. Sudden disruption of a flywheel in motion allows resting inertia to regain purchase, a condition that will almost certainly produce the kind of situation our young founder described in her nightmare.

While every company will exhibit its own unique pattern of decline, here is what we have observed happens inside companies whose founders and leaders no longer demand continuous learning and drive constant experimentation. We call it "innovation anemia" and is its own flywheel spinning in the wrong direction. Here's how it works.

Revenue grows quickly and the old cliche "if ain't broke don't fix it" becomes the prevailing mindset, which for a technology company is ironic since it is so antithetical to how the company most likely began in the first place. Intentional experimentation, once at the heart of the startup, is not prioritized. Thus, the pipeline of customer-value-adding innovations recedes, replaced by a strong planning and program mentality: sell a big program, get rewarded and recognized by the boss, and receive more resources in the form of bodies and budget, regardless of whether they add value.

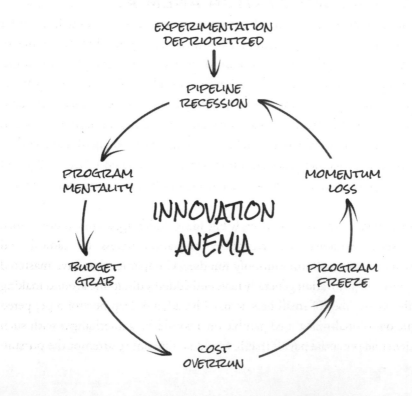

The focus now becomes meeting an enlarged budget. Company expenses then rise faster than sales, which is the antithesis of scaling. That in turn limits organizational effectiveness, requiring even more work to execute the program, leading to requests for more resources. Speedbumps get erected, usually in the form of heavy-handed governance and oversight. But when expenses escalate and grow faster than revenue, cost-cutting is sure to follow. Any potentially valuable innovative initiatives that might still be underway or on the horizon are put on the back burner or frozen, leading to a loss of mobility and momentum, furthering the effects of innovation anemia.

This downward spiral can eventually stop innovation cold and can even destroy the company, no matter how big or successful it once was. To be fair, this cycle happens far more in grownups than in ScaleUps, but we've worked with enough of the latter to detect the precursors to innovation anemia long before the company actually becomes symptomatic. We've found that leaders of companies on a unicorn trajectory understand all of this at a visceral level and remain ever-vigilant for any indication of innovation anemia.

DETECTING INNOVATION ANEMIA

There are several tell-tale signs of innovation anemia. Some companies suffer from an identity crisis, struggling with their innovation DNA, unable to pinpoint their strength and style. Some labor with overly complex definitions and requirements that make innovation inaccessible to the everyman. Others neglect to craft an innovation strategy, leaving them without a means to focus resources effectively. Talent mismatch plagues many companies as they grow and scale, and they often make the mistake of moving "high potential managers"— generally master planners and executors—into roles related to the messy and uncertain world of innovation, where testing and failure are the currency, not revenue.

Then there is the obsession with big ideas, killer apps, and moon shots. Many executives don't even recognize innovation unless it's radical and disruptive, favoring a home-run-only mindset. Companies that have mastered company-wide innovation generally have embedded a discipline around making a significant number of small bets across a broad and deep portfolio peppered with the occasional well-timed gamble on a would-be gamechanger with such an undeniable potential payoff that it would be silly not to attempt the pursuit.

Amazon chairman Jeff Bezos put it this way in his 2015 letter to shareholders:

Outsized returns often come from betting against conventional wisdom, and conventional wisdom is usually right. Given a ten percent chance of a 100 times payoff, you should take that bet every time. But you're still going to be wrong nine times out of ten. We all know that if you swing for the fences, you're going to strike out a lot, but you're also going to hit some home runs. The difference between baseball and business, however, is that baseball has a truncated outcome distribution. When you swing, no matter how well you connect with the ball, the most runs you can get is four. In business, every once in a while, when you step up to the plate, you can score 1,000 runs. This long-tailed distribution of returns is why it's important to be bold.[1]

A little over a year after Bezos wrote that, Amazon bought Whole Foods Market, a move that was viewed at least partially as an audacious experiment in experimentation *for* experimentation, rather than a pure acquisition play. Amazon would be able to experiment in a physical retail space and apply that learning to what we now know as Amazon Fresh and Amazon Go.

That leads us to what is by far the most telling sign of innovation anemia: weak experimentation muscle. In companies both young and old, what we often find purported to be their "innovation method" is in reality a program proposal or planning process focused on delivering projected business results, rather than a more experimental method focused on learning. The innovatively challenged (dare we say dysfunctional?) company places far more importance on data-backed prediction, preferring the illusion of certainty over running simple experiments that cost a tiny fraction of the time and money of an exhaustive data analysis and algorithm-based forecasts.

When it comes to innovation, the mindset cannot be "We know what will work and I'm going to ensure that it does. All we need is the resources to push it through." Rather, it must be "We're not sure this will work, so let's try it out quickly." The former leads to big bets, huge projects, and risky initiatives, while the latter leads to little bets, rapid-fire experimentation, and inexpensive yet valuable insights.

One very practical problem with the big project mentality is that we have a universal tendency to underestimate the time and cost of completing larger, longer-term projects. Nobel-winning economist Daniel Kahneman coined a term for this more than forty years ago, calling it the "Planning Fallacy." (Recall our distinction between strategy as a set of choices to be tested versus a plan to be executed.) We take on far more than we should, routinely exaggerating the benefits and discounting the risks. We overscope, overscale, and oversell. At the same time, we underestimate, underresource, and underplan. As a result, major projects are rarely completed on time, within budget, with the original team, and do not do exactly what they were supposed to do. When it comes to innovation, that big, costly, risky venture can become the very act that not only sparks innovation anemia, but eventually stops innovation cold.

Innovative entrepreneurs know that finding a product/market fit without experimentation with customers is next to impossible. Yet, as the company grows in size and complexity, the muscle memory of the need to innovate can fade, for all the reasons previously cited.

Like many technology leaders, Intuit founder Scott Cook understands the very real dangers of inertia and innovation anemia, which explains why the company institutionalized the principle of "Rapid Experiments with Customers" as one of three pillars of their "Design for Delight" method of innovation.

Rather than offer a comprehensive treatise on innovation or even ideation, our specific aim here is to focus narrowly on the kinetic energy driving innovation—experimentation—and to offer a leaner view of the process, one that can help you keep your innovation engine revving high by reducing the forces of inertia. In our experience, the root cause of inertia nearly always is a shortage of constant, company-wide experimentation.

Experimentation makes innovation possible. It freshens mature products and matures fresh products. It produces significant competitive advantage, so much so that Formula 1 teams face strict limitations on how much testing they are allowed to do, both in-season and off.

A LEANER VIEW OF EXPERIMENTATION

We have no desire to delve into the source and shape of business ideas here. It doesn't matter whether they come from a sudden creative insight while taking a walk along the shore, an observation of customers who use a product in an unexpected way, an artificially intelligent analysis of the exhaust emitted from a vast pool of data, or insights emerging from hundreds of A/B tests entailing ten thousand API calls. We are concerned here with the *implementation* of ideas, because the most interesting part for a would-be unicorn isn't the idea itself; the most interesting part is what should be done with the idea to produce scalable, sustainable business value.

The short answer is *experiment.*

THE EXPERIMENTATION FLYWHEEL

We have the advantage of being able to blend several significant experiences with experimentation over the past two decades: from being an integral part of an organization that today runs well over three thousand experiments a day (Toyota), to working closely on enterprise strategy with one of the top three most valuable companies in the world (Amazon Web Services), to extensive application of user-centered design methodology featuring rapid iterative prototyping (Design Thinking), to frequent thought-trading with MIT's experimentation expert Michael Schrage, author of *Serious Play* and *The Innovator's Hypothesis.* We can pull from, mash up, and distill the best experimentation practices into a universally applicable protocol for constant experimentation.

Enter the Rapid Experimentation Flywheel, a high-impact, lightweight, continuous cycle of business experimentation. *Lightweight* means cheap in terms of resource load. *High-impact* means experiments that address company strategic challenges. Lightweight is very important because there are only two ways to increase the momentum of any flywheel: increase the moment of inertia by increasing the wheel's mass or increase how fast it spins. Doubling the weight of a flywheel doubles the energy, but doubling the spin velocity *quadruples* the energy. The lighter and more compact the flywheel, the faster it can spin.

As with any flywheel, pushing at any point of the Rapid Experimentation Flywheel starts the spin. But let's start at the top.

Irrespective of origin—a strategy priority, a data analysis, a customer support function, a formal customer listening and observation effort, an experiment, or a rare and unexpected sudden flash of creative inspiration—let's say a **Fresh Opportunity** to create future customer value presents itself. It could come in the form of a customer problem or pain point, a stated need, a customer request or suggestion, a competitor analysis, a new trend in user metrics, a customer experience mapping exercise, a new insight from an experiment, or a formal company challenge.

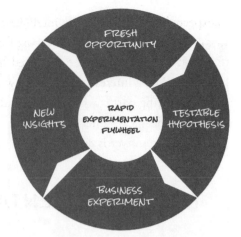

If it's big, compelling, or important enough, it produces an immediate need to generate a **Testable Hypothesis**. This is best defined as a belief that can be disproven about creating customer value, the basic structure of which is the if/then format, and that includes some measurable business outcome that will determine whether the hypothesis is true or false.

That measure must represent something the business cares about. In other words, you need a way to assess the value you believe you will create and someday capture. A good Testable Hypothesis drives an urgent need to run a **Business Experiment**, defined as a fast, cheap, easily repeatable, and scalable test of the hypothesis. The purpose of running a Business Experiment is to discover **New Insights** that in turn produce more Fresh Opportunities to create future value for customers.

Best-in-class innovators document every experiment as any good scientist does. The reason we know, for example, that a company like Toyota runs well over a million operational experiments each year is that they can be found on a document in a central database, which doubles as a global knowledge resource. You don't need a sophisticated tracking system, but if you're going to build a culture of experimentation, you need some way to monitor and measure the effort. A simple four-square template like the one shown below works well as a starting point.

TOOLKIT: RAPID EXPERIMENT FOUR-SQUARE

FRESH OPPORTUNITY	TESTABLE HYPOTHESIS
How might we create value for customers? What is the source of this opportunity? What is most compelling about this opportunity (e.g., size, impact, etc.)?	What is our falsifiable belief about the opportunity? (We believe that if we do X, then customers will do Y.) What do we want to learn? What business outcomes will be affected?
BUSINESS EXPERIMENT	**NEW INSIGHTS**
What simple, quick, cheap, and scalable experiment will test our hypothesis? What is the target metric? Is the experiment easy to replicate?	What did we guess would happen? What actually happened? Why the difference? What is our next step?

The Rapid Experimentation Flywheel provides a simple systems approach that fosters company-wide innovation through a high-velocity learning cycle. Now, some may say that the secret to organizational innovation is "culture." We wouldn't argue that point at all. It's just that "the system" lies at the root and gives rise to culture. You cannot change a culture without changing the underlying system. The system bats last.

UNPACKING THE RAPID EXPERIMENTATION FLYWHEEL

Before taking a closer look at each of the push points on the Rapid Experimentation Flywheel, it is worth noting that business experimentation is a breed apart from scientific experimentation. Science experiments focus on proving a hypothesis centered on some fundamental truth about the natural world. They happen in a sterile laboratory, a closed and strictly controlled environment. Business experiments, on the other hand, are carried out in the volatile, uncertain, complex, ambiguous (VUCA) world of commerce. And while they obviously revolve around hypotheses, they have a much different focus, one related to *economics*. We believe that one big reason more companies don't embrace constant experimentation, or abandon it once they have found a product/market fit and begin to scale rapidly, is that they forget that the core purpose of business experimentation is *investment*: investment in innovation, and investment in the very future of the company. Markets constantly shift, new ones are created every day, and customers are nothing if not fickle when it comes to what they desire at any point in time. In a VUCA world, constant experimentation is the only way to keep up with the pace of change, the only way to *lead* change.

Michael Schrage makes the point about investment being the experimentation raison d'etre in *The Innovator's Hypothesis* by drawing an analogy to Warren Buffet's approach. Buffet is a unicorn many times over—a "decacorn"—not because he is extraordinarily brilliant or has a crystal ball, but because he is a bargain hunter. Buffet knows that it takes no genius to buy a dollar's worth of value for a dollar; the genius is finding a way to buy a dollar's worth of value for fifty cents. Business experimentation has the same economical intent. That's what separates it from pure scientific experimentation.

Business experimentation is a hunt for New Insights into customer value creation on the cheap. It's not about proving or disproving an elaborate hypothesis, but about discovering a scalable inroad to innovation as quickly, cheaply, and as easily as possible. There has never been a great innovator who was not first a great experimenter. Nearly every game-changing innovation can be traced to a simple experiment, and most modern, digitally native companies were founded on a series of simple, fast, and frugal experiments with real customers and users "in the wild."

Fresh Opportunities

The proliferation of increasingly intelligent mobile devices, e-commerce, social media, internet of things (IOT), and cloud-based software services has led to an unprecedented explosion in the number of customer touchpoints and interactions a company sees daily. Everything and everyone is connected. The sheer volume of data exhaust emitted is staggering and provides information to be analyzed in search of patterns that might point out business problems and opportunities. Supercomputer power and machine learning have become integral parts of the innovation arsenal. The playing field for business experimentation is expanding exponentially.

But data alone is not a complete substitute for closely observing how customers engage with your product, even if that observation relies on a digital footprint for tracking and measurement. The reasons are simple. First, even the most sophisticated data analysis yields predominantly historical correlations, but correlation is not causation. Second, computers can't frame, question, and probe as well as humans can. At least not yet. Third, computers are not wired to care. At least not yet.

User-centered design begins with empathy: data alone cannot offer the kind of deep, empathic understanding of human need that comes from spending quality time with customers: watching, questioning, listening. That's where the best and freshest opportunities come from.

Fresh opportunities for experimentation abound. Sometimes they are right in front of us. We just need to improve our eyesight a bit. In the Toyota world, this principle is so central that it is a formal element of the company's Tao or "way," and one of three tenets comprising Toyota's core value of continuous improvement. It's called *Genchi Genbutsu*, roughly "go look, go see." The actual language in the original Toyota Way document reads: "We practice Genchi Genbutsu . . . go to the source to find the facts to make correct decisions, build consensus, and achieve goals at our best speed." If you will recall, this is exactly what the Lexus team did when they observed the American luxury buyer for several months before even thinking about vehicle design. They *became* the luxury buyer (for a while, anyway).

In the Amazon world, the same basic principle is referred to as "working backward"; meaning to start with understanding the customer's problem, and work backward from that to create new solutions.

In helping biotech leader Amgen begin a formal adoption of Design Thinking in 2016, one of our first objectives was to gain a deeper and more empathic understanding of patients on Amgen regimens. At the time, it was against legal policy to directly contact actual end-users, so we took a broader view, choosing to spend the day with patient proxies: those suffering from diseases Amgen targeted but who were taking competitive pharmaceuticals. We watched, interviewed, videotaped, and took pictures for as long as an individual would allow. As you can imagine, data on usage, dosage, and compliance was readily available, but none of it produced the kind of deep understanding and insights we gained from synthesizing our in-field observations. Dozens of fresh opportunities for experimenting and improving the patient experience presented themselves, more than enough to keep us busy for several years.

Had you been strolling through a shopping mall in Northern California forty years ago, chances are you might have been approached by a man introducing himself as Scott, a programmer for a fairly new item called a personal computer, asking you if he could watch you install his product, which he called Quicken. Intuit cofounder Scott Cook is one of the most insightful executives you could ever hope to spend time with, and working with his company was one of the most enjoyable engagements, undoubtedly owing to the organization's embrace of lean thinking.

"Adoption is driven much more by understanding the customer's psychology than it is by technology," Scott advises. "The technology is there; what's missing is an understanding of how customers actually think and work." From Scott's early belief in mingling with customers to find fresh opportunities sprang Intuit's formal practice, called "Follow Me Home." Executive chairman of the board Brad Smith once shared how even when he was CEO he would personally spend some sixty hours each year peeking over the shoulders of users in their small business segment, watching and learning not only how they used Intuit software, but how they worked in general: what they paid attention to, what influenced their action, and, inevitably, how they thought.

The more you watch, the more you understand. It doesn't matter how much data you have collected or how robust your artificial intelligence algorithm is; to consistently discover Fresh Opportunities to experiment and innovate, try getting out more. Get to know your customers better. Fun fact: there is even a Get to Know Your Customers Day four times a year in the U.S., observed on the third Thursday of each calendar quarter.

To further unpack the Rapid Experimentation Flywheel, let's use a real-world example: the Enterprise Strategy group at Amazon Web Services (AWS).

Amazon has a strong culture of experimentation, with a unique set of principles, processes, and practices that work together as a high-speed innovation system. AWS shares that culture. The Enterprise Strategy group is a rather elite team of digital transformation experts—former CIOs, CISOs, CTOs, CDOs—that in previous roles led successful large-scale cloud migrations in legacy Fortune 500–level corporations. The group's charter is to help replicate that success for AWS enterprise clients by drawing on their real-world experience to guide and advise on cloud adoption strategy.

One key challenge the Enterprise Strategy team faced was helping enterprise clients take the first step. Nearly all of the enterprise clients struggled with that. It was a clear and present problem, and often an urgent need.

When you've led a successful migration at scale, it's easy to forget the early problems and pains, stalls and stumbles, and lack of confidence and certainty. Most members of the team had led just one large-scale digital transformation, which translates to a single data point that may not necessarily be the best or broadest base from which to offer advice. It's tempting to focus on the recipe for success and gloss over the difficulties. And whatever worked well in your kitchen may not work as well in someone else's. To improve their effectiveness as an advisory group, the AWS team needed to better understand their customers.

Pre-COVID, current and future enterprise customers would regularly visit Amazon's Executive Business Center (EBC) in Seattle at the invitation of the account team. During day-long visits, a prospective customer would be treated to an overview of the AWS offerings, which included spending ninety minutes with some of the Enterprise Strategy team. Rather than treat that time as a one-way sales presentation, the team saw it as a fresh opportunity to not only better understand customers, but also to help customers understand what the appropriate first step *for them* might be.

Working backward, the team looked at verbatim comments from post-EBC surveys. One theme came through loud and clear: "Enterprise customers find it difficult to know for sure what the right step is in moving their business to the cloud." The next step was to translate the problem into a How Might We question, which we introduced in our discussion of Strategic Speed.

Crafting a good How Might We question is an art. We like to think of the process of arriving at a good one as *framestorming*. The goal is to transpose a problem statement into a statement of opportunity. There are several reasons for that. First, problem statements worded in negative terms—"It's difficult to do X" or "It's unclear how to do Y"—are too limiting in terms of coming up with possibilities to pursue and experiment with. Second, they almost presuppose an unhelpful solution—"Make X easier," "Make Y clearer."

A good How Might We question strikes just the right balance of positivity and scope. It suggests a number of different hypotheses to test, yet is not so broad that it offers no strong guidance. It offers a means by which a number of different ways to approach the opportunity can be evaluated. And it has a bit of inspiration built in, so that people want to engage fully in taking on the challenge.

After considering several different versions, the actual wording chosen was, "How might we enable enterprise customers to quickly discover, choose, and take their best first step toward the cloud?" In other words, the team wanted to help enterprise clients overcome inertia and start their own cloud migration flywheel spinning.

Testable Hypothesis

It's amazing how many definitions and interpretations exist for *hypothesis*. The common theme in all of them is *testability*.

A good Testable Hypothesis in the context of business is a *falsifiable* belief about how to create *measurable* value. Testing might easily refute your hypothesis. Crafting a falsifiable hypothesis is not easy, because it is not natural or intuitive. While accepting a 2016 Pathfinder Award for his contributions to the future of flight at Seattle's Museum of Flight, Amazon's Jeff Bezos confirmed as much when discussing the core Amazon leadership principle of "Be right a lot," putting it this way:

Humans, as we go about life, are mostly very selective in the evidence we let seep into us. We like to observe the evidence that confirms our pre-existing beliefs. People who are right a lot work very hard to do that unnatural thing of trying to disconfirm their beliefs.[2]

This lands us on the doorstep of failure. In that same year, Bezos addressed failure, innovation, and experimentation in his letter to shareholders:

One area where I think we are especially distinctive is failure. I believe we are the best place in the world to fail (we have plenty of practice!), and failure and invention are inseparable twins. To invent you have to experiment, and if you know in advance that it's going to work, it's not an experiment. Most large organizations embrace the idea of invention, but are not willing to suffer the string of failed experiments necessary to get there.[3]

If you're halfway worried that your hypothesis might be refuted by an experiment, then it's probably a good one. The nice thing about experimentation is that there really is no failure, because the goal is not success, the goal is to learn. Think of your most powerful, most meaningful learning experience. For most people, it didn't involve overwhelming success, certainly not at first, but rather a difficult struggle and a good bit of failure.

Most people were taught how to construct a basic formal hypothesis in junior high school science labs. We learned about cause and effect, which we had instantly learned years earlier, when for the first time we fell down the stairs or ran too fast or touched the hot stovetop. We learned how to word a hypothesis in order to spell out the relationship between action (cause) and outcome (effect) with a simple if/then format: "We believe that if we do X, then Y will happen." We learned that if we couldn't actually test out the hypothesis, we needed a new and better one that was testable. We learned that our hypothesis needed to be specific and precise, ideally focusing on one discrete outcome. Finally, we learned that we had to have some measurable way to confirm or refute our hypothesis. All of which is to say that we don't have to learn anything new; we just need to recall and refresh the knowledge we perhaps have left dormant for a time and point it toward the business opportunity we want to address.

The salient differences between our school-age experiments and business experiments concern learning objectives and measurable outcomes. Business experiments are intended to produce new, vital, and often surprising insights into how to create meaningful value for customers, and the measurables include desired business outcomes like quality, cost, speed, experience, revenue, margin, usage, engagement, etc.

The AWS Enterprise Strategy team's hypothesis: "We believe that if we provide our enterprise customers with a guiding framework, then they will be able to determine the right first step for their cloud migration strategy in less than 90 minutes." The team also believed that the best way to deliver that framework might be through a visual canvas. Prototyping began immediately.

Rapid iterative prototyping is a discrete step in Design Thinking, but we hold the view that a prototype *is* a hypothesis. When you build a prototype, you're producing a tangible hypothesis. Irrespective of whether it's paper, clay, or code, when you are constructing a prototype, you are constructing a hypothesis. If you haven't constructed a hypothesis about what you're building, you're building something other than a prototype. Perhaps assembling a finished product. If you write out your hypothesis and do nothing with it, it's simply a sentence.

Multiple design sessions generating a progression of eight iterative versions allowed the team to arrive at a preferred Testable Hypothesis in the form of a prototype framework eventually called the AWS Cloud Strategy Canvas, ready for testing. (The images that follow show a sampling of interim versions. Image 1 shows the first iteration (page 74). Image 2 shows an intermediate iteration (page 75). Image 3 shows the testable version (page 76).)

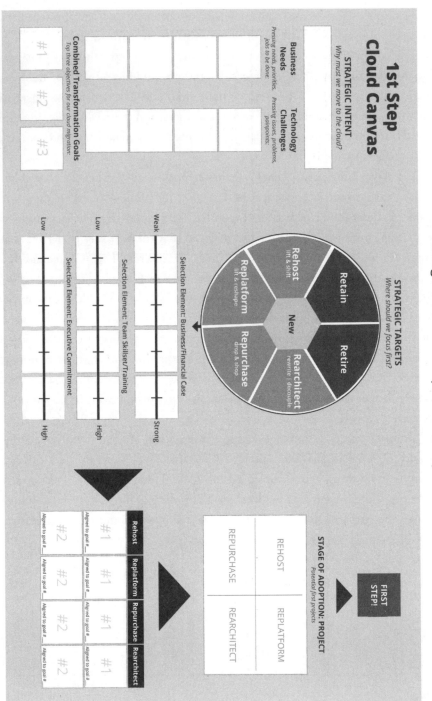

Image 1. Version 1.0. (not testable)

Image 2. Version 1.4 (not testable)

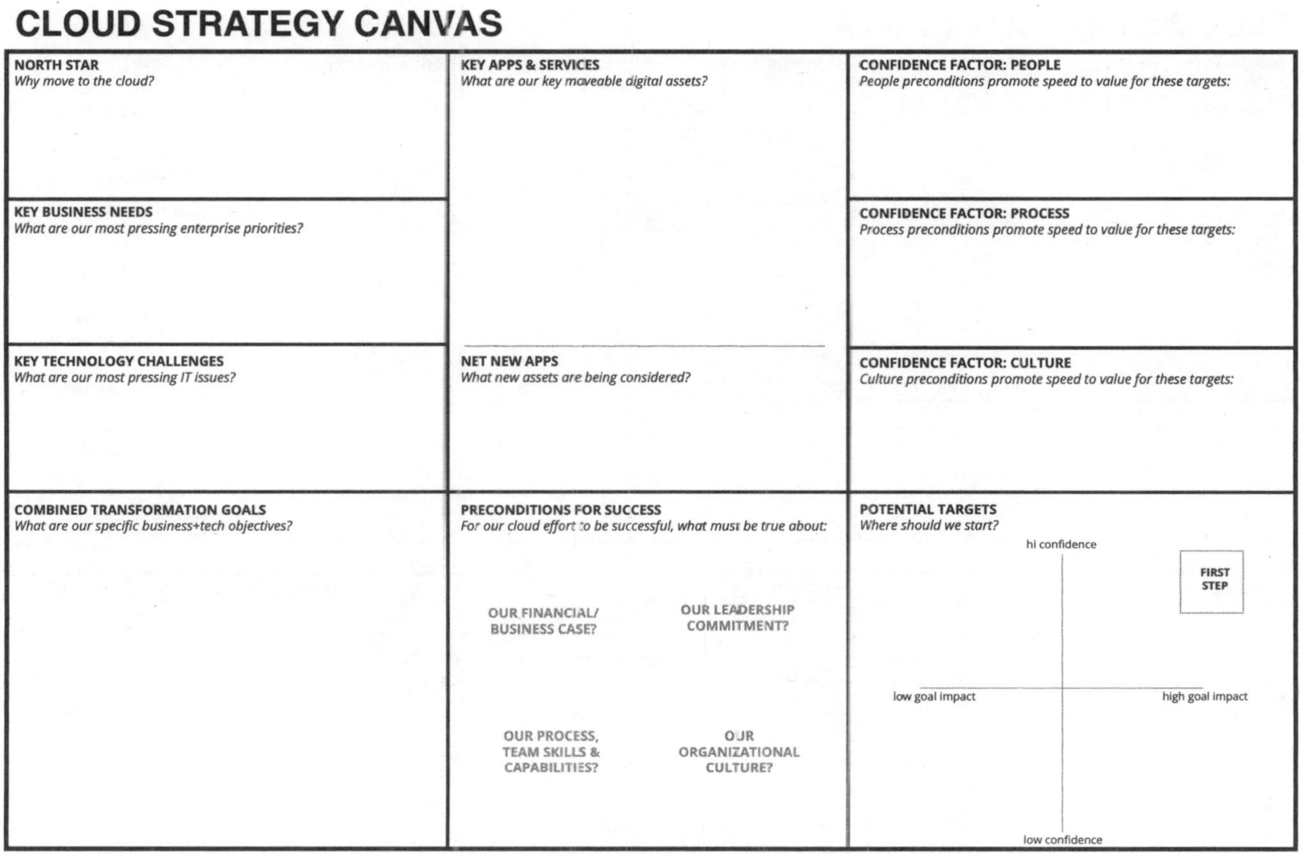

CLOUD STRATEGY CANVAS

NORTH STAR
Why move to the cloud?

KEY BUSINESS NEEDS
What are our most pressing enterprise priorities?

KEY TECHNOLOGY CHALLENGES
What are our most pressing IT issues?

COMBINED TRANSFORMATION GOALS
What are our specific business+tech objectives?

KEY APPS & SERVICES
What are our key moveable digital assets?

NET NEW APPS
What new assets are being considered?

PRECONDITIONS FOR SUCCESS
For our cloud effort to be successful, what must be true about:

OUR FINANCIAL/
BUSINESS CASE?

OUR LEADERSHIP
COMMITMENT?

OUR PROCESS,
TEAM SKILLS &
CAPABILITIES?

OUR
ORGANIZATIONAL
CULTURE?

CONFIDENCE FACTOR: PEOPLE
People preconditions promote speed to value for these targets:

CONFIDENCE FACTOR: PROCESS
Process preconditions promote speed to value for these targets:

CONFIDENCE FACTOR: CULTURE
Culture preconditions promote speed to value for these targets:

POTENTIAL TARGETS
Where should we start?

FIRST
STEP

hi confidence

low goal impact — high goal impact

low confidence

Image 3. Version 1.8 (Testable)

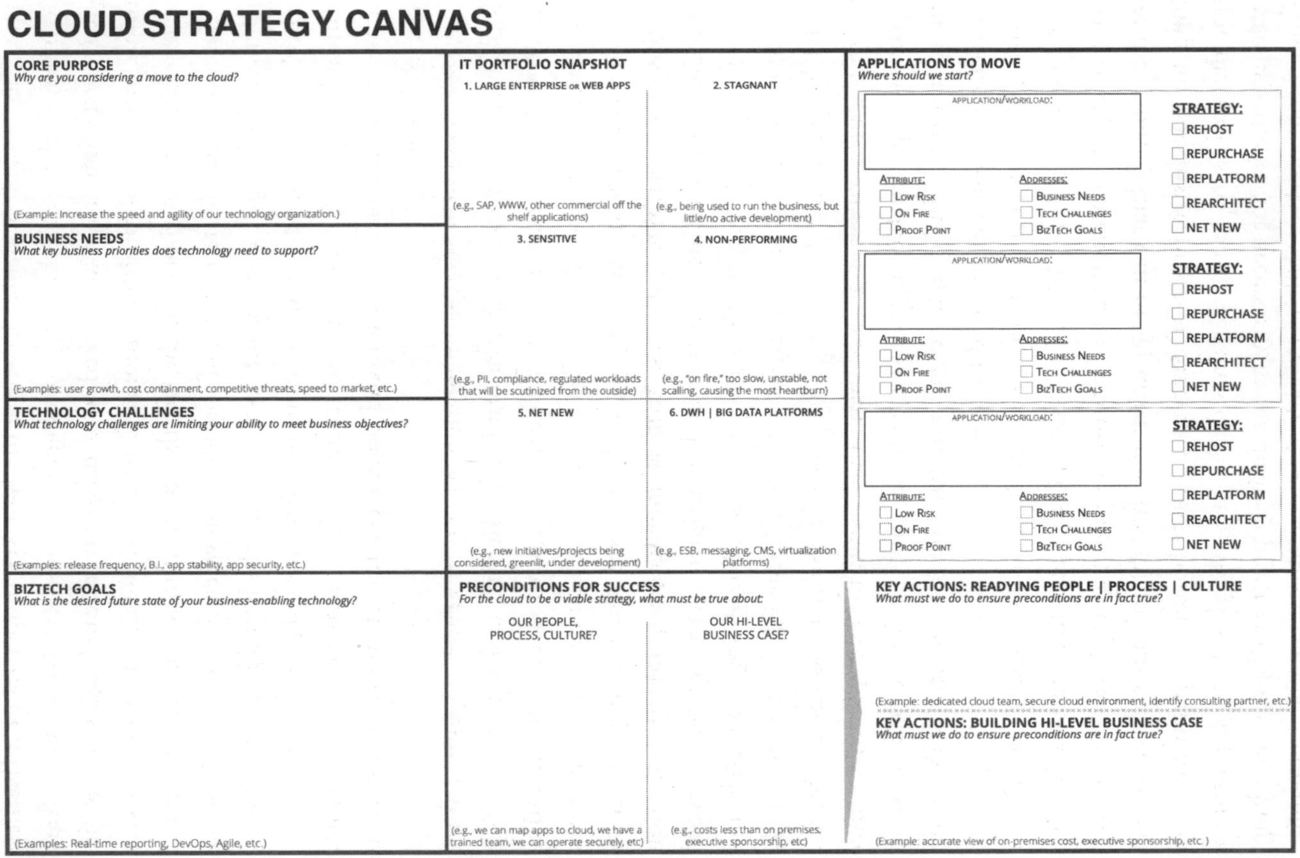

CLOUD STRATEGY CANVAS

CORE PURPOSE
Why are you considering a move to the cloud?

BUSINESS NEEDS
What key business priorities does technology need to support?

(Example: increase the speed and agility of our technology organization.)

TECHNOLOGY CHALLENGES
What technology challenges are limiting your ability to meet business objectives?

(Examples: user growth, cost containment, competitive threats, speed to market, etc.)

BIZTECH GOALS
What is the desired future state of your business-enabling technology?

(Examples: release frequency, B.I., app stability, app security, etc.)

(Examples: Real-time reporting, DevOps, Agile, etc.)

IT PORTFOLIO SNAPSHOT

1. LARGE ENTERPRISE or WEB APPS	2. STAGNANT
(e.g. SAP, WWW, other commercial off the shelf applications)	(e.g. being used to run the business, but little/no active development)
3. SENSITIVE	4. NON-PERFORMING
(e.g. PII, compliance, regulated workloads that will be scrutinized from the outside)	(e.g. "on fire," too slow, unstable, not scaling, causing the most heartburn)
5. NET NEW	6. DWH	BIG DATA PLATFORMS
(e.g. new initiatives/projects being considered, greenfill, under development)	(e.g. ESB, messaging, CMS, virtualization platforms)

PRECONDITIONS FOR SUCCESS
For the cloud to be a viable strategy, what must be true about:

OUR PEOPLE,
PROCESS, CULTURE?

OUR HI-LEVEL
BUSINESS CASE?

(e.g. we can map apps to cloud, we have a trained team, we can operate securely, etc.)

(e.g. costs less than on premises, executive sponsorship, etc.)

APPLICATIONS TO MOVE
Where should we start?

APPLICATION/WORKLOAD:

ATTRIBUTE:
- [ ] Low Risk
- [ ] On Fire
- [ ] Proof Point

ADDRESSES:
- [ ] Business Needs
- [ ] Tech Challenges
- [ ] BizTech Goals

STRATEGY:
- [ ] REHOST
- [ ] REPURCHASE
- [ ] REPLATFORM
- [ ] REARCHITECT
- [ ] NET NEW

APPLICATION/WORKLOAD:

ATTRIBUTE:
- [ ] Low Risk
- [ ] On Fire
- [ ] Proof Point

ADDRESSES:
- [ ] Business Needs
- [ ] Tech Challenges
- [ ] BizTech Goals

STRATEGY:
- [ ] REHOST
- [ ] REPURCHASE
- [ ] REPLATFORM
- [ ] REARCHITECT
- [ ] NET NEW

APPLICATION/WORKLOAD:

ATTRIBUTE:
- [ ] Low Risk
- [ ] On Fire
- [ ] Proof Point

ADDRESSES:
- [ ] Business Needs
- [ ] Tech Challenges
- [ ] BizTech Goals

STRATEGY:
- [ ] REHOST
- [ ] REPURCHASE
- [ ] REPLATFORM
- [ ] REARCHITECT
- [ ] NET NEW

KEY ACTIONS: READYING PEOPLE | PROCESS | CULTURE
What must we do to ensure preconditions are in fact true?

(Example: dedicated cloud team, secure cloud environment, identify consulting partner, etc.)

KEY ACTIONS: BUILDING HI-LEVEL BUSINESS CASE
What must we do to ensure preconditions are in fact true?

(Example: accurate view of on premises cost, executive sponsorship, etc.)

Business Experiment

Simple. Fast. Frugal. Scalable. These are the four key properties of a Business Experiment. Taken together they distinguish a Business Experiment from a science experiment. Matt worked as a part-time research assistant at the National Institutes of Health's National Cancer Institute during his senior year in college, and he can vouch for the fact that none of these four characteristics was given even the slightest degree of consideration when devising experiments.

Simple, fast, frugal, and scalable tests accelerate the Rapid Experimentation Flywheel, producing a steady stream of New Insights and more Fresh Opportunities. *Simple* means easy to replicate. *Fast* means hours or days, not months. *Frugal* means a few thousand dollars per test at most. *Scalability* is next-level though!

Scalable, cloud-based experimentation has taken center stage as a force multiplier of innovation. SaaS platforms like Tricentis and Optimizely (see interview with Alex Atzberger) have made rapid, automated, continuous testing in the cloud at scale possible, accelerating the pace of innovation like never before. Increased speed, reduced cost, and decreased risk multiply the other three Business Experiment qualities. Artificial intelligence–powered simulation has produced software development and experimentation capability several orders of magnitude greater than even the best of traditional research and development processes. It's entirely possible that linear R&D may be wholly replaced by networked T&S—test and scale—in the not too distant future. Much of the unicorn set is already there; they know, for example, that rather than consuming valuable engineering resources running simple A/B tests, it's far more scalable to build lightweight infrastructure for non-tech staff to run A/B experiments without the need to code.

Still, confusion surrounds business experimentation—what it is, what it isn't. As for what it isn't, Albert Einstein spelled it out quite succinctly: "No amount of experimentation can ever prove me right; a single experiment can prove me wrong." That can be an unsettling thought for business executives looking for conclusive proof of concept through business experimentation. Again, the goal is to learn, to gain valuable new insights from exploring a testable hypothesis, not necessarily to conclusively prove or disprove anything. Customers and markets will be the sole determinants of whether something "works" or not. The most we can hope for from a good business experiment is shortening the odds of creating meaningful value, some degree of confidence that our hypothesis does not represent a completely unworkable idea, and a prompt to take the next creative step.

We often get some form of "Then why bother?" when we explain this basic principle of experimentation, especially to non-product-focused executives (not necessarily founders) of rapidly growing technology ScaleUps. The answer is that we really have no choice if we want to continue to grow, scale, and innovate, because the risks and costs of not experimenting are simply too high. We gently remind them of how the company was in all probability founded. We might even remind them of the "great stumble" high-flying Netflix took when in 2011 it ran counter to its own culture of experimentation in favor of running full steam ahead with a sweeping go-to-market stroke: separating the DVD rental business from the emerging streaming video business without a single test. Customers were angry, analysts were stunned, and the resulting 50 percent plummet in stock price reflected both sentiments. The Netflix brand took a big hit, the company lost thousands of customers and billions in market cap, and cofounder Reed Hastings had to make a public apology. All because testing a critical assumption (what should have been a worrisome What Must Be True) in some small way was deemed too expensive or unnecessary, or both.

A small cohort from the AWS Enterprise Strategy group ran controlled experimental agendas that included ninety-minute modules with customers using the Cloud Strategy Canvas over several weeks, in parallel with ongoing day-long EBC meetings using the standard agenda. It was good old A/B testing as most people know it, and low-tech at that. Different levels of facilitation were employed to test how self-guided the Canvas was. Tests were run with several different customer profiles as well, including CEO, CTO, CIO, and assorted other levels of senior executives in charge of IT, DevOps, Strategy, and Innovation.

With over a dozen tests completed, the team felt they had amassed enough evidence to reflect on how well the experiments worked, what they had learned, and what to do next.

Voice of the Operator

INTERVIEW WITH ALEX ATZBERGER[4]

Alex Atzberger is the CEO of Optimizely, a digital experimentation platform that helps businesses conduct website testing at scale, enabling developers to optimize the customer experience. As CEO of Episerver, he led the 2020 acquisition of Optimizely. The new entity was rebranded Optimizely.

Alex, business experimentation is obviously a major part of what you offer as a company. What is your overall perspective on the subject?

For me it's both a philosophy and a practice. It's a whole mindset of being a learning culture, of not being afraid to fail, being able to understand how to build a good hypothesis and test. And giving your team a way to do that with the right tools. As a personal practice, oftentimes as a CEO I say, "Look, we have a new business idea. I'm not sure if it's the right direction. How fast can we find out if this is a good or bad idea, and how can we get some data?" A lot of it is about velocity. It's probably our most important operating goal, and the same is true for our customers. I talk to their leaders all the time, and it's "How quickly can I get the information I need to this or that?"

When you look at what we can do for our customers, it's clear that they have been able to capture a great deal of value in terms of growth by actualizing this mindset, of just quickly trying things out and learning by testing everything. The abundance of data now available makes that all feasible, where it wasn't a few years ago. Being digital is so much of the customer experience today, a primary touchpoint. It becomes super easy to quickly understand what may or may not work, which speeds up innovation and decision-making and ultimately growth.

When it comes to creating that learning culture, what are some of the things you do?

Culturally, we talk a lot about values, especially the behaviors that embody those. We have these five values, and we designate leadership time to discuss those. What behaviors do we as an organization need to embrace around those? One is to keep asking ourselves, Are we actually doing what we tell our customers they should be doing: experimenting? And are we applying it ourselves? We have made some acquisitions where the company culture is not experimental, and none of the people have ever really done this sort of thing before. They would just build and launch and then fix it when things went wrong. Which they did a lot. So we have to insist on it. I talk about it constantly in all-hands meetings. It takes time to permeate the organization. But it is making a difference. Where people used to come to me and ask, for example, if they can have this or that in the top navigation of our site, now they find out for themselves through experiments and data and don't even come to me anymore. That's what I like to see. That's how I know we are making progress.

Is there a common experimentation methodology used across Optimizely?

We have a five-step process that we have actually published a short playbook on. Of course, it begins with a research step where you collect relevant customer data, both qualitative and quantitative. Next we look at that data and identify the problem we want to solve for customers, then settle on a goal and metric for an experiment. Then we create a hypothesis that states our belief about what needs to change, what the outcome will be, and why. Finally, we roll out the experiment to a small subset of users, then review results to see if the outcome has proven or disproven our hypothesis. We want to share the results internally and define next steps with data-driven decisions.

Perfect, that lines up nicely with what we do. What do you find is your biggest cultural challenge around experimentation?

There is a tension around not wanting to do little tests all the time versus being a part of a big project. There can be this bipolar feeling that yes, I want to experiment, but let's do it with a big idea. I've pulled some big projects because I just didn't see an angle of how to use experimentation on something. I think the first thing that you can do as a leader is just ask the team, "Have we looked at it differently? Have we actually tried to define a much smaller project that would give us some data?" There are always times you may have to make decisions in the absence of data, and that's judgment, but for business ideas, looking for evidence needs to come first. Then we can make a better decision. And then what would the data look like that would inform us if it's really a better decision or not? The only way I know how to get to that is through running an experiment, or experiments.

As CEO, are there any specific focal points that are your top priorities?

Yes. One of the things I continually test with the team is how we pitch our solutions. Because that's a very simple thing to test. And you don't say, "This is the pitch, it's not going to change." You say, "Look, this is going to be changing as quickly as we get feedback." I'm forever driving to make it better and better. I think too many times people decide to be perfect on the first go. It doesn't need to be perfect; it needs to be better through trying new approaches, soliciting feedback, listening, and learning what we can do to improve it for the next time. I think this whole notion about incrementalism as a means of transformation is a powerful concept. I get exposed to big-budget decisions that are black and white, yes or no. A lot of people want a big, giant, one-shot transformation. The math just doesn't pencil as well as taking one thousand smaller, faster, cheaper steps that let you get better each time. Oh, and with one thousand times less risk.

New Insights

There are two kinds of insights. The first kind are those *Aha* or *Eureka* moments that neuroscientists refer to as "sudden insights." These are the brilliant flashes of creative genius that seem to come out of nowhere at strange times and places after we have struggled unsuccessfully for a time, thrown up our hands in surrender, broken away, and engaged in some routine activity completely unrelated to the problem: showering, dozing, driving, daydreaming.

Albert Einstein arrived at his theory of special relativity (E = mc²) while riding a streetcar and gazing absent-mindedly up at the clock tower in the city center of Bern, Switzerland. Legendary designer Milton Glaser came up with his iconic "I ♥ NY" while sitting in a taxi, stuck in Manhattan traffic. Author J. K. Rowling got the idea for Harry Potter while staring out the window of her stalled train traveling from Manchester to London. And most people know the story of 3M's Arthur Frey coming up with the idea of a new adhesive for Post-it Notes while sitting through a dull sermon in church, casually musing over a better way to bookmark his choir hymnal.

These big breakthrough moments cannot be reliably replicated, so they cannot be harnessed as an innovation discipline. Neuroscientific research has yet to decipher the inner workings of the right brain processes occurring in the hippocampus responsible for our sudden creative insights. All we know is that the process can't be sped up or pushed to work harder or more intensely.

The second kind of insight is more useful, and while it is often included as an integral part of a Fresh Opportunity, it is the most valuable fruit of a Business Experiment. Four Seasons Hotels holds a 33 percent advantage in revenue per room-night—the key performance measure in the hotel industry—over their nearest competitor (Ritz Carlton) due to founder Isadore "Issy" Sharpe's insight that most people staying in hotels would rather not be in a hotel. They would rather be in the comfort of their home, or in the convenience of their office, where they are most productive. Sharpe's perspective is why Four Seasons was the first to put hair dryers, bathrobes, and toiletries in hotel bathrooms: it feels like home! They were the first to offer 24-hour room service, because it feels like raiding your refrigerator at 2 AM. They were the first to have a real working desk, a two-line phone, and on-demand secretarial support: it feels like the office.

The New Insights phase allows us to review the results and capture learnings from our Business Experiments, and when it comes to carrying out those activities, one of the most effective methods comes from the U.S. Army: After-Action Reviews. According to MIT's Peter Senge, founder of the Society for Organizational Learning, "The Army's After-Action Review is arguably one of the most successful organizational learning methods yet devised."

According to the U.S. Army's Leader's Guide to After-Action Reviews (AAR), "An AAR is a professional discussion of a training event that enables soldiers/units to discover for themselves what happened and develop a strategy for improving performance. They provide *candid insights* [emphasis added] into strengths and weaknesses from various perspectives and feedback."[5]

In other words, AARs are all about learning. The framework is simple and can be applied to any intentional activity, be it group or individual. The Leader's Guide to AARs outlines four steps:

1. Review what was supposed to occur.
2. Establish what happened.
3. Determine what was right or wrong with what happened.
4. Determine how the task should be done differently next time.

A few minor changes allow us to adapt an AAR to a Business Experiment:

*   What did you guess would happen?
*   What actually happened?
*   What accounts for any difference?
*   What was the biggest surprise?
*   What is the next step?

The framework of AARs is widely used outside of military and paramilitary organizations, and the method goes by different names in different companies and contexts: lessons learned, morbidity/mortality conference (hospitals), validated learning, standup meetings, retrospectives, reflections, etc.

At Toyota, for example, one learns the art of *hansei* (pronounced hahn-say). Hansei is the Japanese word for "reflection," but with a meaning more like "introspection." Hansei finds its roots in Eastern philosophy and religion, but it is a profound skill to be mastered. Japanese school children are taught from the start how to perform hansei, and it is a vital part of learning and improving, performed regularly, as a discipline, irrespective of performance. In other words, it doesn't matter whether you got a grade of A or F on your homework, test, or report card, you conduct hansei in all cases to better understand the process that led to the specific result.

No matter what these assess-and-review exercises are labeled, they all share the common purpose of generating (hopefully surprising) New Insights, which can be used to make better choices about creating new value. But here's the thing: most of us don't reflect often enough, or consider disciplined reflection a tool worthy enough to use on a regular basis as an integral part of a larger process. Usually, we reserve a postmortem for when something goes wrong, but too often the goal is simple fault-finding, not deeper learning. And if it's a case of overwhelming success, we mostly just celebrate with a fist bump, high five, back slap, or some other version of "attaboy." But there is no real learning in that, because whether you miss a mark under or over, there's a gap there that demands better understanding. If we want to learn and improve, that is.

For the AWS Enterprise Strategy team, the goal of arriving at a clear first step in a move to the cloud inside the ninety-minute mark was hit over 75 percent of the time, enough to confirm the hypothesis. The key insight emerging from an AAR exercise was indeed a bit surprising: once enterprise customers briefly experienced the logic behind the Cloud Strategy Canvas, they expressed a "got it" response, stating that they "could take it from here," reserving the right to bounce their digital transformation decisions and progress off the Enterprise Strategy team in the future. To the Enterprise Strategy team, this meant that the Cloud Strategy Canvas was scalable: by providing a lightly scripted, self-guiding framework, a one-to-many solution could be offered, enabling the thousands of AWS customers access to Enterprise Strategy guidance at scale. The extra added benefit was that among the test cases involving a CEO, there was a double-win effect, at once conferring a level of confidence in their digital transformation team and relieving them of tactical involvement, in turn speeding up the effort.

The final step in the New Insights phase is making a decision about next steps. (See the fourth step in the AAR.) When the New Insights step refutes the Testable Hypothesis, the decision is usually between abandoning the Fresh Opportunity or continuing with testing. The decision generally depends on the strength of the evidence, the perceived future value of the fresh opportunity, and whether other Testable Hypotheses have been, or can readily be, generated.

When the New Insights step supports the Testable Hypothesis, the decision is generally to either develop and test a higher resolution hypothesis/prototype, or, in the case of completely unexpected New Insights that suggest a new and better hypothesis, pivot in the direction of better.

For the AWS Enterprise Strategy group, the decision was to continue developing and testing, which involved integrating their early results into the organizational culture using a company construct in the form of a press release and frequently asked questions (PRFAQ), which will be covered in the next section.

TOWARD A CULTURE OF CONSTANT EXPERIMENTATION

Look below the surface of any strong and distinctive culture and you will most assuredly find several non-negotiable items that define what matters most: how work is to be performed, how we treat each other, and, as McKinsey founder Marvin Bower put it, "how we do things around here." Non-negotiable means there must be *enforceability*, which rests on *accountability*, in turn requiring *measurement*. If you want a culture of experimentation, make it mandatory, a part of the work, not something special or something you stop "real work" to do. Measure the quantity and quality of experiments, company-wide. It sounds doctrinaire, and perhaps it is, but of all the doctrines one might impose, continuous learning through constant experimentation is certainly one of the least burdensome and most valuable.

If you're looking for a starting point for a current culture with zero experimentation, consider requiring everyone in your company to be involved in at least one documented experiment during the year. If you're looking for a benchmark stretch number, consider requiring everyone in your company to be involved in four experiments per year, one per quarter. The number comes from our involvement with organizations like Amazon, Toyota, LinkedIn, and Netflix that run well over a million experiments each year, many of them using low- or no-tech approaches. One experiment per quarter lines up conveniently with fairly standard twelve-week corporate accelerators as well as quarterly OKRs, which are by design intended to be a stretch in nature.

By requiring experimentation, you automatically create focus and avoid kitchen-sink idea submission and non-productive employee suggestion programs. And you don't need a fancy idea management system. Only ideas embedded in an experiment count. In fact, forget about ideas altogether. Start talking about experiments and evidence instead.

One of the best methodologies for igniting an experimentation culture and establishing a Rapid Experimentation Flywheel is called "5×5" and is the brainchild of MIT's Michael Schrage, who has successfully embedded the X-team practice in several market-leading companies.

5×5 X-TEAMS

Schrage defines the 5×5 methodology this way:

> *Give a diverse team of 5 people no more than 5 days to come up with a portfolio of 5 business experiments that cost no more than $5,000 (each) and take no longer than 5 weeks to run. The willingness to ask simple questions is essential. Simplicity invites ingenuity. The 5×5 offers a fast, cheap, and ingenious method for innovators to revisit—and test—business fundamentals safely. Simple questions about customer segmentation, sales, pricing, performance, and language inspire successful, high-impact hypotheses.*[6]

Having partnered with Schrage on joint client work, it is safe to say the 5×5 methodology works amazingly well. It helps to overcome inertia and frontload a cultural shift. It creates a solid internal market of Business Experiments and inspires cross-functional collaboration. When it becomes an embedded capability and matures to the point of becoming a true competency, it works as a central mechanism to better manage innovation by linking lean and agile experiments to strategic priorities and the exploration of more radical or disruptive opportunities. At the same time, it reduces risk. Remember, it's still experimentation.

The beauty of 5×5 teams is that you can point them in any direction or set them in pursuit of any challenge or opportunity, at any level of the organization. They can be quite specific or completely open. They can be strategic or more operational. They can be internally focused or customer-facing.

The results of 5×5s will speak for themselves: you'll get a rich portfolio of potential Testable Hypothesis tied directly to what you wish to explore, the ability to select the best of the dozens of proposed Business Experiments, and quickly reap the rewards of a Warren Buffet–like approach to discovering New Insights cheaply, with little to no risk and relatively negligible cost . . . all the while mobilizing a critical mass of human creative capital.

Finally, the number 5 is meant to be a guide, more of an ideal than a strict requirement. There is no special magic around it, but more than five tends to be a bit unwieldy and begins to feel like a heavier flywheel to spin up quickly. Fewer than five is fine, especially for more specific, operational opportunities.

Schrage offers a handful of winning attributes common to successful X-teams:

1. Focus on potential business impact
2. Alignment with strategic priorities
3. Compelling hypotheses
4. Pleasant surprises
5. Scalable next steps

The fifth element, scalable next steps, picks up on our discussion of decisions in the New Insights phase of the Rapid Experimentation Flywheel.

SCALING UP EXPERIMENTS

Not every successful experiment results in an immediate productization, standardization, or company-wide internal adoption. Nor should it. The best innovators look at a basket of successful experiments in various stages of development like a venture capitalist looks at investing in young companies in various stages of growth. Deciding if, and how much of, an investment is warranted depends on weighing the risk versus reward, the best early gauge of which is a good bit of diligence. Against what criteria will you decide whether an experiment is allocated resources for taking it to the next level, or to the market, even if that market is internal?

Three practical tools have a successful track record in the field.

Toolkit: PR/FAQ

For a value creation concept at Amazon to see the light of day beyond early experiments is no easy feat. Actionable New Insights must be deemed worthy internally. At Amazon, customer obsession is a leadership principle, and every effort is made to present things in a familiar and thus easily consumable form for customers, including internal customers. PowerPoint is not such a format, so it isn't used. At all. In fact they've banned it, not because it's a bad tool, but because even the best PowerPoint depends on the presenter for success, and not everyone is a great presenter. In its stead are six-page narrative documents, which tell the story of a Fresh Opportunity independent of the storyteller's dazzle, or lack thereof. One such narrative form was referred to a few pages back, called a PRFAQ.

Press releases to news media are generally a few descriptive paragraphs, and a single page in length. In terms of length, the press release part of Amazon's PR/FAQ is no different. What's different is the frequently asked questions (FAQ) component, which anticipates questions and objections from both an external (customer) point of view as well as an internal (company) one, and makes up the remainder of the six-page narrative format.

PR/FAQs are for internal Amazon consumption only. While the customer's perspective must be included, customers never see a PR/FAQ, and neither does the media, traditional or social. They only see the outcome of a greenlit one.

The overall PR/FAQ format is straightforward:

- Headline
- Subhead: one line explaining the headline
- Summary paragraph
- Problem paragraph
- Solution paragraph
- Quotes paragraphs (customer and internal)
- Get started paragraphs
- External (customer) FAQs
- Internal (company) FAQs

The FAQ part of a PR/FAQ comprises the majority of the six pages. External FAQs are those that a customer or consumer of the concept might ask when considering purchase or usage. They flesh out the details of the offer. Internal FAQs, especially those for revenue-generating concept, anticipate pushback and pressure testing the likes of what a contestant on *Shark Tank* might face, or the diligence a company might have to live through at the hands of a potential investor: total addressable market (TAM), resource requirements, financial outlook, risk profile, critical dependencies, key processes, and other elements of long-term feasibility.

Once a PR/FAQ is drafted, a meeting is held with key stakeholders to review it. Feedback, both general and specific—including choices related to phrasing or wording—is fielded. Revisions are made and further review meetings are held. Depending on the level of the concept, this can involve many reviews and revisions before a go-ahead is given. For new products that require significant investment, the acceptance rate of a polished PR/FAQ is low.

The PR/FAQ narrative form is effective as a method for scaling up and potentially launching offerings based on the results of Business Experiments. It does, however, require ditching PowerPoint as the go-to communication vehicle, something that most companies do not have an appetite for.

We had the opportunity to be closely involved in drafting the AWS Enterprise Strategy team's PR/FAQ, and we have included a modified version of it here, sans the FAQs component (see sidebar). Once the PR/FAQ was given the go-ahead, the AWS FirstStep program featuring the Cloud Strategy Canvas was launched both externally and internally. Scalability was achieved via a self-serve approach: AWS cloud customers of all sizes could download the canvas and use an accompanying facilitation/completion guide.

AWS LAUNCHES TOOLKIT TO HELP COMPANIES TAKE FIRST STEP INTO CLOUD

New Guided Discovery Process for Initiating a Technology Transformation

SEATTLE—June 1, 2019—Today, Amazon Web Services, Inc. (AWS), an Amazon.com company, announced AWS FirstStep, a program that helps enterprises that are beginning to adopt the cloud identify the initial projects that are most important to showing the value of a cloud strategy. Built from the experience of existing enterprise migrations, AWS FirstStep is comprised of a series of guided exercises that navigate companies through the questions and choices that they will encounter when starting to use the cloud. Upon completion of the program, enterprises will have developed a clear set of first steps needed to validate the technical, business, and organizational requirements of their cloud adoption strategy.

Most companies that have undertaken a major move to the cloud started by learning and experimenting with the migration of a single application. This smaller step allowed them to gain confidence with the technology, economics, and skill sets that are part of a bigger step into the cloud. But with hundreds or even thousands of applications running within most enterprises, companies often struggle with where exactly to start. Instead of speculating what would be the best "Cloud test," enterprises wanting to begin using the cloud are looking for expert guidance on how to pick the right areas to focus on that will accelerate their technology transformation.

AWS FirstStep helps enterprises cut through the early debates, doubts, and roadblocks and create a personalized plan for how to demonstrate the value of using the cloud based on the best practices of thousands of customer migrations. Using an AWS-led workshop format, company leaders align their business objectives and technology challenges to cloud-enabled capabilities. The outcome produces a clear set of first steps for an organization to begin experimenting with the cloud in the areas of app migration, skill development, and cost savings. These first steps are also developed to inform the eventual business case for a full migration or large-scale adoption of cloud services.

"Companies beginning to work with the cloud consistently ask us what they should do first in order to show value and inform their future roadmap," said Phil Potloff, global head of enterprise strategy for AWS. "AWS FirstStep has become our most effective tool for helping these enterprise customers pinpoint the cloud projects that will show early success and become pivotal in shifting the organization's thinking about how to use the cloud."

Instead of traditional strategic planning models and lengthy project requirements documents, AWS FirstStep utilizes lean innovation principles and rapid prototyping techniques that are designed to create targeted tests and prompt action. The hands-on, time-boxed exercises used in AWS FirstStep feature a new tool called the Cloud Strategy Canvas, a large visual map guiding companies to consider the beginning of their cloud adoption journey in a structured way, and enabling them to identify the critical risks and preconditions for success.

"We had a few teams experimenting with AWS for a while, and frankly I think we wasted a lot of time feeling our way in the dark trying to figure out how the cloud fit in our technology strategy," said Scott Spradley, CTO of Tyson Foods. "We went through the AWS FirstStep process and had immediate clarity as to where we should be focusing our efforts. The Cloud Strategy Canvas in particular helped make our challenges explicit in a very visual way. At the same time, it facilitated important decisions and gave us specific options and pathways within the AWS ecosystem."

AWS FirstStep is now offered at no charge to enterprise customers who are currently working with AWS to develop their own cloud adoption strategy and can be coordinated through local account teams.

Toolkit: Innovation Brief

Splitting the difference between a PR/FAQ and a PowerPoint presentation is the Innovation Brief, an example of which is shown on page 93. Like it sounds, an Innovation Brief lays out the key blocks of information required to move results of early experiments forward, written with the intent to gain go-ahead:

- **Key Opportunity**
  Why is a new approach or concept warranted?

- **Empirical Evidence**
  What insights, data, or evidence supports pursuing this opportunity?
- **Tweetable Headline**
  What short message sells the high concept?
- **Target Customer**
  For exactly which customers are you creating new/more value?
- **Customer Problem**
  What is the unmet customer need? What is the customer's desired outcome?
- **Tested Solution**
  What experiments have been run? What were the results?
- **Defensible Advantage**
  What makes the solution unique?
- **Key Benefit**
  What is the biggest customer benefit?
- **Value Proposition**
  Fill in: (Concept name) is a (description) for (customer type) that (key features), enabling (key benefits), unlike (existing/competing options).
- **Testimonial Quotes**
  What external and internal positive feedback have you captured?
- **Goal Alignment**
  What Objectives/Key Results (OKRs) are supported?
- **Key Dependencies**
  Upon what key stakeholders and/or third parties does market success depend?
- **Business Gain**
  What is the measurable positive business impact (financial, engagement, etc.)?
- **Resource Requirement**
  What development resources (people, money, technology, etc.) are needed?
- **Critical Risks**
  What is the riskiest element of the concept? How will you remove that risk?

The beauty of the Innovation Brief is in the name: it's brief and provides an at-a-glance summary of a potential innovation. You don't have to read a six-page

INNOVATION BRIEF

KEY OPPORTUNITY	EMPIRICAL EVIDENCE	TWEETABLE HEADLINE
Why is a new approach or concept warranted?	What insights, data, or evidence supports pursuing this opportunity?	What short message sells the high concept?
TARGET CUSTOMER	**CUSTOMER PROBLEM**	**TESTED SOLUTION**
For exactly which customers are you creating new/more value?	What is the unmet customer need? What is the customer's desired outcome?	What experiments have been run? What were the results?
DEFENSIBLE ADVANTAGE	**KEY BENEFIT**	**VALUE PROPOSITION**
What makes the solution unique?	What is the biggest customer benefit?	(Concept name) is a (description) for (customer type) that (key features), enabling (key benefits), unlike (existing/ competing options).
TESTIMONIAL QUOTES	**GOAL ALIGNMENT**	**KEY DEPENDENCIES**
What external and internal positive feedback have you captured?	What Objectives/Key Results (OKRs) are supported?	Upon what key stakeholders and/or third parties does market success depend?
BUSINESS GAIN	**RESOURCE REQUIREMENT**	**CRITICAL RISKS**
What is the measurable positive business impact (financial, engagement, etc.)?	What development resources (people, money, technology, etc.) are needed?	What is the riskiest element of the concept? How will you de-risk it?

narrative, and you don't need to sit through, or sort through, a multi-slide PowerPoint deck. The Innovation Brief can be used for both new products and new internal solutions. Customers can be defined as any potential user of the offering, and the "market" can be internal, defined as the organization, whole or in part.

	Experimentation & Early Vetting	Business Case & Lean Testing	Limited Pilot Testing	Go To Market
Purpose	❑ Initial experimentation with a hypothesis or concept to determine if there is merit for deeper investigation and/or investment	❑ Share Innovation Brief with whole SLT ❑ Low FTE investment to support further testing ❑ Define measures/KPIs	❑ Robust MVP/Pilot that can scale ❑ Test the concept at a larger scale ❑ GTM strategy	❑ Deploy Go To Market strategy
Work to Produce	❑ Opportunity identification ❑ Hypotheses generation ❑ Rapid experimentation ❑ Learning capture ❑ Capabilities alignment ❑ Innovation Brief	❑ Innovation Brief drill down; pitch deck ❑ Integration into corporate strategy ❑ Define timeline, stages and KPIs ❑ Higher-res AB, Vaporware, MVP tests	❑ Dev to Scalable MVP ❑ Pilot Testing ❑ Sign on Initial Partners ❑ Update business plan, financials, resources ❑ Test stage gate KPIs ❑ GTM brief	❑ All work described in GTM brief ❑ Monitor performance, retention, churn, support
Do not proceed until...	❑ Innovation Brief go-ahead ❑ Vote of 1 SLT to proceed w/minimal dev assignments	❑ All above complete in full ❑ MVP tests pass KPIs ❑ Vote of SLT to proceed with minimal dev assignments	❑ All above complete in full ❑ Pilot tests pass required KPIs ❑ Vote of majority SLT to proceed with full development	
Investment Level (FTE + Capital)	~1-2 FTE	~3-5 FTE	~$TBDk investment	~$TBDm investment

One auto-tech ScaleUp used a version of the Innovation Brief as the starting point and basis for an experimentation-based, stage-gated yet accelerated new product development process, which looked similar to the diagram above (details have been omitted for confidentiality). Note that as the development effort progresses, deeper dives are taken into each part of the Innovation Brief—which evolves into a Go-to-Market brief—through eventual market launch.

Toolkit: Innovation Score

One question remains. Suppose your leadership team has a dozen seemingly equally attractive PR/FAQs or Innovation Briefs—or the equivalent measure of diligence—in front of them. How will they decide which to move forward, or in what priority? As most people know, securities and investment portfolios use a measure of risk, called *beta*, to guide similar decisions. Is there an innovation equivalent?

One such measure is an innovation score. By surveying hundreds of managers in companies of all sizes and kinds, including venture capital firms, and blending that feedback with a historical study of successful innovations both public and within companies with whom close work on experimentation and innovation was performed, we discovered three key factors that explain nearly all of the variance in the data:

- **FIT.** The Fit factor is a measure of potential organizational impact that answers the key question: *Does this concept represent a good fit for my company, group, or team?*
- **INGENUITY.** The Ingenuity factor is a measure of potential customer impact and answers the key question: *Does this concept solve a problem in an innovative way?*
- **SCALE.** The Scale factor is a measure of potential customer impact that answers the key question: *Will the market exponentially reward us with a return on our innovation?*

Each of the factors has five criteria.

Fit

- Future success is compelling and measurable
- Clear alignment to company strategy
- Complements a strong brand
- Leverages current capabilities (technology, process, expertise)
- Chosen playing spaces (product/service, customer segments, etc.) are open and attractive

Ingenuity

- Solves a pressing customer problem or pain point uniquely
- Features a "wow" factor or experience for users
- Represents a unique and defensible competitive advantage
- Does not require inventing/developing completely new capability/technology
- Highest risk assumptions that must be true for success are easily tested

Scale

- The addressable market/use case is large enough to support desired business gain/revenue.

- The addressable market/use case is likely to grow/continue growing at a significant rate.
- The business/revenue model represents compelling value for customers.
- The business/revenue model represents the opportunity to scale quickly.
- Success can be leveraged with opportunities for related future offerings.

While analysis reveals that the three key factors are nearly equal in weight, experience shows that different organizations prefer to weight the 15 criteria to suit their priorities. Additionally, scoring mechanisms can be tailored to suit needs and preferences. The Innovation Score is offered here as a starting point for creating a common "core score," enabling you to evaluate and compare potential innovations, prioritize and allocate investment resources, and help predict eventual impact and success of concepts for which experimental evidence exists.

CONSTANT EXPERIMENTATION RECAP

The antidote to paralyzing corporate inertia is Constant Experimentation. Without a culture of experimentation, even the most promising of potential unicorns can be lulled into riding the current wave of success until it crests without new ways to create future value for customers. Innovation momentum favors spinning up a lightweight, high-velocity flywheel of simple, fast, cheap, and scalable business experiments over big, heavy innovation management programs. The fruit of constant experimentation is a steady stream of valuable new insights from which new offerings can be developed. A handful of effective methods and tools enhance the ability to scale experimentation. The takeaway lesson is simple: never, ever stop experimenting. Unless, of course, the dream is to live the Entrepreneur's Nightmare.

CHECKPOINTS

☐ Does senior leadership favor experiments over ideas?

☐ Is constant experimentation a required core competency?

☐ Are fresh opportunities and new insights consistently pursued through experimentation?

☐ Do you have a common method for rapid experimentation with customers?

☐ Do you have a standard approach for advancing early experiments toward innovations?

Principle 3

ACCELERATED VALUE

Instant gratification takes too long.
—Carrie Fisher, Actress

Suppose for a moment that you're a potential investor seated at a conference table in a small Palo Alto meeting room in the late summer of 1998, listening to two young Stanford University PhD students pitch their concept for a completely new and novel way to search for information on the internet, which they've just published as their doctoral thesis. Instead of ranking results based on how many times your search terms appear on a page, their algorithm, which they call PageRank, analyzes the relationship between websites and determines the most relevant web pages for your search based on how many other internet pages link to it.

The two founders believe this "wisdom of the crowds" method will vastly improve the quality of online searching, to the point of rendering conventional search engines obsolete. Their concept is compelling, and the rather Spartan simplicity of the user interface—essentially an empty box to type into—is truly elegant. You like their mission, "To organize the world's information." You even like the name, Google. As they explain it, it's a play on the mathematical term *googol*, the name for a number with one hundred zeros. Clever.

Imagine now that they tell you that you have to wait two or three minutes to get those amazing results.

You're out. Nobody likes to wait for value.

THE FRICTION FACTORY

Easy. Simple. Fast. Few companies can boast customers regularly describing their interactions with the company using these or similar words. In fact, the norm is often the exact opposite: *hard, complicated, slow.* As customers and consumers, it doesn't seem to matter how brilliantly any given product meets our needs or solves our problem; when the ability to realize value from the solution becomes burdensome, we leave. If search results on Google took even ten seconds, we would switch search engines in a heartbeat. Google knows it, which is why the first thing they show us isn't just how many results they returned, but how many results in *how much time . . .* which they make a point of informing us is always under one second. The velocity of value delivery separates the great from the good, the would-be unicorns from the also-rans. The question is, why do some companies achieve speed and agility in delivering value to customers, while others struggle endlessly?

The short answer is *friction,* the omnipresent physical force produced wherever moving parts rub against each other. To continue with our Formula 1 car analogy, friction is quite literally where the rubber meets the road. Friction can win or lose a race, and regularly does. Make the wrong choice of tire or misjudge the timing of a tire change, and friction will play a big role in the outcome.[1] Friction is necessary to optimize speed: too much slows you down, not enough prevents grip, control, and safety. Friction is a powerful restraining force, and restraining forces always rule.

As customers, we've all been victims of friction. You know you're friction's victim when:

- You saunter into a big box store and can't locate the item, aisle, or even general direction in which to search without having to hunt for and ask for help.
- You eventually get to where your desired item is supposed to be only to find the item out of stock.
- You have to punch in five different numbers on an endless phone tree to be connected to a human being, only then to be put on hold for what seems like eternity.

- You can't stroll through a new car lot to browse this year's models without being pressured to buy something today.
- Implementing a shiny new software platform that is supposed to change your world takes six months instead of the three promised by your smooth and persuasive account executive.
- It's so hard to navigate that platform that you can't use it without contacting tech support, who then happily informs you that you have to submit a support ticket, which may or may not be resolved this week because they're backlogged.

Any time we queue up or compete for a scarce resource—time, space, attention—friction plays a big role. Consider for a moment the extent to which the internet has eliminated friction: We live in a world of frictionless abundance. We can now find out almost anything about anyone without any red tape within seconds and a few keystrokes—what used to take police detectives days or weeks to find out, and only after multiple approvals. We can buy or watch anything we want at any time with a single click, never leaving the couch. When the COVID pandemic hit the workforce, the lack of friction in needing to be in a specific place at a specific time allowed the economy to thrive on remote work. The lack of friction enabled geographic independence; at the same time, friction played a hand in shaping both the job market and the entire software subscription economy.

Friction, then, isn't all bad. The trick is understanding that friction has both positive and negative effects, and it is only through balancing both that we can optimize personal experiences. For example, the U.S. Federal Reserve Board (the "Fed") uses friction in the form of interest rates to regulate the economy, to prevent overheating or inflation, or to stimulate growth. The U.S. Transportation Security Administration (TSA) founded after 9/11 purposefully adds friction to the security screening process at airports, requiring travelers to comply with an exhaustive list of procedures, making it much harder to pass through unchecked, all in an effort to improve safety, identify potential threats, and prevent dangerous and deadly events. At the same time, the most burdensome of these procedures—unclothing, unpacking, reclothing, repacking—can be avoided by becoming a TSA "known traveler," which while having its own friction tax, in the long run adds two-sided value, making the jobs of both TSA and travelers much easier.

Here's the thing: we are masters at manufacturing *unnecessary* friction. Pull back the curtain of even some of the most successful companies, and you're likely to find a patchwork of silos and systems all designed to *push product*, not necessarily enable customers to easily and quickly *pull value*. As Charles Perow noted in his classic book *Normal Accidents*, systems designed for one purpose but used for another will inevitably fail. Avoiding normal accidents—such as a delay in customer value delivery—often mandates at least a partial systems makeover, which isn't easy. That's why native value-pull systems like the Toyota Production System remain competitive standouts. The friction factory is so efficient that it is nearly impossible to make it through a typical day without encountering some degree of unnecessary friction. The cost of friction is high, while both expectations and the upside of a frictionless customer experience are rising.

According to one estimate, businesses in the U.S. lose over $75 billion[2] annually due to poor customer experience.[3] Salesforce reports that less than 30 percent of business-to-business customers say that their suppliers are providing an excellent customer experience, and more than 80 percent of business purchasers want a consumer-level experience, regardless of how they interact with their vendors and sales contacts. What's more, two-thirds of those surveyed have already switched vendors to achieve that.[4] A study by Qualtrics found that companies earning $1 billion annually can expect to earn, on average, an additional $700 million within three years of investing in customer experience, and subscription software companies in particular can expect to increase revenue by $1 billion.[5] Few CEOs would shrug their shoulders at the promise of doubling a billion-dollar business in thirty-six months. Finally, a survey of nearly two thousand business leaders going into 2022 revealed that their top priority for the next five years will be customer experience (46%), beating out product (34%) and price (20%).[6]

Friction in business nearly always manifests itself in customer pain points and critical moments that, like a tire choice or change in a Formula 1 race, can make the difference between winning and losing. Losing customers can be lethal for any business, but especially so in the subscription economy. It stands to reason that since building a SaaS business to deliver an improved customer experience has become one of the most important factors driving digital transformation in business today,[7] reducing senseless friction wherever possible can only improve the odds of success.

We will dive into how to do just that, beginning with understanding where friction comes from, then transitioning into a brief examination of how companies and their customers fall out of sync when defining and delivering value, and finishing with a field-tested tool for successful value realignment.

SOURCES OF FRICTION

Whenever people and products come into contact, friction occurs. The key is understanding where unnecessary friction is coming from. There are two major sources, each producing effects that negatively impact the customer experience.

Source 1: Vertical Thinking

At the heart of the friction challenge is the difficulty of thinking and operating horizontally in a mostly vertically structured world. Take a look at most any organization chart and you'll find a tree, which everyone knows grows vertically. The customer's company is just as vertical as yours. But the customer experience is *horizontal*.

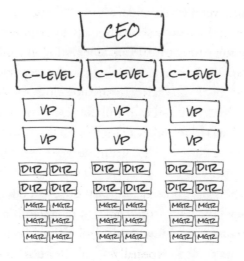

ORG DESIGN: VERTICAL

CUSTOMER EXPERIENCE: HORIZONTAL

DESIRED OUTCOME ⟶ SEARCH–SELECT–SECURE MEANS ⟶ OUTCOME DESIRED?

Vertical thinking is behind various moments that make customers cringe:

- **Mixed messaging.** Marketing says one thing, but the rest of the operation does another. Sales promises best-in-class responsiveness, but customer support tickets are backlogged for days. The best-case scenario here is a mild case of confusion or disillusionment for customers; worse case, churn. Mixed messaging isn't limited to saying one thing and doing another: when what a company is saying or doing today conflicts with what it said or did yesterday, that's also mixed messaging.

- **Disintegration.** When one company function delivers a noticeably different experience than another, it's a head-scratch for customers, and an otherwise seamless experience can be automatically diminished. We see this a lot when looking under the hood of software ScaleUps, where one part of the company was formed at a different time, without a solid change management effort aimed at cultural consistency. Inconsistency in the customer's experience due to different microcultures of different functions—especially when those functions should be, and are intended to be, integrated steps in the value chain—erodes confidence, disconnects the customer, and ultimately destroys trust.

- **Excessive touch.** Closely related to, and perhaps a side effect of, disintegration is the ever painful dance we as customers must do whenever we need help, usually from the customer support department. Banks and telecoms are notorious for this: you need help beyond the generally useless phone tree or website FAQs. Whether by phone or chat, we dutifully enter all of the requested information—name, account number, PIN, etc.—just to get to a live human. If by chance we are lucky enough to be put on hold for anything under five minutes, we are finally connected. The first question we are asked: "To whom am I speaking?" The dance continues, forcing us to provide all of the same information we already entered. It would be comical if it weren't so serious, especially for B2B customer support issues. We worked with one ScaleUp's tech support team that literally called part of their process "the email dance," a back-and-forth with customers they engaged in just to understand the trouble. In one instance we counted forty-eight emails over five days. We helped them solve it old-school style: after two emails, pick up the phone, schedule a Zoom . . . do something face-to-face. Limit excessive touching, but provide a better experience.

Horizontal thinking for a horizontal experience makes more sense. Fortunately, we are beginning to see more horizontal thinking in high-growth ScaleUps, in the form of cross-functional "growth teams" composed of pre-sales, sales, customer success, support, marketing, product, and engineering, all organized around key products instead of departmental silos. This helps to eliminate the vertical thinking that generates multiple handoffs and unnecessary friction that eventually affects customers.

While the horizontal cross-functional or multi-discipline team structure may seem radical, it isn't: the same essential design is found in major motion picture production, surgical teams, special forces teams, continuous-play sports teams (soccer, hockey, lacrosse, basketball), and of course, Formula 1 pit crews. In all of these domains, time is the constraint, and a much too precious one to think vertically.

Source 2: Customer Apathy

When James David Power III—J. D. "Dave" Power—sat down with his wife, Julie, at the kitchen table in 1968 to stuff and stamp hundreds of envelopes containing a quarter as an incentive for recent car buyers to complete something called a Customer Satisfaction Survey, little did he know that his efforts would transform business and usher in a new era, the "Voice of the Customer." His idea was to provide carmakers with feedback from customers on their purchase experience and initial satisfaction with their new vehicle in the first ninety days of ownership. Not a single U.S. automaker took him up on his offer. Just one company showed interest, a Japanese import with a rapidly growing share of the American small car segment: Toyota.

Toyota saw the value of having an objective third party capture the opinions of their customers, as well as share those opinions publicly. Toyota paid $8,000 for the very first J.D. Power & Associates report (the associates were wife Julie and their three young children), called the "California Import Car Buyers

Study," which compared import and domestic brands along several factors and numerous attributes. It helped put both companies on the map, and Toyota became J.D. Power's best customer, subscribing to the ever-growing suite of syndicated products year after year. J.D. Power & Associates was one of the first as-a-service businesses, decades before the term was even coined.

Detroit automakers—Chrysler, Ford, and General Motors—essentially laughed at the concept. No one in "the Big Three" wanted to be told that their products and processes could be better, and for several decades all three resisted the research, choosing instead to deny, disparage, and discredit the data. They collectively chose to shut both eyes and ears, proactively ignoring the voice of the customer, to their eventual detriment.

We call that *customer apathy,* the polar opposite of customer empathy. In a 2012 article about J.D. Power & Associates, trade publication *WardsAuto* wrote that during his 1980s stint as president of General Motors, when Jim McDonald discovered that GM ranked near the bottom of the Power surveys, he cursed out loud, "To hell with J.D. Power!"[8] Ignoring and thus being unaware of what your customers think about your products and processes is a recipe for losing customers. That's never good, no matter what your business model is.

While voice-of-customer surveys are a staple of most companies today, getting closer to customers physically and virtually remains an ongoing challenge. Too many leaders choose to "manage the score" and not their store, so to speak. They're content to peruse the latest survey results, charge the company with raising the score, and be done with it . . . without providing a method or means to do so, mind you. Steve Blank had it right in his seminal customer development book *The Four Steps to the Epiphany*: Get out of the building. It's been over a decade since Blank wrote that, and the ubiquity of the cloud allows us to leave the building without getting out of our chairs. But it remains a point of resistance.

There is no logical reason to avoid immersing oneself in the customer experience, with data and, when possible and appropriate, beyond the data. Watch customers interact with your product. Watch for critical events: where they lean in, where they lean out, where they struggle, where they give up, and where they experience the all-important moment of joy when they succeed.

Customer apathy is behind a few operational gaps we see in many companies that make it difficult to deliver an exceptional customer experience:

- **Customer = Segment.** Unfortunately, this is a prevalent and detrimental mindset derived from a lack of understanding about who the customer really is. If customers are viewed simply as a given type or size of account or market segment, no true understanding of the customer is possible. Segmentation is important for strategy, and of course necessary for a good product/market fit, but it is non-differentiating from the customer experience perspective. The reason is simple: segments do not reveal anything about the true needs of customers. Viewing customers one-dimensionally as a member of a conventional market segment—that is, small business, mid-market, enterprise—limits understanding of exactly *who* in each of those broad and behaviorally indistinct categories is buying and using our products, and more importantly, *why*. Ideal customer profiles (ICPs) and personas are a good start, depending on how they are developed and purposed, but any ScaleUp eyeing the unicorn club must go beyond product/market fit to the more challenging phase of finding go-to-market fit with customers to ensure they become *retained* customers.
- **Missing Maps.** When the territory is unfamiliar, uncertain, or unclear, it helps to have a map. Often those maps are missing or sorely in need of engineering or refinement, especially as the business begins to rapidly scale upward. As new products are developed and launched and operations become more complex and difficult to manage, growth alone cannot compensate for the sense of directionlessness that can creep into the company's collective consciousness. Tools like empathy maps, customer journey maps, and product roadmaps all help to align strategies with operations.
- **Fuzzy Metrics.** We covered Objectives and Key Results earlier, with respect to the importance of top-to-bottom, side-to-side, measurable short-term goals that enable a given strategy to be effectively deployed. OKRs generally focus internally on what needs to be done operationally. They do not, and are not intended to be, key performance indicators (KPIs) of a customer-focused business. The navigation system in your car may help you get from point A to B on your immediate journey, but it does not tell you how well your car is

running. Most companies do a good job of setting and monitoring KPIs; if they didn't, it wouldn't be too long before they wouldn't need to worry about them at all. Recurring revenue and retention/churn metrics are obviously important and absolutely required, but they are lagging indicators, often trailing by months or quarters. To avoid impact down the road from something happening today, we need metrics that tell us what's happening now . . . *with customers*.

Leading indicators can be developed from usage data, support history, customer relationship management (CRM) data, onboarding logs, customer satisfaction/loyalty survey data, engagement measures, training document downloads, user interviews . . . the list goes on. But one key metric must be tracked constantly: time-to-value (TTV). TTV can be generally defined as how long it takes for customers to reach that first *aha* moment when they achieve a desired outcome with your solution. It is a "core score," a top priority for any service business, and the best determinant of whether the principle of *Accelerated Value* is being put into practice. If there is one leading indicator to obsess over daily, this is it. We will examine this concept further in a moment, but the point here is that it is critically important to continually take the pulse of the customer with clear metrics, listening for a strong and steady heartbeat.

As you stand back and squint at the friction factory, one common thread runs throughout: unnecessary friction stems from an inward, self-centered view of the business organized around its own ideas and interests.

To friction-optimize any operation, the exact opposite approach is required: an outward focus on, and organization of work around, customer-centered value.

A LEANER VIEW OF VALUE

Optimizing friction in order to accelerate value to customers requires a mindset shift: from *push* to *pull*. Pull is a defining aspect of lean. It's not about moving potential customers through an ideal purchase funnel, sales process, or consumption chain; it's about enabling them to succeed in accomplishing whatever they're hoping your solution will help them do. Value is no longer simply about an economic transaction, it's about a transformation. It's about building a deeper and more trustful relationship with a customer over time, even if that relationship is digital in nature and carried out through a sophisticated bit of technology.

Putting the principle of Accelerated Value into practice can be thought of as minimizing the friction between two constantly moving gears: Value Defined and Value Delivered. From our experience in working with ScaleUps, we have come to realize a common alignment issue: too much space between indicates a gap in need of closure to avoid loss. We call this the Value Gap. As AWS sales and marketing chief Matt Garman said at the 2019 re:Invent conference, "The biggest obstacle to growth is the failure to understand and align with customer-desired business outcomes."[9]

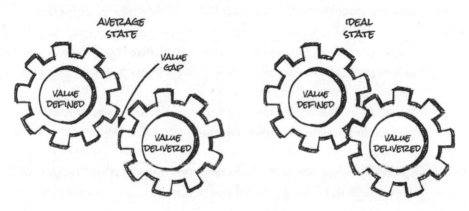

This leaner view of value requires first the understanding that no customer really wants a given product; rather, they want to get their most important jobs done and need a way to maximize their effectiveness in doing so, preferably in a manner faster, cheaper, and simpler than how they're doing it now.

VALUE DEFINED

One of the things that drove Matt crazy when he first began working with Toyota was an internal, informal mantra that went something like, "People don't want our products and services, they want solutions; when it comes to solutions, simple is better, elegant is better still." The statement was a curious one.

First, there wasn't a clear definition of elegant anywhere in any company documentation. The dictionary didn't help very much, because the definitions of elegant and elegance were circular. It was easier to understand what elegant *wasn't* by observing the nature of ideas that were killed: anything (from a customer's perspective) confusing, excessive, wasteful, unnatural, hazardous, hard to use, or ugly could be inferred to be inelegant. Ideas and solutions that made it to commercialization, even if the market was internal, tended to achieve the maximum intended effect through minimum means. That sort of unusual effectiveness was a good enough working definition of what elegant meant in practice.

That left the first part of the statement unclear. When demand for your products and services is at an all-time high and you're growing so fast that you're hiring thousands of new employees around the world each year to staff new factories and facilities to distribute those products, it's hard to argue that customers don't want them. What could that possibly mean? A bit of digging told the story.

In the August 18, 1923, edition of the *Reno Evening Gazette*, a local plumbing company ran an advertisement in column six on page eight that read:

When you buy a razor, you buy a smooth chin—but you could wear a beard. When you buy a new suit, you buy an improved appearance—but you could make the old one do. When you buy an automobile, you buy speedy transportation—but you could walk. But when you buy plumbing, you buy cleanliness—for which there is no substitute![10]

Nearly twenty years later, in the December 1942 edition of the *Somerset American*, the Provident Mutual Life Insurance Company ran a nearly identical advertisement:

Hardware stores report that over one million men bought one-quarter inch drills in one year. Not one of those million men wanted the drills. They wanted quarter-inch holes in metal or wood. People who buy life insurance don't want life insurance; they want monthly income for their families.[11]

The drill and hole metaphor stuck. In 1947, Dale Carnegie Institute trainer Percy Whiting published a book titled *The Five Great Rules of Selling*, referencing the drill/hole metaphor and crediting Leo McGivna of New York City's *The Daily News* for the concept:

> *Last year over one million quarter-inch drills were sold—not because people wanted quarter-inch drills but because they wanted quarter-inch holes. When you buy an automobile you buy transportation. When you buy a mattress you are buying comfortable sleep. When you buy carbon paper you are buying copies.*[12]

These stories and quotes clarified what the Toyota mantra meant. Later into the Toyota relationship, an article appeared in the December 2005 issue of *Harvard Business Review*, in which Clayton Christensen, Scott Cook, and Taddy Hall published an article entitled *Marketing Malpractice: The Cause and the Cure*, crediting the drill/hole metaphor to Christensen's marketing professor, Theodore Levitt, writing:

> *The great Harvard marketing professor Theodore Levitt used to tell his students, "People don't want to buy a quarter-inch drill. They want a quarter-inch hole!" Every marketer we know agrees with Levitt's insight. Yet these same people segment their markets by type of drill and by price point; they measure market share of drills, not holes; and they benchmark the features and functions of their drill, not their hole, against those of rivals. They then set to work offering more features and functions in the belief that these will translate into better pricing and market share. When marketers do this, they often solve the wrong problems, improving their products in ways that are irrelevant to their customers' needs.*[13]

Christensen et al. would go on to introduce a new and better way to think about products and markets that looked at needs from the customers' perspective:

> *The structure of a market, seen from the customers' point of view, is very simple: They just need to get things done, as Ted Levitt said. When people find themselves needing to get a job done, they essentially hire products to do that job for them.*

The marketer's task is therefore to understand what jobs periodically arise in customers' lives for which they might hire products the company could make. If a marketer can understand the job, design a product and associated experiences in purchase and use to do that job, and deliver it in a way that reinforces its intended use, then when customers find themselves needing to get that job done, they will hire that product.[14]

The article told the now infamous "milkshake" story of how Christensen's team got to the bottom of why early morning commuters were buying McDonald's milkshakes—and *only* milkshakes—to go. Research revealed that the "job" people were hiring the milkshake to do was not so much about hunger or flavor as it was about boredom. The milkshake beat out all the competing options—bagels, donuts, bananas, Snickers bars—for getting the same job done, mostly because it broke up the monotony and kept someone busy for the twenty-plus minutes it took to sip a shake through a straw. Secondarily, they wouldn't need to worry about getting food again before noon.

Soon after the *Marketing Malpractice* article came out, the notion of products being hired for a specific job became known as Jobs-to-Be-Done Theory (also called Jobs Theory) and was formally introduced to the world in that form by Anthony ("Tony") Ulwick in his 2006 book *Jobs to Be Done: Theory to Practice*. As Ulwick tells it, he had introduced Christensen years before to the concept of market segmentation based on jobs people hired products to do, ala the drill and hole metaphor. (See our interview with Tony Ulwick.)

Toyota, like many customer-obsessed companies, had subscribed to this way of thinking long before it was a "theory," in all likelihood due to the dismal failure of their initial entry to the U.S. market in the late 1950s with the market misfit Toyopet Crown, which had simply not been up to the target customer's job-to-be-done. Toyota was forced to return to the drawing board and suffer a delay of nearly half a decade before another passenger car could be produced suitable for the American driver.

That early failure was a valuable lesson learned and never forgotten: only customers can define value, and that value centers on the problem they're trying to solve or the objective they're trying to reach. True value is about the Job with a capital "J": the customer's Job-to-Be-Done. Customers are hiring what a company provides for a specific reason or reasons, and the better the understanding of, and alignment to, those reasons, the better the opportunity to help customers get their Job done and get the results they need. The customer's Job is the best and brightest guiding star in the business universe.

It may sound dramatic, but entire industries have gone extinct by failing to define value properly. A favorite example is the story of ice.

For almost the entirety of the nineteenth century, the ice industry amounted to a single, mostly seasonal job: ice harvesting. Special saws were used in winter to cut large blocks of ice from frozen ponds and lakes, then load them onto horse-drawn wagons and haul them to homes of wealthy individuals, ice houses for storage, or barges and trains for shipping to warmer, ice-barren regions. The ice industry spurred rapid growth and expansion in a range of other industries, including meat, produce, and fish that previously were restricted to local consumption. Ice harvesting created a "cool culture," and most households had an icebox for storing perishables. The ice harvesting trade became a global market, peaking in 1900. Then it vanished almost overnight.

Harvesting was replaced by a new technology, ice manufacturing, which had slowly been developing in the late 1800s. Ice plants with mechanically powered chilling facilities that could produce ice blocks quickly and cheaply all year round put the ice harvesters out of business. Ice factories sprung up in every sizable city, and ice manufacturing enjoyed a profitable existence for nearly a quarter century. Then it vanished almost overnight.

In 1924, Frigidaire introduced a new technology called refrigeration. Refrigeration replaced ice manufacturing, absorbed ice making, and made cold storage—in the form of electric freezers and refrigerators—affordable household conveniences.

Here's the thing: none of the ice harvesters became ice manufacturers. And none of the ice manufacturers became refrigeration companies. Neither group could see that it was not ice, or the service that delivered it, that customers were really paying for. Rather, it was the job they needed ice to do: *keep perishables fresh.*

History repeats itself. Blockbuster, Kodak, Borders, Netscape, Tower Records, typewriters, fax machines, VCRs, pay phones . . . the list goes on.

Conclusion: the Job endures, but the means by which the Job gets done are replaceable.

That century-old plumbing advertisement had it right.

The Jobs Rubric

The Job that we hired Jobs Theory to do here is to define value from the customer's perspective to maximize acceleration of value.

We have worded the above Job carefully. It has two major components: a Job (define value from the customer's perspective) and a desired measurable outcome (maximize acceleration of value).

Note how closely this mirrors the structure of OKRs—Objectives and Key Results—which we discussed earlier in the book. In fact, Mural's chief evangelist Jim Kalbach in *The Jobs to Be Done Playbook* defines a Job as "the process of reaching objectives under given circumstances."[15] We could easily have used customer OKRs, but why introduce yet another nomenclature? Instead, we have synthesized the two concepts.

The differences are nuanced, and at the highest level we are really talking about a "What?" and a "So what?" or "What do you want to do and why do you want to do it?" There are many books and articles written far more in-depth and focusing much more on the nitty-gritty of Jobs Theory. Most are written from an innovation perspective, to help startups find a product/market fit. Most ScaleUps, though, and certainly potential unicorns, have already found that fit, and are seeking a better go-to-market fit. The Accelerated Value principle addresses the latter, and our main focus is on the Value Gap.

We want to keep it simple, using an easy rubric:

JOB-TO-BE-DONE	DESIRED OUTCOME
(Main Objective)	(Key Result)
Verb + Object + Circumstances	*Delta + Measure + Focus*
Example:	Example:
Protect important information from exposure	Minimize loss of confidential company data

Notice that this structure does not mention or even suggest a solution. In the example above, a company might retain a security firm, subscribe to a SaaS security platform, build an internal security team, require special clearances, install physical identity measures, or employ sophisticated encryption . . . all viable solutions.

A Job-to-Be-Done is a customer's main objective. It can and should be stated very simply using a verb, an object of the verb, and a word or two about the circumstances, context, or situation. In the example above, the verb is *protect*, the object is *important information*, and the circumstances or context relates to *exposure*.

A Desired Outcome is a measurable key result. It can and should be stated very simply using a change vector or delta, the measure itself, and a few words to add clarity and focus. In the example above, the delta is *minimize*, the measure is *loss*, and the focus is *confidential company data*.

Keep this framework in mind when defining value from the customer's point of view:

- Like an OKR, a clear start and stop are required; you should be able to answer the question "Was this achieved?" Steer clear of stating Jobs with words like *maintain, support, help, manage*, and the like, simply because it will be difficult to know when the Job-to-Be-Done is, well, done.
- The Job-to-Be-Done and Desired Outcome should be independent of timeframe; meaning, the Job-to-Be-Done will still be here twenty-five years from now. Past, present, or future, a Job-to-Be-Done remains essentially unchanged.
- The Job-to-Be-Done is not the customer's job title or description, nor is it a simple to-do item or task. *Go to the grocery store* is not a main Job-to-Be-Done, but *get groceries for the week* is.
- Avoid conflating the Job-to-Be-Done with the Desired Outcome; remember that the first is an objective, the second is a result. It may help to think of Desired Outcomes as needs—designers certainly do! Irrespective of what you call them, they require insight only gleaned from spending time with customers. The majority of Desired Outcomes are not immediately obvious or well-articulated by customers. They can be inferred from observation, but should be confirmed through interviews, stories, and experiments.
- Never forget that customers are far more loyal to the Job-to-Be-Done than to your product or service. If something better, faster, simpler, and/or cheaper comes along, they will shift over to that solution, assuming switching costs aren't prohibitive or painful.

From Proposition to Promise

One final note on Value Defined concerns the standard business practice of creating a value proposition. We included it as a key part of the Innovation Brief in our discussion of Constant Experimentation. It always helps to have a one-line "what + so what" statement ready as a pithy answer to the inevitable question: What does your company (or product) do? In general, the value proposition goes something like this:

- (Company/product name) is a (description) for (customer type) that (key features), enabling (key benefits), unlike (existing/competing options). Hypothetical examples:
  - HearNoEvil is a portable music player for audiophile music lovers that plays music files in lossless formats, enabling improved quality unrivaled by other compressed file players.
  - Brandstar offers the only automotive consumer data that accurately predicts future purchasing behavior, enabling advertisers to know where buyers' hearts, minds, and pocketbooks will actually be.

We suggest going a step further to create a "Value Promise" for each specific customer and their Job-to-Be-Done. This helps break up a one-size-fits-all value proposition into something that is a bit more Job-tailored. Using the example in the rubric above, we can simply blend the Job-to-Be-Done and Desired Outcome to create a one-line Value Promise that reads like this:

Anubis protects your important information from exposure so your chances of losing confidential company data are minimized.

This format sounds and feels more like a personal promise to an individual and creates an expectation of a successful Job-to-Be-Done completion and Desired Outcome achievement. And if we know anything about customer satisfaction, it is the delta between expectation and outcome.

Give the Value Promise a try. We find that in addition to one universal value proposition, it helps to have several Value Promises, each tailored to a unique Job-to-Be-Done performer, whether buyer, customer, or end-user.

Voice of the Operator

INTERVIEW WITH TONY ULWICK[16]

*Anthony Ulwick is the founder and CEO of Strategyn,
a growth strategy and innovation consultancy, and
bestselling author of* Jobs-to-Be-Done: Theory to Practice.

**Tony, you've written that you and the late Clayton Christensen
collaborated on what is now known as "Jobs Theory." Can you
share a bit of how all that came about?**

Well, I read *The Innovator's Dilemma*, this was around 1997, and I
thought, well, what we [Strategyn] do solves that dilemma, right?
Eventually one member of my sales team reached out to Clay,
and he took a meeting with us. We went up to Harvard in 1999. I
remember well that it was in the fall and the campus was beautiful.
I presented him with Outcome-Driven Innovation [ODI] because
that's what we called it, that was our process. We talked about how
it's based on the notion that people buy products to execute some
underlying process.

He was intrigued, and we subsequently met a number of times
and talked more about the process, the approach. He introduced
me to his Innosight team and suggested that we work together,
which we did for about two years. My main focus was on jobs to
be done. Their main focus was really on disruptive innovation. That
was the basis for the relationship. We both published articles and
books. At some point they became more focused on jobs and we
kept talking about "the underlying process people are trying to
execute." He said, "That isn't that sexy. You should call it the job."
That became the job-to-be-done. Here we are all these years later.
It's a dumb name for a theory, but that's what it's called.

What is the current state of Jobs-to-Be-Done and ODI?

At the high level there are really two camps. ODI was derived really as a process for innovation, the goal of which in my opinion is to conceptualize a product that you know will win in the market before you even start developing it. In order to know it's going to win in the marketplace, you have to know in advance that it's going to get the target customer's job done better, simpler, and more cheaply, or as you say, more elegantly.

The other camp came about sometime around ten years ago, 2012, 2013, somewhere in there. Many more companies started getting involved with jobs-to-be-done and they gave it a different twist, more on the marketing side, the demand generation side. I have to say it comes to some degree from Clay's milkshake story, because in it he's saying that if you really know why people are buying the product, you can sell more of that product. So it's less about innovation, more about positioning what you have in such a way that more people want it, because it's helping them with the job that they're trying to get done.

Another way to say this is the ODI focus is on helping the job executor get the job done better, while the focus of the demand first group is to convince the buyer that it can get their job done.

What are some of the typical challenges companies experience when attempting to put Jobs Theory into practice?

It starts at the beginning, defining a market in a unique way. We don't define a market as a vertical or an application or a technology, or really any of the conventional segmentations. We define it as a group of people that are trying to get the same job done. You have to figure out who you're creating value for . . . the job executor . . . and then ask and answer: What job are they trying to get done?

The mistake is taking a product-first mentality. You can't say, I'm a kettle maker and people buy my kettle to heat water. Okay. They do, but they're doing it as part of a bigger job, which is to create a hot beverage for consumption. If you don't get to that point, you'll never understand what the customer's trying to do. Defining the market through that lens is challenging! A mindset shift is required for people to really grasp this. And a lot of it goes back to basic definitions.

We have data that tells us 90 percent of product teams don't agree on how to best divide a market. Over 95 percent say that there isn't an agreement on what a customer need actually is. Much of it is just getting these basics down. What a need is, what a market is, what a segment is. If you don't have alignment around what a market is and what a need is, you're certainly not going to have alignment around the solution and making sure it has that product/market fit. Defining needs as outcomes sounds simple, but it's extraordinarily hard.

Who's doing a great job of, er, Jobs Theory?
Well, there's one company that nailed it. The Medicines Company. They were acquired by Novartis last year at a 41 percent stock premium. We worked closely with Clive Meanwell, the CEO. His company is viewed as extremely innovative. What they were able to accomplish is using ODI at scale, meaning they not only applied it to their external customer facing products, but they applied it to their internal business processes as well. So they were just running extremely efficiently on all cylinders. And that I think is the ultimate measure of the value of outcome-driven innovation. It's creating a valuable company.

It sounds like that mind shift you mentioned occurred, company-wide.
That's exactly right. It starts with a change in mindset, and Clive was the first to have the new mindset. I remember when we first met, he stopped by in our San Francisco office and we sat and chatted for a bit and he "got it" right away. That's powerful. He

drove it through the whole company. And it's pretty rare in my experience that a CEO would even attempt to do that, or has the time to think about it, much less have the inclination to change an entire thought process. But he did and the results speak for themselves. That's the power of Jobs Theory.

VALUE DELIVERED

We live in a world of services. Even manufacturers of tangible products understand that future success in the form of repeat, expanded, and referral business is dependent on the ability to service and support the physical goods they sell to customers.

We have customer relationship management software company Salesforce to thank for two world-changing service innovations: a new software category and the formalization of a function dedicated to preventing customer abandonment and ensuring that customers get their Jobs done. The first became known as software-as-a-service (SaaS), the second was called Customer Success.

Salesforce had good reason to focus resources on Customer Success: although they were a double unicorn five years after their 1999 launch, nearly 100 percent of their customers canceled in the first year. There is perhaps no clearer indication of a customer's inability to pull value from a product or service than that. Today, any company with that level of churn wouldn't have a prayer of seeing a billion-dollar valuation; if it did, it wouldn't be a unicorn, it would be a black swan.

The practice of Customer Success was born to remedy all of that. Much has been written about Customer Success, and successful companies have sprung up dedicated to it. In 2015, Nick Mehta, CEO of Gainsight—one of those companies—published a bestselling book titled *Customer Success*, containing ten "laws." By 2021, those laws were in need of revision, mostly due to evolving customer and market changes. In a short e-book called *10 New Laws of Customer Success*, the authors had this to say:

> *It is no longer enough to have a customer journey—you must have one catered to each individual. You must simultaneously consider their most urgent needs*

*and their long-term goals. The traditional, linear lifecycle didn't make sense
for today's customers. A linear engagement model or customer journey from
Marketing to Sales to renewals fails quickly.*[17]

We agree. Thus, the main focus of the Accelerated Value principle is
mapping, pinpointing, and understanding the gaps in value as an effective
approach to accelerate value.

The best place to start is with the current delivery of value, then work
your way backward in reverse engineering fashion using the Jobs-to-Be-Done
framework to rethink value from the customer's point of view. This helps you
move toward a more horizontal way of thinking and uncover opportunities to
reduce churn and improve retention. The goal is to improve the most critical
measure of Value Delivery as noted above: *time to value* (TTV). To the extent
that we can shrink the time it takes for customers to realize value, everyone
wins.

Let's take a closer look at this leading indicator before introducing a practical
approach to Value Delivery.

Why TTV Matters

We began this book with the story of how we helped Gainsight reduce their
TTV by 66 percent. We began our discussion of Accelerated Value by making
the point that if a Google search took a few minutes to return results, we would
not be talking about Google today. That's the nature of consumer products
and e-commerce; we need near-instant gratification. B2B products are more
complicated, involve more customer interaction, and take longer in general to
deliver value. Today, "product-led growth" (PLG) is behind a current trend that
borrows from B2C software platforms and e-commerce, and generally amounts
to a tiered product, the lowest tier of which promises more of the instant value
delivery characteristic of consumer products.

TTV is fairly self-defining: it is the time it takes a new customer to
realize value from a product. And remember, value is defined as a completed
Job-to-Be-Done and Desired Outcome. If nearly 10 percent of newly subscribed
customers are canceling after the first month (the way those of Salesforce were
before they institutionalized Customer Success), it's a strong signal that TTV
exceeds thirty days, and needs to be reduced. Unless and until value is delivered

to customers, getting them to stick around and even buy more is going to be like trying to push water uphill.

Suppose two competing subscription SaaS companies offer similar solutions. The first offers a one-year contract, but the onboarding and implementation take ten months, leaving sixty days to deliver value and have a chance at renewal. The second company offers a six-month contract, and customers are up and running in sixty days. All other things being equal, it should be clear who wins the business.

If TTV is defined as the time it takes customers to realize value, it makes sense (for B2B companies) to come to an understanding and alignment with them on their list of Jobs-to-Be-Done and Desired Outcomes right up front, because then the clock can be concretely set and synced to those markers. Validate that alignment with customers, using a detailed list of Outcomes, so that the Value Delivery motion can be logically timed and balanced in a leaner and more iterative way. Reducing Desired Outcomes to broad process buckets—onboarding, enablement, implementation, first project; typical post-sale process steps—leaves you with a TTV clock that starts ticking in the customer's mind at contract signature, sometimes even before.

Unfortunately, we see this approach too often. Too many companies assume that making good on the promises made in the marketing messaging and the sales process is enough. It isn't, for all the reasons we discussed earlier in the Value Defined section. Agreement with customers on what they consider measurable value and ensuring that those measures are delivered, made apparent, and checked off must be done before any thought of renewal can be entertained. On average, those things are not usually done, or if they are, they aren't the standard, and that inevitably leads to a Value Gap.

Fortunately, Value Gaps are fairly easy to close with the right methods and tools, such as a Value Gap Analysis (see Voice of the Operator: Mind the Value Gap) and Customer Value Mapping, which we will describe in-depth next.

Voice of the Operator

MIND THE VALUE GAP: WHY COMPANIES FAIL TO SCALE CUSTOMER SUCCESS[18]

by Samma Hafeez
VP, Sales/Customer Success Center of Excellence, Insight Partners

If you have traveled to London, you might be familiar with the oft-used expression "mind the gap," a warning boldly imprinted on nearly every London Underground platform to remind riders to take caution and avoid the gap between the subway platform and train when boarding. Multiple preventative safety measures have similarly been introduced over the years to prevent rider injuries, allowing the Tube (the Underground's colloquial name) to retain one of the best safety ratings in the world—a major feat for an urban transport system that is over 150 years old and spans more than 250 stations.

How can we adopt similar safety protocols to protect our businesses from catastrophic churn? The sad reality is that very few churn incidents occur by mere happenstance; the metadata on SaaS churn points to a patently clear pattern: companies are failing to mind the Value Gap.

What exactly is the Value Gap?
The Value Gap is best explained using the late Clay Christensen's "jobs-to-be-done" framework. According to Christensen, customers hire products and services to deliver specific outcomes or perform specific "jobs" in a more optimal way (i.e., faster, better, or cheaper). When a given product or service doesn't satisfactorily complete a desired job, skepticism and negative thinking start to creep in. Left unchecked, customer trust and faith in the vendor quickly erode. Once customers feel disgruntled about an experience or sense

that their desired outcomes are unlikely to be achieved in the near or foreseeable future, they default to plan B. If we fail to read the writing on the wall, the gap between the metaphorical platform (customers' expectations, anticipated value) and the subway train (the customer experience or outcomes we actually deliver) becomes irreversible, widening to a point of no return.

If your company is serious about growth, it's time to get serious about closing the Value Gaps along your customer and user journeys.

How can companies close the Value Gap?

Conduct a formal customer Value Gap analysis (VGA) on an annual basis. No matter how impressive your various retention numbers are, it behooves you to develop a mature discipline that routinely exposes your blind spots. As the fitting platitude goes, an ounce of prevention is worth a pound of cure.

How do you conduct a customer Value Gap analysis?

A customer VGA leverages quantitative and qualitative methods to help you understand what jobs your customers are hiring your company to do and where you are falling short. It can help identify the root causes of churn, along with the emotional and rational motivations that result in downgrade or termination requests. Coordination failures and communication breakdowns across the customer lifecycle are flagged, process or documentation gaps that stall progress or result in haphazard engagements are discovered, and ways to better match talent to task and reduce enablement or skill gaps can be determined.

If you want to perform a robust VGA, devote a full quarter to complete the exercise, as several teams and individuals will need to be consulted throughout the process. The ideal time to perform a VGA is typically the first half of the year to allow findings to inform your strategic and budgetary plans for the subsequent year. A

VGA is typically managed by an operational leader who has the authority, influence, and ability to round up key stakeholders and synchronize different workstreams.

Follow this ten-step process to conduct your next customer value gap analysis:

1. **Secure executive sponsorship.** Without a formal endorsement from your leadership team, this exercise is unlikely to bear fruit or result in any material changes for your customers.

2. **Assemble a cross-functional task force.** To uncover all the possible Value Gaps across the customer lifecycle, you will need individuals from marketing, sales, professional services, customer success, customer support, operations, and product to engage in some capacity.

3. **Define clear workstreams in a project plan.** A project plan provides management with clear visibility into who is working on what while allowing everyone to understand how they fit into the big picture and stay on task.

4. **Gather and analyze various customer data sources.** It is important to understand when and where your customers and users are getting stuck or frustrated.

5. **Learn from customers who churned.** Take a microscopic look at the data for customers who downgraded or canceled over the last twelve to eighteen months. Look for early warning signs you may have missed. Call lost customers to gather candid feedback and ask what you could have done differently, and if they are realizing value with another solution.

6. **Learn from customers who renewed or expanded.** Remember to learn from your happy customers! This is an opportunity for your company to identify key moments in value throughout the customer lifecycle and determine how to reproduce and scale those experiences in the future.

It is just as important to discover what is working as it is to discover what is not.

7. **Observe your customers in action.** Schedule time to observe a representative sample of customers using your product or filing a support ticket to discover how different users behave, what they expect your product to do, and where they forfeit their sessions, drop off, or raise their hands for help.

8. **Identify quick wins.** As you synthesize your newly gathered insights, focus on near-term quick wins. You don't want to lose sight of immediate opportunities to minimize churn or boost retention.

9. **Design and run an MVP.** While you find those quick wins, don't lose sight of the long game. Design a minimum viable solution that addresses high-risk value gaps and then go test it.

10. **Refresh your customer empathy and journey maps**. With your newly acquired learning and MVP results in tow, don't miss out on the opportunity to reflect on what good looks like. Update your customer empathy and journey maps so they remain evergreen and serviceable for your internal teams.

What is the ROI of a VGA?

Closing customer Value Gaps directly translates into higher gross and net retention performance. And there is no ceiling to net retention. By delivering value earlier and earlier in the customer journey, we can significantly reduce renewal dread while initiating upsells and expansion opportunities more effortlessly.

Don't allow your customers to fall off the edge of the train platform. Improve your safety protocols today by running a customer Value Gap analysis and hanging a safety sign in your home or corporate office to remind yourself and your teams to mind the Value Gap.

THE CUSTOMER VALUE MAP

Everyone loves maps. Road maps, trail maps, subway maps, value stream maps, customer journey maps, treasure maps. They ground us, orient us, guide us. Where would we be without them? But what if the terrain doesn't look like the map? What if the ground has shifted, and keeps shifting, so the current map doesn't work very well?

In working together several years ago on an effort to improve the customer experience for a number of important customers, we came to the realization that the traditional customer journey map—usually a nicely designed menu of all the things a company ideally wants a buyer, customer, or user to do or consume throughout their relationship with a brand—was almost obsolete as soon as it was published, for two reasons. First, because a typical customer journey map does not concern itself with the customer's Jobs-to-Be-Done. Second, and in part due to the first, the actual experience customers were having did not reflect the pretty map. During the months, sometimes years, it took to research, draft, refine, and enable others to actually use the map, customers and market forces had changed, often dramatically, in some cases seemingly overnight.

Although it was years in the future at the time we were rethinking customer journey mapping, the COVID-19 pandemic is a good (albeit extreme) example. Suddenly, we were all in unknown territory, and the existing maps didn't work. While key jobs-to-be-done remained stable, we replaced the means used to pursue and achieve them with new ones. Counterintuitively, the pandemic eased and in some cases completely erased many points of friction related to in-person interactions: traveling, commuting, meeting. It also produced a new set of challenges, all of which included new friction and impacted customer experiences.

We wanted something far more useful. It had to be more dependable, more stable, and, paradoxically, more dynamic and easily updated in real time. It had to point us toward areas in need of immediate attention where we were missing the mark in providing value to customers. We considered adapting what in the lean world is commonly called "value stream mapping," but honestly, the term is just a fancy word for process mapping and is generally not focused on the customer as much as it is on discrete process steps that are internal and usually invisible to a customer. We needed something better.

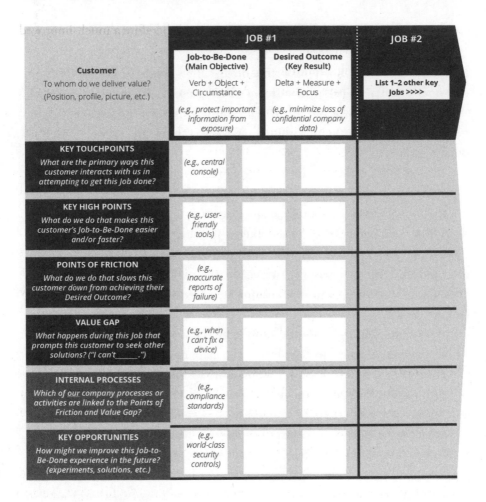

Realizing that the customer's main Job-to-Be-Done is stable over time, a tiny flash of insight produced what we now refer to as a Customer Value Map, an overlay of Jobs Theory on the key inflection points in any customer experience that we use to guide value acceleration efforts. We did not want to lose the notion of a customer journey entirely, but we needed a leaner lens through which to view it—from a *push* to a *pull*. Instead of the common push-focused journey being focused on all the things a customer must do to acquire and use a given solution, we needed to orient the map to the Job a specific customer was hiring that solution to do. Unlike customer journey maps that typically focus on customer steps and actions, we wanted to focus on customer goals and outcomes. Our hypothesis: done right, we would understand better how to achieve a more effortless pull by the customer, and therefore a much-improved experience and ultimately successful Job done.

Instead of using traditional demand generation phases (Awareness, Consideration, Purchase, Retention, Advocacy, etc.), we anchored everything to key customer Jobs-to-Be-Done. We then made sure to reflect current touchpoints, high points, points of friction, and gaps in value delivery. We also wanted to pinpoint key internal processes and activities that were linked to the specific customer's Jobs-to-Be-Done. Finally, we wanted to capture opportunities and ideas to accelerate value vis-à-vis Jobs-to-Be-Done and Desired Outcomes.

Armed with all of this, we could emerge with a solid list of fresh insights that provided a point of origin to begin closing the gaps and guide the effort to accelerate value. A good map shows you where you want to go and the various routes for getting there, but it only works when you know exactly where you are.

Our current basic Customer Value Map framework is shown on page 128.

TOURING THE CUSTOMER VALUE MAP

Navigating the Customer Value Map is simple, and completing it in a team setting requires little special facilitation. As long as everyone understands the basic principles of Jobs Theory, the rest is fairly self-explanatory.

Let's take a quick tour.

The Customer Value Map is really just a matrix that begins with the customer whose experience we want to map. Personas and profiles, if they exist, are helpful, but we like to invite actual customers to these sessions; first, because it is always illuminating, and second, because it saves time having to validate the draft map with real customers in the future. If that's not possible (and it often isn't), we always recommend completing a Customer Value Map for a certain customer type with a team of people who know that customer best.

Either way, we always spend a few warmup minutes completing a basic empathy map for that customer, quickly sketching out their general characteristics and answering several key questions: What is this customer seeing, saying, doing, feeling, hearing, and thinking? This gets people out of their own heads and into the head of the customer. Empathy map templates are widely available, and the one we use is shown on the next page.

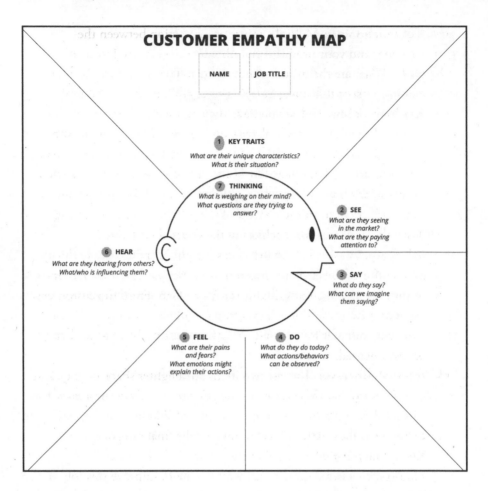

CUSTOMER EMPATHY MAP

NAME   JOB TITLE

1 KEY TRAITS
What are their unique characteristics?
What is their situation?

7 THINKING
What is weighing on their mind?
What questions are they trying to answer?

2 SEE
What are they seeing in the market?
What are they paying attention to?

6 HEAR
What are they hearing from others?
What/who is influencing them?

3 SAY
What do they say?
What can we imagine them saying?

5 FEEL
What are their pains and fears?
What emotions might explain their actions?

4 DO
What do they do today?
What actions/behaviors can be observed?

Once the empathy map is complete, we begin with horizontal thinking, working across the top of the Customer Value Map, left to right, mapping the one to five key Jobs this customer is hiring your solution to do, using the rubric we introduced earlier. In most cases, there are one or two main Jobs, and a few supporting Jobs. Once the top row is complete, we work vertically, completing all of the six left-hand categories before moving to the next Job. We do not work by row, but rather by column, focusing entirely on one Job at a time. This is critical to avoid falling back into old ways of thinking about an experience. Specificity breeds insights; generalization doesn't, at least in this case.

We move down the left-side map navigation sections, respecting the word *key*, focusing on the top one to three responses in the six left-side categories:

- **Key touchpoints.** Multiple points of interaction between the customer and your product undoubtedly exist for any Job-to-Be-Done. What are the primary ones? Which ones does the customer employ most at this point in trying to complete the specific Job?
- **Key high points.** Unless you have the advantages of a natural monopoly, you're not the only game in town, and there are reasons you're successful . . . moments of joy you and your product create for the customer, making their Job easier and/or faster . . . what are they?
- **Points of friction.** We spent a great deal of real estate discussing sources of friction. In the context of the Job, how are you slowing down the customer from achieving the Desired Outcome?
- **Value gap.** In every Job, there comes a point of inflection, a critical moment or problem that can determine whether the customer leaves or stays with your solution. This is a Value Gap. From the customer's point of view, these Value Gaps often sound like, "I can't do X" or "It's really difficult for me to do Y." These are solvable, but they must be documented.
- **Internal processes.** The last two items are a lighter shade of gray, just to emphasize that these are from the perspective of *your* processes and activities that are linked to the Points of Friction and Value Gap. These act as locators and focal points for the final category.
- **Key opportunities.** Using Points of Friction, Value Gaps, and Internal Processes output, what can be done to improve this Job for this customer? What can be built? What simple, fast, and frugal experiments can be run?

When all of the Customer Value Maps are complete (one company we worked with developed ten different maps for ten different customers with ten different teams over the course of just two days), know that you've taken a huge step forward in the effort to accelerate value to customers. A few immediate next steps are in order:

1. **Socialize the maps.** This is not a case of "what happened in the mapping session stays in the mapping session." Those not participating but having a vested interest in the output should be

briefed and allowed to add any input. Having the physical or digital artifact of the Customer Value Map makes it easy.

2. **Prioritize key opportunities.** For each map, collect, cluster, cull, and classify the bottom row, Key Opportunities. Cluster by theme, and cull any that seem duplicates or redundant, as well as any that are simply off the table for the time being. Classify opportunities, using the simplest prioritization schema: *Must Do Now*, *Should Do Soon*, and *Nice to Do Sometime*.

    Remember to view the list with the customer and their respective Jobs in mind. The goal here is twofold: first, to create a master list of potential action items to close the identified Value Gaps, and second, to look for some quick and easy wins to implement immediately. The Customer Value Map never fails to surface a number of considerations that everyone collectively agrees should have been done already (and is surprised that they aren't already in place).

3. **Validate with customers.** If the customer or a close proxy did not participate in the Customer Value Mapping, you'll need to validate with your customers that this is in fact how they see the world. Proxies can be super-users of your product, people in your company in the same role, recent hires from a customer or customer look-alike, and anyone who interacts with that particular customer daily and knows them very well.

We have included a short session guide and agenda here.

TOOLKIT: THE CUSTOMER VALUE MAP SPRINT

Map Key Customer Jobs-to-Be-Done in Less Than a Day

Don't be surprised when that six-month-long customer journey mapping project turns into a year. And don't be surprised that it's dead on arrival upon publication. Customers and markets move so quickly, even a few months can render journey maps obsolete. A better way is to anchor efforts to accelerate value to customers to what remains stable over time: their Jobs-to-Be-Done.

By utilizing the Customer Value Map (find a download link to a digital copy in the Toolkit Resources section), you can quickly map customer jobs, desired outcomes, touchpoints, friction points, high points, critical events, internal processes producing friction, and opportunities to improve value delivery.

If conducting the mapping sessions in person, multiple teams can work at once in the same room. If conducting the mapping sessions remotely, either use features like breakout rooms or take it one customer, one team at a time. The time blocking for a half-day session is shown on the next page.

AGENDA ITEM	TIMING	DESCRIPTION
Empathy mapping	45 minutes	Use the Empathy Map included in the Toolkit Resources section. There are seven categories, so simple math means five to six minutes per section. Don't overthink it.
Customer Value Mapping	2.5 hours	Use the Customer Value Map canvas included in the Toolkit Resources section. Map the top three to five customer Jobs. Move horizontally across the top header (Jobs-to-Be-Done and Desired Outcomes) first, then complete the six categories underneath each Job. Horizontal first, then vertical!
Readout	10 to 20 minutes per team	If you're conducting workshops in person with multiple teams working simultaneously, it's time to level up the room. Quickly run through the highlights of each Customer Value Map. In the interest of time, when reading out the Key Opportunities, have each team focus on just their top two Opportunities.

	JOB #1		JOB #2		JOB #3	
Customer To whom do we deliver value? (Position, profile, picture, etc.)	**Job-to-Be-Done** (Main Objective) Verb + Object + Circumstance (e.g., protect important information from exposure)	**Desired Outcome** (Key Result) Delta + Measure + Focus (e.g., minimize loss of confidential company data)	**Job-to-Be-Done** (Main Objective) Verb + Object + Circumstance (e.g., protect important information from exposure)	**Desired Outcome** (Key Result) Delta + Measure + Focus (e.g., minimize loss of confidential company data)	**Job-to-Be-Done** (Main Objective) Verb + Object + Circumstance (e.g., protect important information from exposure)	**Desired Outcome** (Key Result) Delta + Measure + Focus (e.g., minimize loss of confidential company data)
KEY TOUCHPOINTS *What are the primary ways this customer interacts with us in their journey to getting this Job done?*						
KEY HIGH POINTS *What do we do that makes this customer's Job-to-Be-Done easier and/or faster?*						
POINTS OF FRICTION *What do we do that slows this customer down from achieving their Desired Outcome?*						
VALUE GAP *What happens during this Job that prompts this customer to seek other solutions? ("I can't ____.")*						
INTERNAL PROCESSES *Which of our company processes or activities are linked to the Points of Friction and Value Gap?*						
KEY OPPORTUNITIES *How might we improve this Job-to-Be-Done experience in the future? (experiments, solutions, etc.)*						

ACCELERATED VALUE RECAP

Accelerated Value to customers requires a solid understanding of where and how friction is slowing down the ability of customers to pull value effortlessly from a product. We tend to operate and organize in a mostly vertical way, which creates friction for a mostly horizontal customer experience. Friction comes from not understanding and aligning with our customers' desired outcomes. Defining and delivering value from the customer's point of view is best done using the jobs-to-be-done framework, aka Jobs Theory. Customer jobs remain stable over time; only the means by which they get them done changes. Therefore it makes sense to map those jobs to discover opportunities to close any Value Gaps, thereby accelerating value delivery. A Customer Value Map is an effective tool to accomplish that task quickly to keep pace with customers.

CHECKPOINTS

- ☐ Do customers realize value from your products quickly and effortlessly?
- ☐ Do you have documented Customer Value Maps for all key customer profiles?
- ☐ Do you clearly understand the job(s) your customers are trying to do?
- ☐ Are your products and services aligned to customer/user desired business outcomes?
- ☐ Do you have a prioritized list of opportunities to improve the customer experience?

Principle 4

LEAN PROCESS

There is surely nothing quite so useless as doing with great efficiency what should not be done at all.
—Peter Drucker

Our Insight team has gathered on an October day in New York City at a rented SoHo loft space to kick off a process optimization initiative for one of our portfolio companies as part of our Lean ScaleUp program. It is the first in-person training event since the onset of the COVID pandemic. Today, the teams will experience the power of a lean system in action as they go through the official Toyota Production System simulation.

The goal of this three-hour simulation is to set the proper context for the software implementation process improvement work to come by demonstrating how to boost value—quality, cost, speed, and experience—by making small changes at high leverage points to create a lean system that allows customers to pull value effortlessly. We will build working model cars two different ways.

The first way uses six standalone workstations, parts conveyors, supervisors, and managers, all focused on pushing out product batches as fast as possible to a channel partner—a retailer—who then sells to the end customer. Five minutes to build fifteen working model cars. Results are disastrous: defects, late/lost sales, and an average unit cost of nearly $50, to produce a $10 item. It's not scalable, or even viable.

The second, leaner way uses four conveyance-free workstations under a single roof, one-piece flow, and a pull system to produce and sell all fifteen cars on time, defect-free, for $5.50/unit.

Triple on-time sales with half the resources at one-tenth the cost. Lesson: a lean process scales.

SCALEUP ENEMY #1: WASTE

In many respects, the SaaS economy has lean thinking to thank for its explosive growth: overall cost and complexity of acquiring and managing IT resources is reduced, IT service quality improves, as do speed, flexibility, and agility. In other words, the "iron triangle" of quality, cost, and speed—the old cliche of "pick any two"—is effectively destroyed by the sheer simplicity of the SaaS business model.

As-a-service solutions are by nature leaner offerings: they achieve more with less. They add value by reducing costly burdens that previously plagued customers of legacy enterprise software solutions. Those burdens are properly classified as *waste*, defined simply as the motion of performing work that adds no value for customers, and in fact diminishes it. Waste is and always has been the primary target of lean, and it is the archenemy of companies in the throes of scaling for growth.

The challenge is achieving a level of organizational effectiveness to match the product. As we mentioned in the introduction, ScaleUps struggle with waste simply because growth has outpaced development of the standardized operational processes needed to sustain the business into the future. In our experience, waste in high-growth technology companies exists not because the work being performed is inefficient, but rather because it is *ineffective*, defined simply as the wrong work performed.

Anyone with a military background knows that to defeat the enemy, you must know it well. Let's take a closer look at waste.

MEET THE ENEMY

As enemies go, waste is a rather nefarious one, with the ability to rain excessive complexity down on the entire experience from every imaginable perspective. It bloats your ranks, exhausts your capacity, and drains your resources, leaving you vulnerable to a leaner offering from a competitor.

In his seminal 1988 book *Toyota Production System: Beyond Large Scale Production*, Toyota's legendary chief engineer, Taiichi Ohno, urged leaders to keep an eye on what he called the value-to-waste ratio. He believed, and was able to demonstrate, that only about one-quarter of any work activity actually adds value for customers; the rest is non-value-adding work, split into two categories: incidental work (25%) and waste (50%). Value-added work allows customers to complete their Jobs-to-Be-Done. Incidental work is activity that must be done to deliver that value, but the customer doesn't care about it, nor wish to pay for it. Waste is everything else.

Incidental work will never disappear entirely, but can be reduced. For example, to attend a meeting in person, you need to travel. Unless you're an attorney, no one is going to pay for travel time. No company pays you to commute. So you want to reduce travel time as much as possible.

Waste is the stupid stuff, the things we do that no one, and certainly not a customer, is asking us to do. Peter Drucker's quote captures the essence of waste: "There is surely nothing quite so useless as doing with great efficiency what should not be done at all." It's an important point, because efficiency and effectiveness are not the same thing. The first is about doing the work right, the second is about doing the right work. *Nearly all waste comes from not doing the right work.*

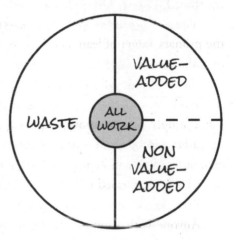

The entire Toyota Production System, and thus all lean methods related to it, is based on the simple goal of looking for and removing excess waste. No one has said it more plainly than Taiichi Ohno himself:

All we are doing is looking at the timeline from the moment the customer gives us an order to the point when we collect the cash. And we are reducing that timeline by removing the non-value-added waste.[1]

Beautiful. Simple. Elegant. Everything else is just detail.

In our work with SaaS ScaleUps on process optimization, the majority of projects entail shrinking "quote to cash" time. In other words, production environments and high-growth technology environments share the same clear goal. Let's turn our attention to the enemy standing in the way of achieving this goal.

According to Ohno, the enemy has seven faces:

Overproduction. Anything done without regard to demand counts as overproduction. That includes something as simple as processing an order before it's actually needed. Uber owes much, if not all, of its success to excising this waste when it pioneered on-demand car service . . . without cars. Likewise, Airbnb has become a wildly successful lodging service without producing a single property.

Overprocessing. When there are too many non-value-added steps to achieve a given outcome, you've got overprocessing. Examples include too many operations to complete a phase of work, the effort needed to inspect and fix defects arising from poor tool or product design, and redundant data entry due to a lack of integration among multiple systems. Amazon banished overprocessing with "1-Click" buying.

Conveyance. The best you can hope for when transporting anything—digital information included—from one place to another is that nothing goes wrong. No offense to transporters the world over, but conveyance is a necessary evil to be reduced wherever possible. The decline of the U.S. Postal Service began with one of the most radically innovative applications ever, now well over a generation old: email.

Inventory. Any time inventory of any kind builds up, it creates pressure to manage, reduce, or eliminate it. A visit to the average car dealership—an experience many consider more painful than a root canal—is a case in point: the buildup of cars is the root cause of sales pressure and unfriendly consumer tactics. New mobility-focused subscription models supported by an all-digital experience such as Faire.com are attacking inventory waste directly.

Motion. Needless repetition of any process (even a lean one) sucks time and productivity. Case in point: signing in to various mobile apps is a big burden. Enter fingerprint and face recognition software, genius bits of technology that eliminate the need to constantly reenter our user names and passwords, which most of us can't remember anyway.

Defects/Rework. Everyone has experienced a defect of some kind: errors, inaccurate or incomplete information, flawed products. It's obviously important to reduce the probability of these things happening. Surprisingly, however, it's not always a top priority. For example, death by medical error or accident is the nation's leading cause of accidental death, exceeding all other causes of accidental death combined. Medical errors and accidents kill approximately as many people each month in the U.S. as COVID-19 did before vaccines became available.[2] This would make medical errors the third-leading cause of death in the last decade. New technology such as digital employee software, RFID, bar coding, and iris/fingerprint scanning are focused on eliminating these critical errors.

Waiting. The late Tom Petty had it right in his song "The Waiting": it's the hardest part. Whether it's an endless, unmoving queue, being stuck in idle while you wait for an approval to proceed, the "spinning wheel of death" as your application decides whether it feels like opening today, or simply a slow download speed hampering your ability to stream every *Seinfeld* episode ever made in HD, we've all experienced waiting and the accompanying sense of helplessness and lost productivity. Netflix completely eliminated the need to wait seven days to watch the next installment of a show you love.

It should be easy to see that removing waste and reducing non-value-added work improves the value-to-waste ratio (VWR). When a given waste form is eliminated entirely in a given domain, it is labeled as radical, and sometimes (depending on quality and cost) disruptive, innovation. To wit, Netflix, Uber, Airbnb, et al.

We are not after radical innovation here. We are after *balanced optimization* of the processes that deliver value to customers. And for that, we do not need to

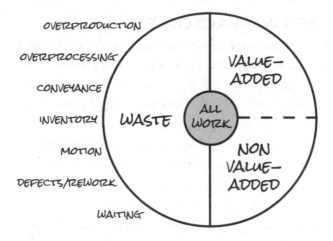

change the world, we just need a reliable discipline to continuously improve the VWR. What makes that difficult at all is the word *continuously*.

Fortunately, the entire principle of Lean Process rests on such a discipline. It is one thing to explain this "work wheel" and the power of removing waste, but it is quite another to understand it. That's why the first thing we do when preparing a team to optimize a given process is to have them experience *all* of these waste forms in a very physical way: through the simulation exercise described earlier. We are advocates of learning by doing and fully embrace the old aphorism, *what I see I forget, what I hear I remember, what I do I understand.*

The understanding we are after is not just how waste destroys value, or how a lean approach rectifies that, but also that a physical, production-focused example is in principle no different from their daily work: they too work in a factory producing a digital product, and *everything* is a series of steps to produce a desired result. Everything they do is part of a process. Every part on an assembly line must flow to the right person at the right time in the right form to allow the downstream function to add value to the work in process, and eventually to channels and customers. The sales and post-sales processes of a SaaS company are no different in that regard. From an initial company contact to the customer's realization of value, information must flow to the right people at the right time in the right form.

No matter how technologically advanced their packaged bit of code may be, they face the same enemy every company does in creating customers.

A TALE OF TWO FACTORIES

We begin the simulation by telling the team the short story of a "toad-like" factory that almost overnight became a "prince" of a plant:

It is 1982, the year of the Wendy's "Where's the Beef?" commercial and Jordache Jeans. The U.S. is still reeling from an oil crisis, and long lines at the gas station to buy enormously expensive fuel has consumers dumping their gas-guzzlers and buying smaller, fuel-efficient imports. Trade restrictions loom, forcing foreign car companies to begin building cars on American soil for the first time.

The General Motors plant in Fremont, California, is plagued by multiple strikes and sickouts by the United Auto Workers, five thousand union grievances on file, absenteeism topping 20 percent, rampant substance abuse, and four drug-related murders. It's GM's worst plant in terms of quality and productivity, with double-digit defects and twice the average assembly time. Eventually, the factory closes.

Enter Toyota, looking to test its production system on U.S. soil. Toyota and GM form a joint partnership in 1983. Toyota injects cash to reopen the Fremont line, which will build cars on a modified platform producing rebranded Toyotas for GM. GM now has access to the top-selling Corolla, rebranded as Chevy Nova. Hailed as a great experiment and entrepreneurial startup, the plant is named New United Motor Manufacturing Inc. (NUMMI). Eighty-five percent of the workers are hired back; 112 union job descriptions are flattened to just three: team member, team leader, group leader. Fourteen levels of plant management are flattened as well. Those with leader designation are flown to Japan to learn the Toyota Production System and kaizen, or continuous improvement. The team is told that they have a "right to succeed" and that the path to enacting that right runs through a new responsibility: Don't just do a job, improve the work.

Operations begin in 1984, and within two years, NUMMI has the highest quality and productivity of any GM plant, building nearly defect-free cars faster. Absenteeism drops down to 3 percent. Worker satisfaction and engagement reaches record levels, with over nine thousand employee-led improvements implemented the first year, another six thousand in year two. Employees now buy and drive the cars they make. The U.S. Labor Department awards NUMMI a citation for stellar union relations. By 1988, NUMMI has won J.D. Power & Associates awards, and former NUMMI engineer John Krafcik has published an article entitled "Triumph of the Lean Production System" in MIT's Sloan Management Review, coining the term "lean" to describe the essence of the Toyota Production System.

To bring that story to life, we will bring the before and after factory to the team to experience firsthand through the same exercise Matt taught to new employees upon their hire at Toyota Motor Sales USA Inc., Toyota's U.S. headquarters.

Before
We have the team experience the Fremont plant first. Here's how it works:

1. We introduce the Make-Alot company, with Morris Better as CEO. We share the corporate philosophy: "The More We Make, The More ($) We Make." We share the company motto: "Push Out As Much As You Can, As Fast As You Can."

2. We explain the operation: We are building working SUVs, complete with electric motors. There are two separate lines, one for the body, one for the chassis. Each line has three separate stations, each operated by one person, for a total of six functions: Body Prep, Glass Assembly, Accessories Assembly, Powertrain Assembly, Wheel Assembly, and Final Assembly/QA. Space between stations indicates geographic distance, so to get parts from one station to the next, we need parts conveyors, three people to cover the six locations. We sell to a channel partner—the retail dealer—who then sells to the customer.

3. We need two supervisors to keep the lines moving fast and to "motivate" the workers to work faster and a manager to make sure the supervisors are doing their jobs. Each worker has a production schedule and is told that if they follow it, good things will happen. We train the workers quickly by demonstrating the job; we don't need their input, we just want them to put the parts together as fast as they possibly can. They only go together one way, so it's not rocket science. They are building in batches of two or more (as fast as they can) at a time, and calling for conveyance when they have completed

a batch. We allow the manager and supervisors to have a short executive offsite, so they can strategize over how to meet the CEO's expectations.

4. Unbeknown to the workers, a customer places an order for one of three different colored vehicles every twenty seconds, fifteen orders total. If the dealer has no inventory, we place the order in the Late Delivery Lane of the dealership.

5. We run the plant for just five minutes. It's loud. It's frantic. Supervisors are shouting at workers to work faster. Workers are shouting for conveyance. Parts are flying, cars are coming apart on delivery, some don't even turn on, others do but run backward. The retail dealer is shouting at the Make-Alot CEO for more cars. The customer is simply shaking her head.

6. Then we debrief. First, a qualitative review: What went wrong? Everything seemed so nice and orderly, everything in its place, and a place for everything. The answers haven't changed in over twenty years of doing this, in dozens of countries, in every kind of company and culture:

    - In a word: chaos
    - Stress from supervisors
    - ALL seven waste forms present
    - No flow, no standards
    - Conveyance is everywhere, but workers can't get conveyance when needed
    - Poor training, horrible management
    - Not enough resources
    - Workers treated like robots
    - No desire for employee suggestions
    - No talent-to-task fit
    - Dealer doesn't get enough cars to sell; those they get don't work
    - Customer doesn't get what they ordered

    Then we look at the numbers—labor cost, work in process, defects, late deliveries, lost sales, total cost, total sold, unit cost, and on-time deliveries. We have lost nearly one-third of the targeted sales. The rest are late or defective, and usually both. We are producing products with a unit cost of over eight times the selling price. Without government subsidy or bailout, we're out of business. We shut down.

The factory layout is on the following page. (Note: retail dealer and customer not shown.)

After

After a short break and brief room reset, we share the good news: a new company is going to reopen the plant, make a few changes, and hire back most of the workers. We then reveal the new plant:

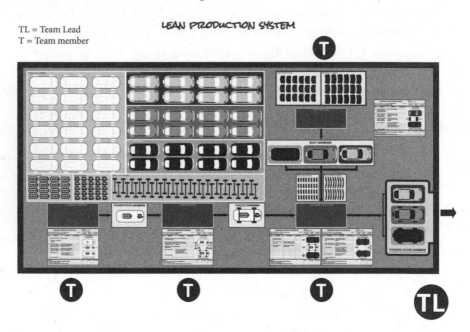

TL = Team Lead
T = Team member

LEAN PRODUCTION SYSTEM

No new equipment, and the same cars will be built with the same parts. We still sell to a channel partner (the dealer), who sells to the customer. But much is missing from the first factory. We coach the team to look at the new operation through the lens of subtraction: What has been removed or reduced? One by one, we unpack the observations about what isn't there:

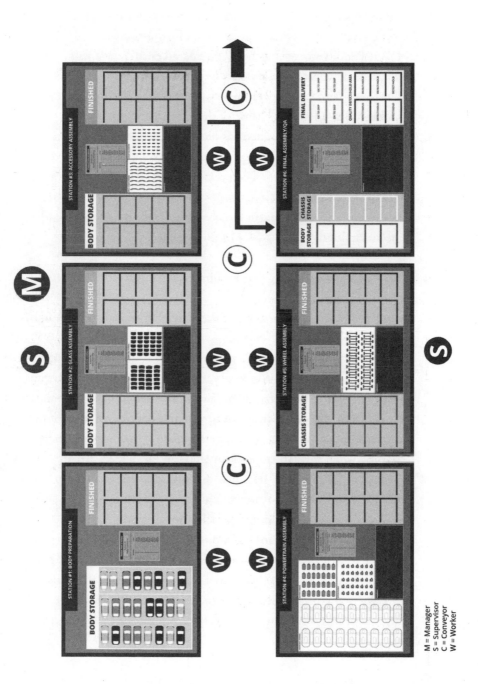

- The six separately housed stations have been consolidated under one roof; conveyance between stations is no longer needed.
- Finished goods storage has been eliminated entirely; we will utilize one-piece flow instead of batches of two or more.
- Four team members instead of six workers; two functions have been combined, based on cycle time of the jobs.
- End-of-line quality assurance has been removed; quality checks are performed at each station.
- Production schedules have been removed; we are no longer in a push system, we are in a pull system.
- Supervisors and the manager are gone, replaced by one team leader who has mastered every aspect of the system.

A few items have been added that require explanation:

- Visual flow indicators; arrows on the factory floor show direction of flow.
- Each station has a *kanban*. Kanban is the Japanese word meaning "sign card." The kanban concept was borrowed from U.S. grocery stores, which run on just-in-time inventory systems. The kanban is a request from a downstream station, which is considered an internal customer. The only time work is performed is when it is requested, meaning when the kanban is empty. It eliminates the waste of overproduction and enables a just-in-time pull system. We explain that it will be difficult not to work ahead if the kanban is full, since our natural tendency is to build slack into the system.
- Each station has a standard operating procedure (SOP). We explain how the role of an SOP in a lean system is different from how most organizations view SOPs. SOPs in a lean enterprise are the basis for kaizen, or continuous improvement. We share the history of continuous improvement, which formally began in 1940. (More on this to come.)

We demonstrate how the entire system keys off a customer order, which the dealer fills. Dealer stock of that vehicle is replenished by the factory. Each station pulls from the upstream station. We select two individuals for two pivotal stations. We explain the role of the team leader: oversee the operation and help when a problem occurs. We discuss the concept of a *poka yoke*, or failsafe device for error-proofing, when performing a quality check.

We explain the concept of *andon*, which is a call for help to solve a problem that could potentially halt production. We share that fifteen customer orders will be placed in five minutes, with a cadence or *takt* time—net available time divided by demand—of twenty seconds. That means job *cycle time*—total task completion time—must be twenty seconds at most in order to be on schedule in a one-piece flow system. If even a few seconds are spent trying to fix a problem, we will run behind; therefore, immediately call for help. It's one of the hardest things for many people to do. Don't "cowboy" it, because the problem may not be solved and it can get worse. The team leader is experienced in all facets of the operations and will not only help solve the problem at the root cause level, but also deliver just-in-time training to the team member. We suggest that if extra time exists because their kanban is full, think about ways to improve the work, explaining that any improvement happens off-line, never in production, and is always experimental.

We then have the team read their SOPs before we train each station on the job, demonstrating some style nuances that don't rise to the level of an SOP; pro tips, as it were. We allow practice time so that everyone is comfortable with the job. The rest of the team is assigned the role of kaizen observers, positioning themselves behind one of the four stations: the job is to simply watch and look for where any struggles may occur and think of countermeasures.

We then run the exercise again. The room is nearly silent, save for an occasional call for help. We never mention anything about philosophy, mottos, teamwork, goals, quality, cost, or speed. We simply explain the system. The system always rules . . . the system bats last.

The results speak for themselves: every qualitative issue is erased. The numbers tell the story (see image on page 150).

Depending on which measure you look at, there is exponential improvement in doing the same work but using fewer capital resources in a different system that makes small changes at high leverage points, removes waste, creates a pull versus a push, and is tied to the customer all the way down the line. This system scales, profitably. And there is ample improvement opportunity.

PROCESS & PERFORMANCE METRICS

ROUND	LABOR COST ($10)	WIP COST ($6)	DEFECT COST ($6)	LATE DELIVERY ($10)	LOST SALES ($10)
Before (non lean)	$140	$150	$148	$70	$40
After (lean)	$60	$12	$0	$10	$0

	Before (non lean)	**After** (lean)
TOTAL COST	$548	$82
TOTAL SOLD	11	15
COST/UNIT	$49.81	$5.46
# ON-TIME	4	14

INSIGHT
PARTNERS

Welcome to the wasteless world of lean process. Let's look at the wasteless way.

THE TAO OF LEAN

Wasteless. Synchronized. Rhythmic. Poetry in motion. These are some of the terms people use to describe the two seconds during which a routine pit stop in a Formula 1 race is performed.

Seldom are words like these used by customers to describe their experience with a company's offerings, or by employees to describe the internal processes of their organization. Still, many organizations hold up a Formula 1 pit stop as the epitome of the qualities they aspire to in delivering value to customers, not the least of which is speed. And more than a few operations have applied the Formula 1 pit stop model with great success, including surgical teams, aviation crew management teams, and software implementation teams. They understand that fans in the stands are like their customers, and are there to see the pinnacle of motorsports. That's what they paid for, and that's how they define value. They see the car and driver as their organization, doing everything in their power to win and delight the fans. As it is for fans, value is in the racing, and anything that detracts from racing diminishes value.

The sole exception is the pit stop, perhaps because it has become a race in itself, a race against the clock, and a highly entertaining show to watch, if only for a blink. A slow or boggled pit stop can make the difference between winning and losing, which is why enterprises in domains other than racing are so interested. As we have said before, value delayed may be value lost.

To be sure, pit stops in Formula 1 racing are a thing of beauty. They have evolved over the years to become unique from those in other forms of racing, and by far the most complex, as is Formula 1 racing in general. Each car is required to perform at least one routine pit stop per race. The entire job is to replace the wheels on the car in order to give the driver fresh tires. The crew must perform eight different functions in five key motions, and each member has a very specific role. The pit crew is not a formal special team, in that everyone on the team (aside from the driver) has other roles in the garage, and all are elite-level mechanics with an engineering background. But for those two seconds, something special happens.

Allow us to geek out a bit here. The relevance will become apparent. Here's what happens.

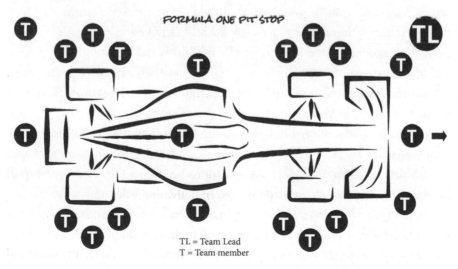

FORMULA ONE PIT STOP

TL = Team Lead
T = Team member

Motion 1: Hit the Mark. As the driver enters the pit lane at nearly fifty miles per hour, his pit crew of twenty-plus highly trained mechanics are poised, seemingly frozen in their respective ready positions. The driver stops the car precisely on designated markers. Even the smallest deviation from those markers adds time; even if only a slight shift in position by the crew is required, that half-second or so in a two-second stop represents a 25 percent loss. To prevent that from happening, two crewmen hold up bright red and yellow visual markers to help the driver line up his wheels precisely on the mark.

Motion 2: Raise the Car. The front and rear jack men are moving into position even before the car stops. Front and rear backup jack men stand ready in case anything goes wrong. As the car comes to a complete stop, an electronic red traffic stop light is triggered, and the two jack men lift the car off the ground. Two additional crewmen move in on either side of the car to stabilize it and hold it still to prevent any jostling from the wheels being changed. They also clean the driver's visor if needed, double as side jack men when the front wing of the car has been damaged, preventing a front jack from being used. At the front of the car, two crewmen on either side adjust the front wing as needed.

Motion 3: Replace the Wheels. Twelve crewmen are required, three per wheel, each assigned to one of the three wheel change steps. The tire gunner operates the wheel gun to loosen the nut holding the wheel to the car. The wheel and wheel gun are high-tech wonders. The wheel nut is integrated into the wheel and requires only three turns to screw or unscrew. The wheel gun is pneumatically supercharged to spin at over ten thousand revolutions per minute. Once the wheel nut is loose, the gun automatically switches spin direction to the tightening mode. As one crewman pulls the old wheel off, another crewman puts the new one on, and the gunner tightens the wheel nut. The car's axles are tapered, making the wheel change easier and faster. The gun is fitted with a button the gunner presses to signal the electronic traffic system that the new wheel is fit properly. If anything goes wrong, the gunner will cross his arms in the air, making an "X."

Motion 4: Lower the Car. As the gunners finish, the jack men pull quick-release handles to drop the lifting pads on the jacks, returning the car to the ground. The front jack man begins to take a long, sweeping sidestep to move out of the way before the car hits the ground, a move made easier by a swivel handle on the jack. Like the wheel guns, the jacks are fitted with buttons the jack men press to signal the electronic traffic system that the car is safely on the ground. The entire crew steps away from the car.

Motion 5: Release the Car. The electronic traffic light turns green once three things happen: the system indicates that the wheels are on safely, the car is safely on the ground, and no override has been triggered by the "lollipop" man—so named for the old practice of holding up a traffic stop/go sign on a pole. As chief mechanic, the lollipop man oversees the entire pit stop, monitors the pit lane for other cars, and ensures that the driver can safely leave the pit area without incident. Another safety mechanic is at the rear of the car as well. Both have buttons that can prevent a green light.

All of that happens in two seconds. A Formula 1 pit stop illuminates the power of a lean process, and the direct outcome of waging a war on waste. Do things go wrong? Yes. Is there room for improvement? Absolutely. But as a vivid metaphor for the removal of waste to enable greater value added for customers, it stands alone.

To draw a parallel between a Formula 1 pit stop and a truly lean process or system is not the stretch it might seem. Even when the comparisons appear slim, there are valuable lessons and practical takeaways all hopeful unicorns can, and should, apply to their own processes.

LEAN LEVERS

A lean process or system is earmarked by several levers that can be pulled to create flow by reducing incidental work and removing waste. To draw a comparison between the lean production system and a Formula 1 pit stop, take a look at page 155, which shows the pit stop layout juxtaposed with that of the lean production system introduced earlier. The basic schematics are similar. In both cases, any activity that does not directly add value has been streamlined or eliminated.

In both cases, every functional role on the team adds value essential to the final outcome. There are other similarities:

- **Flawless Execution.** There is no room for errors in a two-second tire change. If it's not done correctly, the race may be lost. The tire guns have error-proofing designed into them to alert the gunner if something goes wrong. In a lean system, quality is also designed in, and error-proofing is both technological and human-centered: parts only fit one way, and if things go wrong, the team leader solves the problem at the root-cause level. Defects and errors that are knowingly ignored or passed on (called *jidoka* in the lean production system) are unacceptable and can be grounds for disciplinary action.

- **Creating Flow.** The lean system in the training simulation demonstrated reduction in handovers by a factor of six, achieved by eliminating space, time, and motion. Value is pulled effortlessly as needed, not pushed in spite of need. The Formula 1 pit stop has eliminated all handovers, as there is simply no time (or space). The mere act of passing a physical object from one person to another takes half the time of a routine pit stop. As you watch a pit stop, the tires coming off the car come within centimeters of those going on the car. In a lean system, handovers are obviously necessary, but there is a finished Toyota Camry coming off the line every forty-five seconds, so non-value-added motion like handovers must be minimal.

- **Kanban Pull.** Only work that is needed or requested is performed. Nothing else adds value. Building a buffer into processes in a "just in case" way is waste, and incurs cost. The Formula 1 pit crew may work only once in a given race, and only when the race director and driver agree that a new set of tires is needed. There is no regularly scheduled pit stop, just as there is no regular production schedule in a lean system; everything is synced to need.

- **Visual Management.** While it may not be apparent in this book, the lean production system is entirely color-coded: all kanbans are matched to the color of the car being built, SOPs all include pictures, and there are clear direction indicators. A Formula 1 pit stop can only be performed in two seconds if the driver stops the vehicle exactly in the right place. Communication between the driver and the pit crew is entirely visual: the tarmac in the pit lane is clearly marked left, right, and center to help the driver position his car perfectly, two crewmen wear visual markers on their sleeves to indicate where wheels must be positioned, the stop point is communicated visually, and a traffic light signals when it is safe to drive away. Two words spoken takes two seconds—verbal communication here is useless.

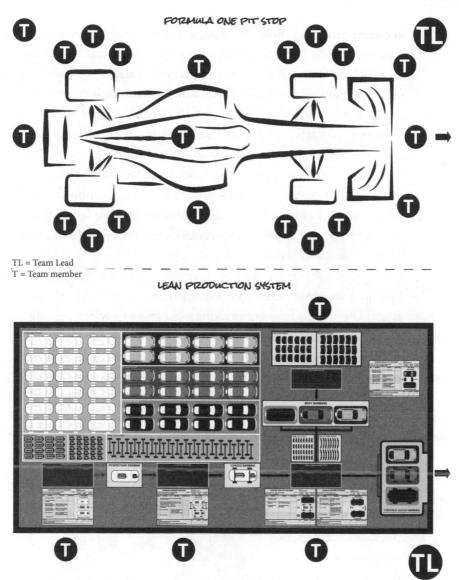

FORMULA ONE PIT STOP

TL = Team Lead
T = Team member

LEAN PRODUCTION SYSTEM

- **Local Leadership.** In both models, an experienced senior team leader versed in all aspects of each position oversees the work. The job is not to supervise or direct the action as much as it is to ensure that things go according to plan, and to help and support if they don't. In addition to oversight, they provide foresight, anticipating potential mishaps.

- **Practice.** Formula 1 pit crews practice regularly, like any other sporting team. It has been said by pit crew members that if they miss a scheduled practice, they notice a dip in performance. If they miss two, others notice. In a lean system, personal mastery is an important principle. It is referred to as "the right to succeed." When we run the lean operation in the simulation previously described, we make sure to give everyone on the team time to practice their roles, gain confidence, and develop their own personal SOP. Marc Andreesen has been quoted as saying, "The gap between what a highly productive person can do and what an average person can do is getting bigger and bigger. Five great programmers can completely outperform 1,000 mediocre programmers."[3]

The two most impactful levers, however, deserve a deeper dive before we turn our attention to exactly how to pull them: *standardized work* and *continuous improvement*.

Standardized work and continuous improvement are at once both principles and practices. They are two halves to a whole, yin and yang, and should not be thought of as separate, standalone concepts. One without the other yields marginal value. Continuous improvement without a standard to work from is like trying to improve your golf swing at the driving range on a foggy day: you have no way to know if the tweak you make produces a better result without data. Standardized work without improvement is destined to quick and certain irrelevance.

The only way that a two-second pit stop can be consistently achieved by ten different Formula 1 teams race after race is through a standardized process: the crew must know exactly what the goal is, what their role is, what to do when, and how best to do it. The only way that dozens of factories across the planet can consistently

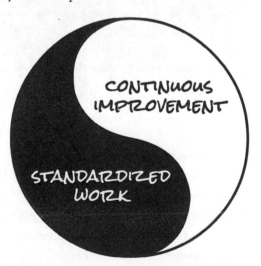

produce quality vehicles and maintain a market leadership position for over fifty years is through standardization. The only way that a Formula 1 pit stop can be reduced to the current two seconds (down from nearly sixty in the 1950s) is through data-driven improvement over improvement, analyzing time and motion, and experimenting with even the tiniest of changes that make a big difference.

And the only way to do that is to begin with a standard.

Continuous Improvement

Continuous improvement as a formal business practice is now over eighty years old. It began during Franklin D. Roosevelt's presidency, under which we experienced both the recovery from the Great Depression and the end of World War II. When U.S. involvement in the European theater looked imminent in 1940, the U.S. manufacturing sector needed ways to not only convert factories and ramp up production—even more than it had been doing to provide support to China, Great Britain, and Russia in their respective battles—but also to rapidly train people to replace the workers who would soon become soldiers. Many of those replacements were women who had never set foot in a factory before. Training was required. New methods were needed.

The Department of War, at Roosevelt's direction, formed an emergency service called Training Within Industry (TWI) to help quickly boost both production and productivity. Three programs were developed: Job Instruction Training, Job Relations Training, and Job Methods Training. Job Methods Training (JMT) taught how to generate and implement ideas through hundreds of small changes that could be made quickly on the front line of production.

The term coined for the method: *Continuous improvement.*

As Donald Dinero correctly points out in his 2005 book *Training Within Industry*, Job Methods Training

> *taught workers to objectively evaluate the efficiency of their jobs and to methodically evaluate and suggest improvements. The course also worked with a job breakdown, but students were taught to analyze each step and determine whether there was sufficient reason to continue to do it in that way by asking pointed questions. If they determined some step could be done better by eliminating, combining, rearranging, or simplifying, they were to develop and apply the new method by selling it to the "boss" and co-workers, obtaining*

approval based on safety, quality, quantity, and cost, standardizing the new method, and giving credit.[4]

Training scaled up quickly, using a train-the-trainer multiplier approach that is still used today in launching a new Toyota plant. Intuit used the method to establish and grow an internal group of "innovation catalysts."

Here's how it worked: Five course developers each taught two trainers, who in turn trained twenty instructors each. These trainers taught and led "quality circles" in nearly seventeen thousand plants across the United States. By the end of the war in 1945, TWI had trained nearly two million people on continuous improvement. Average productivity across all trained factories rose 25 percent.

TWI as a U.S. Emergency Service was discontinued along with other such services at the close of the war. But the approach followed General Douglas MacArthur's occupation forces in Japan as the U.S. began to help rebuild the devastated nation. McArthur saw TWI as a good way to jumpstart the reconstruction effort. Fortunately, one of the original TWI instructors had formed TWI, Inc., and came to Japan to support McArthur's occupational forces. McArthur had help from two other influences: first, complementary training by the U.S. Air Force for the Japanese people operating the supply depots; second, the teachings of Dr. W. Edwards Deming, who arrived in 1950 at the behest of the Japanese Union of Scientists and Engineers to teach Japanese managers the "Scientific Method" of *Plan-Do-Study-Act*.

The message remained clear and constant through all three influences: everyone is responsible for improvement, and there is no end to improvements. The message was culturally consistent with the Japanese belief in personal mastery, exhibited through trade, as well as through performing and martial arts.

By 1953, continuous improvement had become Japan's de facto standard business practice and had been incorporated into nearly every major manufacturing operation in the country. It became known as kaizen, or "change for the better."

As a practice, kaizen has a flywheel of just three steps:

1. Create a new standard
2. Follow it
3. Find a better way

Like any flywheel, stop any one of the inputs of energy and the flywheel will come to a rest. Lean process optimization is achieved only through a cycle of continuous improvement loops. Unfortunately, far too many leaders in far too many ScaleUps take a one-and-done approach, then sit back and scratch their heads wondering why their processes still destroy value for customers.

The first step lands us on the doorstep of standardized work.

Standardized Work

For nearly every process we've ever helped optimize, we discover exactly three versions, the first of which is wholly irrelevant:

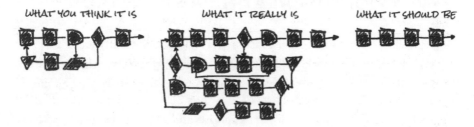

The general root cause of this situation is the lack of true standard operating procedures (SOPs).

Many people cringe at the mere thought of SOPs, thinking that they somehow stifle creativity and personal expression. They're often perceived to be control mechanisms intended to prevent individuals from performing the job in the manner they see fit. We've even seen SOPs viewed as downright oppressive.

In fairness, the skepticism and cynicism probably exist with good reason: in the vast majority of engagements we've had over the last two decades, we've observed standards to be many if not all of those evil things. Most companies miss the point of standardization, confusing it with blanket uniformity—and indeed control.

Alas, most SOPs are drawn up in a vacuum by operating entities not actually doing the work anymore, and render something far removed from reality. They sit permanently in a seldom accessed folder in a forgotten corner of a shared drive, only to be pulled out when some process-minded person takes it upon herself to ask why everyone is doing something completely different every time a new customer is onboarded.

SOPs are about performance. Done right, they are living, breathing documents representing only one thing: the best known method *today*, in the context of work being performed in a specific environment. If you were to look at a given operation in twenty different Toyota plants, for example, it would be done a bit differently, primarily because each plant was built in a different time period, with different technology, by people in different cultures. But within a given plant and discrete operation, standards establish a best practice until such time as a better way is found.

TOOLKIT: CREATING A STANDARD

How do you create a new standard? What defines a good SOP? Whether it's a pilot's pre-flight checklist, a surgeon's protocol, or a SaaS implementation, there are two criteria: clarity and consensus.

Clarity

Draft a standard operating procedure with the assumption that an untrained eye will read and try to follow it. Make it specific and complete to capture relevant knowledge. Make it concrete and representative of the real world. Describe with precision the what, where, when, who, and how. That way, there's no question of what constitutes a problem. However, do not script style. Leave room for individuals to carry out the key steps in a manner that works best for them. The tire gunner on a Formula 1 pit crew can place his hands on the gun based on which hand is dominant; forcing everyone to use a specific hand in a specific order is not helpful or useful in the context of an SOP.

Consensus

Everyone who will employ the standard must agree on it. That forces a shared investigation to ensure that the standard represents the best known method or practice at that point in time. The activity in turn facilitates understanding.

Three basic steps are required to deploy a standard:

1. **Establish a Best Practice.** Make sure it's the best known method. Study your best. Get input and feedback from those doing the work. Get agreement on it.
2. **Document the Standard.** Keep it to one page if you can. Make it visual if at all possible. Use graphics, check sheets, templates. Post it or publish it so everyone will be aware of it.
3. **Train to the Method.** Build a launch plan. Inform everyone. Prepare the needed materials and train end-users and trainers. Monitor the standard for effectiveness and usage.

Keep looking for a better way, and revise the SOP when you find one.

A true SOP has two primary characteristics:

1. It is created by the individuals performing the work; they are the only valid source of subject matter expertise.
2. It is dynamic, meant to be changed when a better method is discovered, tested, and accepted.

A good SOP lets you know where there's a problem. It shows you where to begin the search for solutions. It prevents mistakes from being made twice. It lets you capture and retain knowledge and expertise. And in physical environments like Formula 1 pit stops, manufacturing facilities, and hospital operating rooms, it helps you stay safe.

Voice of the Operator

HOW A FORMULA 1 PIT STOP CAN SAVE AN INFANT'S LIFE[5]

The Great Ormond Street Hospital (GOSH) in London is a world-renowned children's medical institution, housing over sixty different pediatric clinical specialties and carrying the highest rating for care in the United Kingdom. The hospital is famous for being the beneficiary of the Peter Pan copyright, a gift from author Sir James Matthew Barrie in 1929.

GOSH is also the only hospital ever to call the Ferrari Formula 1 pit stop team to help them improve the post-surgery handover process in which an infant must be transferred from the operating theater to a mobile unit for transport to the intensive care unit following intricate and risky heart surgery called an "arterial switch." The procedure is often done in the first two weeks of a newborn's life to correct a congenital heart defect. The cardiothoracic team had become alarmed at the mortality rate, not from the surgery, but from the move to the ICU following it. In one horrifying instance, seven infants died in rapid succession. A study involving over twenty specialists from across the UK revealed a messy, ad hoc handover process.

Two surgeons happened to be watching a Formula 1 race on a Sunday afternoon in 2003 following an exhausting morning involving both an arterial switch and a heart transplant. As they watched the race, it dawned on them that a pit stop—which at the time involved refueling and took roughly seven seconds—wasn't all that different from the post-surgical handover process. The duo fielded a team of GOSH doctors and traveled to Italy to spend time with the Ferrari Formula 1 pit crew.

The GOSH team presented their handover process in pictures and video, which by all accounts left the Ferrari technical race director in a bit of shock. Compared to a pit stop in which every person has a single job, communication is entirely verbal, and the action is tightly sequenced, the handover process seemed haphazard and chaotic: multiple conversations were conducted simultaneously, machines were manipulated in seemingly random order, and no one person was in charge.

When something went wrong, all hell broke loose. It was clear that no one had given thought to a contingency plan, and the action was entirely reactive. The race director explained how a pit crew trains for worst-case scenarios and invited the hospital team to observe a Failure Modes and Effect Analysis (FMEA) session. They learned that the goal with FMEA was to increase the rate of success by lowering the risk of failure to zero. This aligned perfectly with the GOSH team's objectives. They watched and learned how the team used a simple framework for conducting FMEA, calculating a "risk priority number," and generating "countermeasures":

A. PROCESS STEP	B. POTENTIAL FAILURE MODE	C. LIKELIHOOD OF FAILURE	D. IMPACT OF FAILURE	E. ELUDES DETECTION	F. RISK PRIORITY NUMBER	G. COUNTER MEASURE
		1 TO 5 (5 = HIGH)	1 TO 5 (5 = HIGH)	1 TO 5 (5 = HIGH)	C X D X E	

They watched a pit stop process improvement session and learned the value of process mapping, standard operating procedures, and trying to work out what people's tasks should be, in what sequence and with what equipment. Importantly, they learned the value of having a designated team leader.

While not every pit stop practice could be transferred directly to the patient handover process, the GOSH team was able to draft a new standard protocol involving four key phases: outlining roles and responsibilities, establishing a team leader, instituting safety checks, and creating contingency processes.

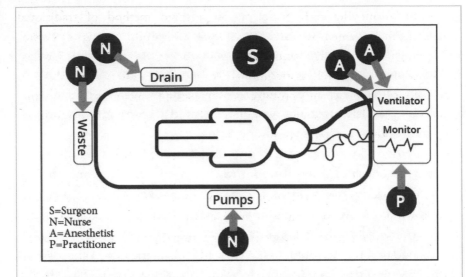

S=Surgeon
N=Nurse
A=Anesthetist
P=Practitioner

The new protocol was tested over a two-year period. Data on technical errors, information omissions, and overall handover duration were monitored. The results were significant: errors related to technology fell by over 40 percent and errors related to information were cut in half. Although saving time was not an explicit goal, overall duration was reduced to fifteen minutes, down from thirty.

The new protocol became standard operating procedure, as did process improvement. The overall hospital reaction was ideal. Instead of staff being satisfied with the new handover process, they said, "This is great, but we can do better."

A LEANER VIEW OF LEAN: THE KAIZEN SPRINT

We will conclude our discussion of Lean Process with a look at the basic methods and tools we use when we work with teams to optimize processes, and use real-world examples of sales, post-sales, and support process optimizations in the SaaS environment to illustrate how they are best applied.

With fast-moving tech ScaleUps, an adapted method of traditional continuous improvement we call a *kaizen sprint* works best, as it is both faster and more effective than conventional process mapping exercises lasting weeks and even months, as well as traditional kaizen events that can last three to five days. Lean kaizen sprints produce an average improvement in quality, cost, speed, and customer experience of roughly 25 percent. We should note that they can be performed remotely as well as in person.

THE DECISION

Like any change, realizing the need to change is a necessary precondition to successful process optimization, as is leadership support for the change. We've yet to meet an operational leader in a high-growth company that couldn't pinpoint some aspect of the business he'd like to improve. In the world of SaaS, every process linked to recurring revenue should be optimized to scale for growth, sooner rather than later.

Does this sound familiar? Your sales team has doubled or tripled in size and sales are growing well, with your customer base growing in number and complexity. Now that larger sales team needs more effective and efficient support to keep pace with growth, so a new sales operations function is needed. Growth is through the roof. You add pre-sales as well as post-sales motions, like customer success and customer success operations. The number of handoffs between functions has increased. Decisions are made ad hoc, often without a thought to future impact. New tools and systems are added, perhaps an additional product is launched or acquired, and you've expanded locations, with each one doing something different. Your sales operations, order management, and legal approvals are now at risk of becoming bloated with redundant processes that lead to contract churn and longer sales cycles. Quarterly revenue targets start to slip as reps struggle to get new business quotes approved and more deals signed. The quote-to-cash cycle balloons beyond a quarter. Implementation times are too long, time-to-value is potentially slowing expansion possibilities, if not causing churn. Support tickets begin to pile up, and response and resolution times expand. Eventually, all this lands on customers, whose experience begins to suffer.

Even if only half of this scenario rings true, it's tailor-made for process optimization. On the off chance that you're a decision maker thinking that a lean process optimization initiative might be a shoulder shrug or for some reason not worth the effort, take a minute to answer the fifteen questions in our Lean IQ Self-Assessment.

TOOLKIT: THE LEAN IQ SELF-ASSESSMENT

Our work with dozens of the world's best-known, tech-forward organizations, as well as many of the most valuable entrepreneurial startups in the world, has identified lean processes as a critical company-wide capability. Research analysis from our engagements enabled us to identify three key factors and fifteen criteria related to lean operations.

Take this short self-assessment, scoring 1 point for every yes, 0 for every no.

FACTOR: VALUE	NO	YES
We have a clear understanding of what our customers truly need and value.		
We design our key processes from the customer back.		
Every person in our organization understands their role in delivering value to customers.		
Problems that may impede customer value are discovered and solved before customers are impacted.		
Our customers remark how easy it is to do business with us.		
FACTOR: FLOW	NO	YES
We have standard operating procedures for all key processes.		
All key customer value-adding activities are aligned to optimize quality, cost, speed, and experience.		
Critical information moves effectively in a timely manner between key functions and process users.		

	NO	YES
Our key value-adding processes enable customers to pull value effortlessly.		
Key process performance indicators are regularly updated and openly visible.		
FACTOR: OPTIMIZATION	NO	YES
We place the highest priority on eliminating all forms of value-destroying waste.		
Continuous improvement and innovation are company-wide capabilities.		
We consistently utilize a problem-solving method featuring rapid prototyping.		
Constant business experimentation is a core element of our daily work.		
Senior leaders actively identify, champion, and participate in continuous process improvement.		
SCORING		
13–15 points: 95th percentile—Maintain process optimization efforts.		
10–12 points: 75th percentile—Close the Value Gap with lean process optimization initiative.		
<10 points: Danger zone—Launch lean process optimization initiative.		

Finally, if you're still on the fence, consider these facts: First, the team you select will work on something *you* feel needs attention—something of concern or that clearly advances a current objective—and concern something within your base of responsibility and control. Second, the team will arrive at a minimally viable solution that can be tested rapidly in a limited way, within thirty business days, without additional capital. Third, the team will work on a problem they all touch, using a solid problem-solving methodology. Fourth, the project will result in a clear value enhancement. Finally, every process optimization project is first an experiment, and there is no broad execution or standardization until the learning is captured and validated with a compelling case for feeding it forward.

BEFORE YOU SPRINT

Once the decision is made to begin the lean process journey, we suggest five preparation steps. We call it 5S Prep, in a somewhat tongue-in-cheek reference to the lean practice for creating and maintaining a neat and orderly workplace known as 5S, for the five Japanese words (which we won't bother to list here) used to describe what is essentially the business version of Marie Kondo's *The Lifechanging Magic of Tidying Up*.

1. Secure facilitation.
2. Set targets.
3. Select teams.
4. Send communication.
5. Schedule sprints.

Secure Facilitation

In our Kaizen Sprints, we use two key tools. The first is a solid framework called the Lean Kaizen Canvas, which we will describe in detail on the following pages. The second is a master facilitator, an objective professional from inside or outside the company trained in team problem-solving methods and group facilitation who will work with you and the team to instill the required discipline. The facilitator owns the kaizen sprint process embedded in the Lean Kaizen Canvas. Your team will actually learn better and progress faster, because a good facilitator knows how to handle obstacles like groupthink and devil's advocates, and can constructively and productively move the team beyond them.

Most software companies today have embedded lean-based agile development capability, which utilizes sprint methodology, so they have all the internal resources they need. We recommend securing a good facilitator early on to assist you with the preparation for a process optimization effort, as well as leading the kaizen sprint.

Set Targets

High-growth technology companies should focus on customer-facing processes and set aggressive improvement targets in the ballpark of 25 percent or higher. This is consistent with typical first project business gains. It's not uncommon to see improvement targets in the 50 percent range; in fact, we introduced this book with the story of Gainsight, which set two aggressive targets at this level. If this seems audacious and somewhat uncomfortable, that's exactly where you want to be. In our experience, anything lower usually amounts to simply working longer and harder. We are after new and innovative thinking that helps close the Value Gap between the current reality and the ideal customer experience, defined as the ability to seamlessly get their main job done.

Typical go-to-market/lead-to-cash target areas in a sales-led growth motion include optimizing lead to opportunity, opportunity to close, sales to post-sales handoffs, kickoff to launch, launch to contract renewal, and customer support. All sponsoring parties should agree on the overall targets before choosing teams charged with achieving them.

Not every target or optimization initiative is suitable for a lean process improvement. Avoid target areas, projects, or initiatives with the following characteristics:

- It addresses "nice-to-do" issues.
- It addresses areas lacking good visibility.
- Results are months away.
- Selected areas are fraught with controversy.
- Targeted processes lack strong interest.
- It addresses subjects beyond the team's control.
- It targets an issue already undergoing change.
- It is being used as an opportunity to execute an already conceived solution.
- It addresses something not part of the daily work.
- It addresses or involves strategic systems-level issues.
- Potentially it involves capital expense (new head count, technology, etc.).

Select Teams

The primary criterion for selecting a team or teams to optimize a process is simple: only people *actually doing the work on a daily basis* should be included. A cross-functional team is required, with each key step in the process represented by someone executing that step, rather than someone managing or overseeing that step. The team owns, and is entirely responsible for, carrying out all aspects of the process optimization project; this is not a case of making recommendations for someone else to implement.

In a sales process optimization initiative, for example, team members might include several of the following individuals and functions:

- Business development representatives
- Account executives
- Sales operations specialists
- Customer support representatives
- Customer success managers
- Implementation partners
- Technical support managers
- Sales engineers
- Product specialists
- Finance
- Legal

Unless you are planning to optimize an executive-level process, a team composed of people with titles like "president" and "chief" is a red flag that you don't have the right people on the team.

As far as size goes, think "two pizza" teams, meaning around eight people. Do not worry about choosing a team leader at this early stage, as one will emerge from the optimization sessions, usually based on the nature of the experiment to be run.

Send Communication

A bit of socialization is in order when launching a first lean process optimization effort. We never recommend a big, splashy program announcement. Your first effort is an experiment, and it should be communicated as such. However, the importance of process optimization, and the specific process and target, must be emphasized. The Japanese use the term *nemawashi*—a practice drawn from the art of bonsai and meaning "preparing to plant"—for the kind of simple but effective communication needed: short answers to the handful of questions that will be running through the minds of team members: *Why are we doing this? What is the goal? What is lean? Why have I been selected? What is expected of me? How do I prepare?*

A simple email message to the selected team members answering these questions should suffice, along with material cut from this section and perhaps a YouTube link to a Formula 1 pit stop.

Schedule Sprints

Once you have chosen the team or teams, it's time to look at calendars. There are two ways to run a kaizen sprint: in-person and remotely.

For an in-person kaizen sprint, you need one full day. Depending on your selection of facilitator, you should be able to take one to four teams through the sprint. Different teams can focus on different targets, but we always suggest doubling up on a target, because the solutions are usually different. When it comes to solutions and countermeasures, we subscribe to the Jeff Bezos "two is better than one" philosophy. The in-person sprint is a working session six hours in length, not including meals and breaks. The last hour of the day is reserved for a team readout to the leadership sponsors, during which the Lean Kaizen Canvas is shared, and executive permission to run the optimization solution test is granted.

For remote sprints, we recommend taking it one team at a time, splitting the equivalent of a full day of work into two three-and-a-half-hour video conferences using collaboration software (such as Mural or Miro), followed by a separate meeting for a team readout to the leadership sponsors. We recommend teams prepare a short presentation covering the same ground as the in-person readout, but in a far more viewer-friendly way.

Let's take a closer look at the Lean Kaizen Canvas.

THE LEAN KAIZEN CANVAS

The Lean Kaizen Canvas provides a framework for a lean kaizen sprint. The canvas represents the evolution of what used to be called an A3 in the Toyota world: a single sheet of paper with an international paper size of A3, the largest sheet of paper that a fax machine would accept when faxing was the state-of-the-art technology for communication. In Japan, they were referred to as kaizen newspapers, because an A3 was a visual artifact of a kaizen project. It is both prepared and read like a Western newspaper, top to bottom, left to right.

The Lean Kaizen Canvas is a modified, blown-up version of an A3, a six foot by three foot physical wrapper around the central scientific problem-solving method used in lean process optimization. The current version integrates the basic experiment format and asks *What must be true?* to surface any worrisome conditions preventing success. It is easily digitized using white board applications. (We have provided a download link to a digital copy in the Toolkit Resources section.)

Like all our other canvases, The Lean Kaizen Canvas is designed to be self-instructive and includes guiding questions, should individuals or micro-teams (two to three people) choose to use it for smaller continuous improvement efforts.

Let's unpack the Lean Kaizen Canvas and incorporate some real-world examples.

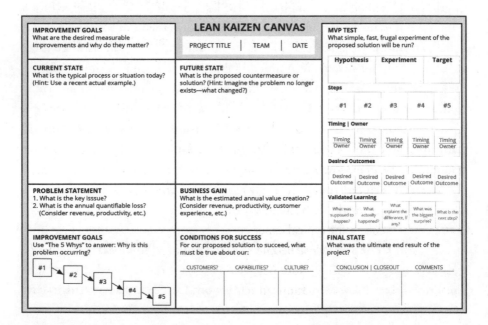

- Company A is focused on reducing sales process cycle time.
- Company B is focused on reducing time-to-value in the post-sales process.
- Company C is focused on reducing response time in the tech support process.

IMPROVEMENT GOALS (30 MINUTES)

What are the desired improvements and why do they matter?

While the big target has been set by the leadership sponsors, there will always be subordinate and supporting goals and objectives that the team may wish to add. Make sure to discuss and capture the answers to the second half of the question, pertaining to why the goals matter. This is the "What, so what?" prompt. You're after the business rationale here.

COMPANY A (Sales Process)	COMPANY B (Post-Sales Process)	COMPANY C (Tech Support)
Reduce the time from "Vendor of Choice" designation to contract signature by 50 percent in order to speed up value capture.	Reduce implementation from 143 to 90 days or under in order to speed up expansion, reduce churn and downsell, and improve customer satisfaction.	Improve ticket resolution time for key and strategic customers 25 percent and CSAT 20 percent in order to minimize risk of downsell and churn.

CURRENT STATE (90 MINUTES)

What is the typical process or situation today? (Hint: use a recent actual example.)

The goal is to describe, define, and grasp the current process, focusing on what is *actually* being done. Be as analytical as you can possibly be. Use a recent example representing the typical experience. Do not focus on outliers, best case, or worst case examples. Most people are familiar with flowcharting methods. Keep it simple: one Post-it Note per step. Do not create a detailed map with separate streams for information and functions; rather, aim for a high-level

COMPANY A (Sales Process)	COMPANY B (Post-Sales Process)	COMPANY C (Tech Support)
Summary	High-Level Process	Summary
Currently, it takes an average of sixteen weeks from the time we have verbal approval as "Vendor of Choice" to contract signature. The two biggest time delays are (1) getting approval on a master order agreement and (2) deal structure alignment, scoping, product, and statement of work.	• Contract signature • Classification in segment • Assignment of team • Schedule kickoffs • Handover to post-sales org • Content/configuration scoping, budget allocation • Technical implementation • Support training • Content configuration completed, tested, approved • Admin training, launch planning • User accepted testing • Execute launch plan, deployment, go live	Currently, it takes more than 108 hours to simply respond to an important customer's support ticket. The critical step taking the longest to execute involves product escalation and the triage of customer tickets with handoffs to engineering.

macro process map of no more than twenty steps. The job is to pinpoint a pain point, not create a flowchart.

The goal is to create an aerial view of the current state from a process perspective, then look down on it to identify the one step that would yield the greatest impact if it could be improved in some way. Years ago, the lumber industry would restore flow to logjams among logs floating down the river by using dynamite. The problem with that approach is that you lose valuable assets. Logjam 2.0 saw helicopters hovering over the logjam to identify the one or two "loggerheads" causing the bottleneck, then lowering a cable claw to straighten them out. You're trying to do the same thing. You're not blowing up your current process; you're looking for the point that would yield the maximum effect with minimum means. Gain consensus from the team on the single step creating a digital logjam.

We should note that this is an unconventional view, and lean purists and six sigma black belts might cry heresy, but we are operating in a world of high-growth technology ScaleUps, where speed and agility, not perfection, are the watchwords.

Irrespective of whether you're conducting the session in-person or remotely, now is the time for a short break. Give the team a chance to change their space, clear their heads, answer some emails. Experience shows, and research supports, that after ninety minutes or so, energy wanes, stress increases, and clarity of thought decreases.

PROBLEM STATEMENT (45 MINUTES)

What is the key issue? What is the annual quantifiable impact? (Consider lost revenue, productivity, etc.)

The Problem Statement is in two parts. The first part is a succinct summary that frames the issue, outlining the single process step the team has identified as their primary focus. The second part is a quantification of the problem's impact on the business. This is meant to be a ballpark view of how much the current process is costing the company each year. Typical calculations include revenue loss or slippage, revenue at risk due to churn, lost productivity due to wasted time, and customer satisfaction–related measures. For productivity calculations, the easiest way to arrive at an annual figure is to take the number of people involved and multiply it by how much time is taken doing non-value-added activities each day to get a daily impact number in hours. That figure can easily be annualized.

An annual dollar figure answers the inevitable question from sponsoring leaders: *How big a problem is this?* Nothing gets management's attention better than a significant hit to the business.

COMPANY A (Sales Process)	COMPANY B (Post-Sales Process)	COMPANY C (Tech Support)
Significant misalignment between master agreement and deal structure significantly delays the contract process. At risk is $1.5 million in Annual Recurring Revenue, and $1.25 million in Services.	The content scoping step does not define the optimal path to first value, which extends Go Live longer than necessary. At risk $1.76 million in revenue; lost opportunity of $2.75 million by not closing fifty-three days earlier. Productivity lost $150,000 due to account managers spending time on discounts, downsells, and delays.	Lack of complete and timely issue resolution inhibits customers' ability to reach their targeted business outcomes and realize value. This leads to downsell and churn. At risk is $76 million up for renewal next year.

ROOT CAUSE (45 MINUTES)

Use "The Five Whys" to answer: Why is this problem occurring?

"The Five Whys" is a simple technique, often attributed to the founding patriarch of Toyota, Sakichi Toyoda. Taiichi Ohno maintained that the Toyota Production System was built on the practice and evolution of this method of problem solving:

> By asking why five times and answering it each time, we can get to the real cause of the problem, which is often hidden behind more obvious symptoms. Why can one person at Toyota Motor Company operate only one machine, while at the Toyoda textile plant one young woman oversees forty to fifty automatic looms? By starting with this question, we obtained the answer "The machines at Toyota are not set up to stop when machining is completed." From this, automation with a human touch developed.[6]

In other words, The Five Whys, at least in this case, enabled Toyota to scale production.

There is no real magic in the number 5. Simple problems can often be answered with a single "why." More complicated problems necessitate peeling the onion a bit more. However, if it takes more than five whys, it's a good bet your problem statement is too broad and needs to be reframed. The Five Whys works very well for difficult and complicated process problems. However, the more complex, multifarious (aka "wicked") problems require more sophisticated approaches.

The reason that problems must be solved at the root cause level is that what appears to be the problem is not, so what appears to be the solution can't be. Think about an iceberg for a moment: 80 to 90 percent of the danger is below the surface. Avoiding what you see on the surface, while it seems like a solution, is not. Problems that are solved at the symptom level may offer temporary relief, but pain will return, and the problem can become even worse. Ibuprofen taken for a migraine may work for a few hours, but the pain may return until the cause is diagnosed and treated.

The method is conducted by asking "why" in a vertical chain, each why digging into the previous one. The test of a good five whys is that logic makes sense in both directions.

Here's a simple example that requires only four "whys." Suppose your child comes home with a D this semester in math class. For many parents and their children, that's a clear problem, which could result in not being able to play varsity sports or failing to gain entrance to a college of choice. Without digging deeper, your solution might be some sort of privilege restriction until the grade improves. However, using The Five Whys can help solve the problem:

"Why did you get a D in Math?" Answer: "I didn't do the homework
   assignments."
"Why didn't you do your homework?" Answer: "I don't like math, Dad."
"Why don't you like math?" Answer: "I'm no good at it."
"Why do you think you're no good at it?" Answer: "I don't understand it."

Root cause discovered, and it didn't take all five Whys! The solution now comes into frame: get help, for which a variety of options exist . . . tutoring, extra time

COMPANY A (Sales Process)	COMPANY B (Post-Sales Process)	COMPANY C (Tech Support)
Why #1: We are not controlling the deal.	*Why #1:* The one accountable for implementation is not enabled to scope content and configuration.	*Why #1:* We don't identify the root cause of an issue quickly.
Why #2: We don't educate the customer early enough.	*Why #2:* We haven't defined a baseline for minimally viable products (MVPs) either internally or between us and our solution partners.	*Why #2:* Lack of effective advanced triage process that matches talent to task.
Root Cause: Sales Reps are not enabled with mindset, training, and tools.	*Why #3:* We don't have a unified implementation strategy focused on Time to Value.	*Why #3:* Lack of dedicated capacity/skill with the ability to define effective and very advanced product triage issues.
	Root Cause: Time to Value is a new priority.	*Why #4:* Advanced and "special team" swarming is not being adopted efficiently.
		Root Cause: No clear ownership.

with the teacher, etc. The logic holds going back up the chain: because your child doesn't understand math, they aren't good at it, therefore they don't like it and don't do their homework, which results in getting a D for the semester.

Using The Five Whys is sometimes like drilling for oil: you may need a few attempts to get it right.

If you're conducting the sprint in-person, it's time for a lunch break. In a remote session, this section concludes the first of two three-hour sessions. If the team has not quite completed either the problem statement definition or the root cause logic, assign it as homework to be completed before the next session. Additionally, assign the homework of populating the Future State section with individual ideas, so that you can hit the ground running in your second session.

FUTURE STATE (60 MINUTES)

What is the proposed solution or countermeasure? (Hint: Imagine the problem no longer exists—What changed?)

This is the fun, right-brain part of the sprint. The goal is to run a one-hour ideation session and emerge with a concept for an MVP that everyone agrees is the best solution. Typical brainstorming rules apply: individual ideas first, then build on those as a team.

Keep in mind that this is focused ideation, and the contributing causes in The Five Whys chain can help provide the team with design principles, providing the criteria by which the best solution can be chosen. Designers use this trick all the time: take each contributing cause and reverse it, so that it

COMPANY A (Sales Process)	COMPANY B (Post-Sales Process)	COMPANY C (Tech Support)
"Tom Brady Armband": Tactical field playbook for Sales Reps and approval matrix, enabling and empowering them to sell value immediately after Vendor of Choice approval, without waiting for internal approval.	Develop and align on an implementation strategy featuring phased implementation and defining MVP examples for specific use cases. Train implementation accountable team on scoping (MVP). Evangelize phased implementation approach pre- and post-sales.	Create a standardized advanced special team (SWAT) swarming ticket response process with high-quality referral/handover to designated engineering team members to reduce response time drastically.

becomes a positively stated result. You then have a collection of design targets. In the D-in-Math example, the best solution should (a) enable understanding, (b) build confidence, (c) make math enjoyable, and (d) improve homework completion.

Don't forget the improvement goals, and don't forget the lean constraints: no capital expense, and the team can test their MVP inside thirty business days.

BUSINESS GAIN (30 MINUTES)

What is the estimated annual value creation? (Consider revenue, productivity, customer experience, etc.)

This is the flip side of the calculations made in the Problem Statement around the business impact of the Current State. How much does the proposed solution gain back on an annual basis? Does it add value over and above the current loss and produce a net gain?

Give the team a fifteen-minute break, as this section concludes the first ninety minutes.

COMPANY A (Sales Process)	COMPANY B (Post-Sales Process)	COMPANY C (Tech Support)
Twenty percent of next year's growth plan: win rate increase; average deal size increase Vendor of choice to signature < eight weeks; overall sales cycle < one hundred days	Regain all lost productivity Regain all potential revenue lost or at risk Potential upsell and expansion Better client experience, engagement, involvement	De-risk renewals; 95 percent on-time renewal transactions; 90 percent-plus forecasting accuracy sixty days prior to quarter end Free up customer success manager; time better utilized on renewal activity

CONDITIONS FOR SUCCESS (45 MINUTES)

For our proposed solution or countermeasure to succeed, what must be true about our customers, capabilities, and culture?

This section is unique to the world of process optimization and incorporates everything we shared in our discussion of Strategic Speed around Reverse Engineering. As with Strategy Design, the discussion of assumptions and potential barriers to success is generally some of the richest dialogue among the team. Unlike strategy, however, we don't need to concern ourselves with a discussion of chosen playing spaces or potential competitive reaction. Here the focus is on what must be true about what customers truly value, what must be true about the capabilities needed to implement the MVP, and what must be true about the organizational culture. List anything that gives you pause or worries you about testing the MVP, and build it into the experiment in order to gain a higher confidence level.

COMPANY A (Sales Process)	COMPANY B (Post-Sales Process)	COMPANY C (Tech Support)
Most worrisome condition for success: it must be true that management will accept and empower a certain risk level, mitigated by reps using a standardized playbook and pre-constructed approval matrix.	Several conditions for success must be true: (1) customers must see value in phased implementation and "value drip"; (2) no negative business impact on our solution partners; and (3) implementation cannot be viewed as "complete" after MVP goes live.	The most worrisome condition for success is availability and skill level of individuals on the advanced triage special team.

MVP TEST (45 MINUTES)

What simple, fast, and frugal experiment will yield proof of concept?

This section incorporates everything we shared in our discussion of Constant Experimentation. All lean process optimization solutions and countermeasures are designed to be minimally viable products/processes (MVPs) and tested before any standardization or full implementation. Reference the Constant

Experimentation principle and create a testable hypothesis, craft a business experiment including a success metric, and draft a brief project plan outlining the key steps and point persons, as well as desired outcomes for each key step.

COMPANY A (Sales Process)	COMPANY B (Post-Sales Process)	COMPANY C (Tech Support)
Hypothesis: If we enable/empower sales reps with a playbook plus approval matrix train to sell value immediately after Vendor of Choice, we will dramatically decrease time to signature. *Experiment:* Test in third quarter: pick ten deals that are slated to close in Q3, train those reps, compare to the current process. *Target:* Vendor of Choice to Signature = eight weeks.	*Hypothesis:* If we define and deploy a strategy to split implementations into phases, we can improve Time to First Value. *Experiment:* Select three test clients or prospects that are about to close, apply phasing strategy to scoping approach, execute phased implementation, compare to normal process. *Target:* Time to First Value under ninety days.	*Hypothesis:* If we improve information sharing and quality of handover materials to engineering, we will reduce the mean time to resolution. *Experiment:* Execute on all qTest issues that are sent to R&D over six weeks, compare to normal/baseline triage resolution time and CSAT. *Target:* Reduce time to SWAT status by 50 percent

This concludes the actual sprint part of the kaizen sprint. The remainder of the Lean Kaizen Canvas can be completed following the MVP test. The Validated Learning section aligns with the New Insights element of the four-square template we shared in our discussion of Constant Experimentation, and can be completed at the close of the MVP test.

So that we don't leave you hanging, here are the MVP test results.

COMPANY A (Sales Process)	COMPANY B (Post-Sales Process)	COMPANY C (Tech Support)
Average time from Vendor of Choice to contract signature = forty-six days (six weeks). >50 percent reduction.	Time to first Value (MVP) of eighty-seven days.	17X improvement in issue response time (108+ hours reduced to less than seven).

FINAL STATE

What was the ultimate end-result of the project?

The Final State section closes out the Lean Process Optimization project. Capture conclusions, any closeout items necessary, and comments. Recall our discussion of Constant Experimentation regarding hansei and include any reflections, suggestions, or thoughts not captured elsewhere on the Lean Kaizen Canvas.

We recommend a short "final impact readout" with leadership sponsors, during which you can share your Validate Learning and Final State comments. With any luck, this will be the first step on the journey toward building company-wide Lean Process optimization capability.

Given the success of the experiments in the examples above, all three process optimizations were first strengthened, piloted more broadly, then standardized.

THE JOURNEY TO LEAN PROCESS MATURITY

The question of how long it takes to embed a lean capability into an organization is a common one. The question itself is heartening, because we often see lean process optimization and improvement treated as a side hustle or a one-off to address some burning issue. One-and-done is anathema to continuous improvement.

The impact of lean continuous process optimization is hard to argue with, as is its scalability. Once a team has done a lean kaizen sprint and learned the simple framework captured on the Lean Kaizen Canvas, there is nothing stopping those eight to ten individuals from using that framework on other efforts, thereby transferring knowledge and capability. The same goes for each subsequent effort. Once people have done a few optimizations using the framework illustrated here, they don't need to set aside a whole day to conduct a sprint. If you think about it, the framework is entirely modular.

The journey to full maturity is best compared to that of agile development, which is based on lean thinking. Depending on the size of the product development organization, transformation to a fully embedded capability across the organization can take a year or more. Just as it would not make sense to do a couple of product releases using agile methodology, then revert to a waterfall approach, it does not make sense to do one or two lean process optimizations and then revert to the non-lean, low-frequency approach to value delivery.

The basic maturity model is simple, as the story of TWI during World War II points out: train a core group through the active learning process illustrated here, recycle that effort with new teams and targets, further enable hand-raisers wishing to become facilitators, continue to engage in lean process optimizations, then rinse and repeat until it becomes the de facto way to incrementally improve and innovate. Competency is achieved when you can't *not* continuously optimize.

As to the specifics of how best to do that given your unique company culture, it's best to look inward at successful examples of similar past efforts to adopt and home-grow a new capability. Try to identify what made those efforts successful, and use those factors as key elements of the formula for the path of least resistance.

In other words, study your best and go from there.

LEAN PROCESS RECAP

Waste is defined simply as work that no one wants, needs, cares about, or even asked for. It is the fourth restraining force and archenemy of all efforts to scale for growth. It impedes the free flow of value to customers and slows the capture of value *from* customers. Lean process optimization is the antidote because it specifically targets waste, with the goal of eliminating everything that lengthens the time from order to cash. A lean process is like a Formula 1 pit stop, a two-second activity performed by highly trained individuals, each with a single, precise role, in a standardized way, and constantly improved to save tenths of a second. Optimizing processes in fast-paced, high-growth companies is best achieved through a kaizen sprint, a modern approach to continuous improvement based on standardized work. A simple framework for process optimization is the Lean Kaizen Canvas, which embeds the scientific problem process and offers what can be a self-guided approach.

CHECKPOINTS

- ☐ Is high priority placed on eliminating all forms of value-destroying waste?
- ☐ Do key customer value-adding activities optimize quality, cost, speed, and experience?
- ☐ Do you have standard operating procedures for all key processes?
- ☐ Is continuous process improvement a company-wide capability?
- ☐ Do senior leaders actively champion and participate in process optimization?

Principle 5

ESPRIT DE CORPS

Never doubt that a small group of thoughtful, committed people can change the world. Indeed, it is the only thing that ever has.
—Margaret Mead

You have just been handed a $175 million check to launch the venture of a lifetime. It's a rocket ship of a project, and you have three years to get it off the ground and into full flight. The ability to set strategy and innovate is paramount, as the project requires you to develop new technology, new capabilities, and new systems. You'll be able to hand pick your team from the best of the best, but you'll need every ounce of your leadership skills to bring them over the goal line. Your backers urge you to take whatever risks are necessary to make it work.

There's just one caveat. "Don't fail," they tell you. "Move fast, but don't slip up." Suddenly, the golden opportunity becomes a complex problem to solve.

Your name is Brian Muirhead, and you've just been chosen to lead flight systems for the Mars Pathfinder project at NASA's Jet Propulsion Lab. Your mission: design, build, launch, and land on Mars an all-new, state-of-the-art, low-cost, remote-control, all-terrain land rover that can crawl over the red planet and reliably beam back images, collect samples, and discover scientific data.

Oh, and that $175 million? It's a mere fraction of the billion-dollar budget for the previous Viking mission to Mars, which took over three times as long as you've been given.

And it failed.

A LEANER VIEW OF LEADERSHIP

Strategic Speed. Constant Experimentation. Accelerated Value. Lean Process. If these four operating principles were easy, natural, or intuitive, we would not need to write a book about them. But they aren't. Making any one of these principles operational will lift performance to some degree. In fact, one might argue that the rise of the unicorn class is due at least in part to the value placed on software that automates at least some element of one of the four principles. Dozens of companies have sprung up, for example, to sell cloud-based software that helps your business to set and track OKRs, to perform rapid testing on websites and products, to deliver and capture greater customer value, and to automate business process workflows.

Operationalizing *all four* principles, however, results in *top* performance. That's no easy feat, and it requires us to practice what we preach and ask, What must be true for a high-velocity technology company to put all four principles into play in a synergistic way? The obvious answer is the fifth and final principle in our S.C.A.L.E. model. The real question is, What must be true to establish esprit de corps? The answer is less obvious: a specific kind of team leadership, a leaner brand called Grease and Glue.

GREASE AND GLUE

Grease and Glue is not our term, it's the rather sticky one we learned from Chief Engineer Brian Muirhead of NASA's Jet Propulsion Laboratory, who led the flight systems development for the successful Mars Pathfinder project in NASA's "Faster, Better, Cheaper" era of the mid-1990s.[1] Being handed a $175 million budget in mid-1990s dollars is in the ballpark of $350 million today, equating to a generous but not outrageous late-series funding round for a promising ScaleUp. But the level of complexity involved in designing, building, launching, and landing a space exploration vehicle from scratch inside four years is at least an order of magnitude greater than that of scaling up or even taking public a subscription software company. An operational leader is needed who can recruit and build a high-performing team that is up to the challenge of hitting aggressive targets under daunting constraints, can instill a sense of unity, and can pull off a massive mission with all the world watching and every expert in the media betting against you. Brian was and is such a leader, and he dubbed his secret sauce "grease and glue" leadership.

Leadership is by nature a broad and weighty subject. Every year, a new crop of books and speeches is delivered on the general topic of leadership. We have lost count of the number of leadership styles comprising that overall market, and we have zero desire to contribute to the list. We find Grease and Glue to be an accessible and useful metaphor for the two essential roles of an operational leader charged with steering a high-growth technology company in the throes of scaling up. It is a much leaner view of leadership, and fit for purpose. There must be something to it, because Brian Muirhead's team brought the Mars Pathfinder project home on time and well within budget. It was launched on December 4, 1996, and millions of people tuned in exactly seven months later on July 4, 1997, to watch images of the red planet beamed back by the tiny *Sojourner* rover. The entire mission cost less than it did for Hollywood to produce the blockbuster *Titanic*, which opened the same year.

The Grease role is all about removing the restraining forces of drag, inertia, friction, and waste. (In Brian Muirhead's case, quite literally.) Our discussion to this point has explored the Grease role. Left to explore is the Glue role, which is all about developing the connective tissue needed to build unity among individuals and keep them working as a high-performing team able to meet a pressing challenge using the four guiding principles. In other words, the Glue role holds everything together.

The difference between Grease and Glue leadership and other, more complicated approaches has much to do with the current work environment. Organizations are looking for the extra effort and innovation that come from fully committed and engaged individuals. The quality of leaders plays a unique and critical role in gaining this commitment. At the same time, the world is becoming "de-jobbed" at an accelerating rate due to a variety of factors, not the least of which are the ubiquitous role of technology and the global market pressures requiring speed and flexibility in responding to customer needs. The result is that tech firms of today are far more team-based than ever before, something further exaggerated by the COVID-19 pandemic and its aftermath. The modern model is much more like soccer than football, characterized by cross-functional ensembles composed of individuals with complementary skills focused on passing a moving ball, rather than running set plays dependent on a quarterback. The game is now much more fluid and dynamic, with everyone on the team sharing responsibility for winning.

Counterintuitive as it may seem for a rapidly growing ScaleUp, the Glue role for leaders of teams is critical to achieve the collaboration required to keep pace with the speed of change. The Glue job centers on building esprit de corps.

SPIRIT MATTERS

French for "team spirit," esprit de corps as a formal business concept dates back to a list of fourteen management principles put forth by Henri Fayol in his 1949 book, *General and Industrial Management*. Fayol spent his entire career in a mining company, eventually becoming managing director and leading the company to prosperity from near ruin. Esprit de corps was last on the list of fourteen. As Fayol explained it, "Harmony, union among the personnel of a concern, is great strength in that concern. Effort, then, should be made to establish it."[2] Fayol argued that fostering a harmonious and unified team spirit creates an atmosphere of mutual trust and understanding, and out of that trust comes value.

Military historians are quick to point out, however, that esprit de corps as a unifying concept in the armed forces predates the business context, going as far back as the late 1800s.[3] Indeed, most people associate esprit de corps with military (and paramilitary) organizations, most of which define esprit de corps quite simply as "devotion and enthusiasm among members of a group for one another."[4] The principle has been studied more in that context than in any other, with research focusing on the transformation of diverse individuals into a cohesive unit capable of accomplishing a mission under threat of extreme danger.

Given the public perception of military groups as hardened, rough-and-ready bands of brothers with a "mission first" focus, it is at least somewhat curious that a rather intangible and emotional quality such as harmony would figure so centrally. But a peek at how esprit de corps is institutionalized reveals a different story.

To begin with, "mission first" is only half the story. The full phrase used by several branches of the military is "mission first, people always." Second, the manner in which esprit de corps is both taught and developed in military leadership training is in reality the inverse: people first, mission always. Instilling esprit de corps begins by establishing a trusting connection at the individual level first. Focus then turns to the collective team effort toward a common mission. Former military personnel now in business leadership roles build team unity in the very same way. (See our interview with former U.S. Army combat engineer Dan Page on page 199.)

This corresponds with recent research into the interpersonal behaviors that make for superior leadership in any domain. In his bestselling book *Social: Why Our Brains Are Wired to Connect*, UCLA psychologist Matthew Lieberman argues that the likelihood of being viewed as a great leader is five times greater when strong relationship skills like empathy and communication are paired with an equally strong focus on achieving results. Leaders demonstrating strength in only one area—either relationships or results—have just a one in eight chance of being viewed as great leaders. For those strong in both, the odds are better than 70 percent. Unfortunately, less than 1 percent of leaders score high in both areas.[5]

Understanding that esprit de corps requires a bifocal approach is important. However, nearly every scholarly treatment of esprit de corps in organizational literature focuses on either the individual or the collective aspect, failing to link the motivations of individuals with the results of the team. The emotional aspect of esprit de corps makes many senior executives uneasy, especially those laboring under the old-school adage, "It's not personal, it's business." The new-school version must be, "It's personal *and* business."

But to be fair, it's not as easy as it sounds. Our brains have something to say about it.

Lieberman's research into the neuroscientific aspects of leadership underscores that of the Nobel prize–winning behavioral economist Daniel Kahneman in his 2013 book, *Thinking, Fast and Slow*. In short, it seems that the brain has a tough time being relationship-focused and results-focused at the same time. The neural networks responsible for the two different activities are located in different regions of the brain. Goal-focused activity happens in the outer surface, whereas social thinking happens in the middle of the brain. The two networks seesaw back and forth, but don't collaborate. In other words, relating to people makes it harder to focus on results, and vice versa.

But just because we are not able to use both processes simultaneously doesn't mean we can't create a culture that prioritizes a balanced, bifocal application of both modes in an effort to build esprit de corps. A good time to do that is when a fledgling startup with a solid product/market fit enters the ScaleUp phase, before all the additional layers, functions, and headcount start to dilute the natural, organic esprit de corps that pervades the proverbial startup in a garage. Once lost, recapturing that "one-company" unity is possible, but never losing it in the first place is a better and easier option.

Nearly a half-century of combined operating experience and field advisory work with every breed of organizations imaginable (including military and paramilitary) allows us to state with confidence that no specific formula exists for creating and instilling an ethos of esprit de corps. At a higher level of abstraction, however, three broad but distinct ingredients do exist from which every organization must concoct its unique blend: an *individual factor*, a *collective factor*, and a *force multiplier*.

The third provides the context for the first two, as diagrammed in the model here. (Credit to former U.S. Army combat engineer Dan Page for the Venn diagram metaphor; see page 199.)

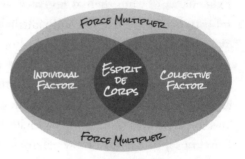

Anyone who plays or follows sports should be able to see the key elements of any sporting event reflected in the esprit de corps model. The pressure of winning under clear rules within a short and finite period of time is built in. Tennis legend Billie Jean King was quoted as saying "pressure is a privilege" so often that it became the title of her autobiography. "Usually if you have tremendous pressure, it's because an opportunity comes along," she wrote. "Most of the time . . . if you really think about it . . . usually it's a privilege."[6] She was talking about the weight of expectation. We have all felt the adrenaline rush from pressure to perform, and as King maintains, it's a matter of what you do with it: some choke, some chill, others charge.

That brings us to the individual and collective factors. If your player is having a bad day in a critical matchup—possibly succumbing to the intense pressure—there will be no win unless they either leverage the pressure to reverse the momentum, or, in the case of team sports, the collective factor makes up the difference to save the day.

For sports fans, the blend and balance of the three ingredients makes for great drama, which is why the come-from-behind or "Cinderella" story is such a frequent plot line in movies, television, and books. It's also why those who follow sports love watching and become emotionally invested. "Die-hard" fans actually experience the fight-or-flight response from adrenaline release following an intense event, as well as aggression from the release of performance-enhancing hormones such as testosterone.[7] A mild form of addiction occurs, because dopamine is released in the pleasure center of the brain, resulting in the desire for more.[8] For all of these reasons, we will refrain from using sports examples for our business model.

To better illustrate how this model works, take the case of the typical college lecture on, say, organic chemistry. A passing grade in this very difficult class is the force multiplier, but there is no esprit de corps, because the collective factor is missing. Students are seated individually in the lecture hall with no interaction. When the class moves to the eight-hour lab, however, a new dynamic takes over. The force multiplier is now the goal of producing a certain level of yield with an acceptable purity within a compressed period of time. There is much to be done, so students must work in groups of three, each member having an individual role which, if performed poorly, carries the potential for group failure. Esprit de corps is now present.

A similar difference exists between a mature company and a nascent startup. In the latter, a strong sense of natural esprit de corps characteristic of many startups arises from a powerful force multiplier: fear of failure and potential loss of seed capital, often that of the founding team and a few angel investors. The founding team is unified in their pursuit of a product/market fit, working around the clock at a furious pace to ensure success. Individuals trust each other, and a collective passion for the idea pervades the shared pursuit of a common goal.

In a successful, mature organization, however, a strong sense of esprit de corps is less common, reserved only for those with strong Grease and Glue leaders who inspire those in their charge with a compelling force multiplier: a vivid picture of the future supported by measurable ambitions that are both audacious and arduous, impossible to reach without all hands working in unity, in turn requiring a strong interpersonal bond.

In the remainder of this book, we will unpack the nature of these three main ingredients of esprit de corps by sharing what we have discovered to be among the most powerful flavors of each: *pressure* as the force multiplier, *trust* as the individual factor, and *people/culture fit* as the collective factor.

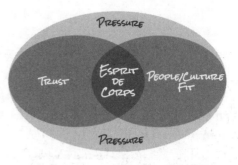

PRESSURE: A FORCE MULTIPLIER

We introduced this book by sharing the story of Gainsight, a customer success SaaS that set and achieved two ambitious goals that helped them reach unicorn status. We then shared the moon shot Winning Aspiration of Toyota's Lexus division to displace market leaders BMW and Mercedes within two years. Then we looked at a two-second Formula 1 pit stop that can win or lose the race and discussed the rationale behind setting aggressive improvement targets for process optimization efforts. Finally, we began our discussion here with the story of the Mars Pathfinder team that completed a seemingly impossible mission and set a new bar for space exploration. The force-multiplying power of positive pressure in the form of a stretch goal is proven to inspire and guide both individual and collective action.

But not all forms of pressure are created equal. One could easily argue that all goals carry with them the very real possibility of being downgraded or abandoned by those who set them. Perhaps an involuntary, external threat provides a better force multiplier. It is one thing to be faced with the challenge of winning in even the most hypercompetitive of domains—business, sport, government—but it is entirely another to, for example, engage in a fight to survive the existential threat of a deadly force majeure.

FORCE MAJEURE

In the early afternoon of August 5, 2010, a typically hot South American Thursday became a nightmare that would last sixty-nine days for the thirty-three copper-gold miners who suddenly found themselves trapped under 700,000 tons of rock 2,300 feet below the surface from a massive cave-in at the small San José Mine in the Atacama Desert near Copiapó, Chile. A rock the size of the Empire State Building had collapsed the mine, imprisoning the team of thirty-two miners and their foreman. For the next seventeen days, no one in the world above knew whether anyone had survived. Rescue operations that would eventually involve NASA and the Chilean Navy began immediately. But the situation looked grim.

Underground, no souls were lost, and no serious injuries were sustained. Tons of collapsed rock eliminated any hope of exit. It took hours for the dust to settle to the point that movement was possible. When it did, the men made their way to the mine's safety refuge, a 540 square-foot metal-doored space carved into the rock with two long benches and stocked with food, water, and a few oxygen tanks for miners to take regular "breathers." Under normal circumstances, it had better ventilation than other parts of the tunnel, but most of the ventilation shafts had been damaged or destroyed. The food stores only had enough for forty-eight hours: twenty cans of tuna, four cans of beans, one can of salmon, two cans of peas, one can of peaches, ninety-six packets of crackers, eighteen liters of juice, sixteen packets of flavored condensed milk, and ten liters of potable water. Most of the food was long past its expiration date. Ample but industrially polluted water used in the mining process was stored in large tanks throughout the tunnels. All electricity had been lost, rendering the ventilation fans inoperable. Sounds of crumbling rock filled the dark void, accompanied by constantly dripping water from the ceiling of the tunnel. In the days to come, the miners would suffer from heat, fatigue, hunger, thirst, dehydration, infection, hallucinations, and unbearable stress. The fear of death by starvation was palpable. Circumstances went beyond pressure. They were the stuff of torture.

The advantage (if it can be called that) of a life-threatening crucible like the one facing the thirty-three trapped miners was the instantaneous creation of, and universal commitment to, a common goal: *survival*. The *what* and *why* were eminently clear; the urgent issue was *how*.

To answer that question, thirty-two men focused intently on the thirty-third miner, fifty-four-year-old shift foreman Luis Urzúa.

SUPER GLUE

Under normal circumstances, Chilean mining operations are quite hierarchical. Those with special skills are superior in rank to general laborers. The mining shift foreman is equivalent to a military commander, and questioning an order carries a penalty. A few conditions among the trapped miners put those traditions to the test. First, five members of the group were contract workers, not mine employees. Before the mine collapsed they were considered outsiders, because they did not report to Urzúa. Further, although Urzúa had more than twenty years of mining experience, he had never coordinated a disaster recovery, and in that regard he was untested. By all accounts it took every bit of his leadership skills to keep his team together and alive.

During the first team huddle in the refuge following the cave-in, Urzúa stepped into the Glue role—Super Glue, to be more accurate. A topographer by trade, his first step was to get a lay of the land. He set up a command post outside the refuge in a small pickup truck, sketched a rough map to help orient the team, marked their location, and began to craft an exit strategy. Over a mile of tunnels could be explored to search for escape. Helmet lanterns could be used sparingly for light. Machinery and motor vehicles could supply limited power, light, and even water from vehicle radiators. Backhoes could take limited runs at blocked tunnels.

His second step was to inventory the skills in the group. In addition to general laborers, there were complementary special skills among the men, including an electrician, machine operator, mechanic, driver, medical worker, hydraulic engineer, manager, supervisor, and soccer player: a former Chilean soccer star now worked with the miners.

Urzúa immediately sent a few drivers in pickup trucks to investigate possible ways out, but limited visibility resulted in a crash. The men didn't give up, though, and while all possible exits, including a ventilation shaft, were blocked, they had plenty of tunnel to work with. The refuge could not house all thirty-three men, so Urzúa formed three groups, with two groups setting up camp higher in the mine. Separate areas for work, sleep, and lavatory were designated.

His third task was rationing the food. Not knowing how long it might take to be rescued, they rationed food under the assumption it would be several days. At first, the men ate a small portion of food just once a day. But a few days into the ordeal and with no sign of help, they went to one small bite of food the equivalent of a half spoonful of tuna or salmon every forty-eight hours. Eventually, they would eat once every three days. The potable water didn't last long, so milk and semitoxic water from the many work tanks in the tunnel became the substitute.

Urzúa let it be known up-front that in the event of rescue, he would be the last to leave, and he reinforced the notion that his role was not to give orders, but to keep the team together, to survive and leave alive. He suggested, and the men agreed, that a democratic process should guide all decisions, with a simple majority winning in the case of disagreement. All preexisting intrateam hierarchy evaporated quickly, save Urzúa's de facto leadership role. The former soccer professional likened the way the men worked to a soccer team, with each man assigned a small task suited to his skill: mechanics took care of vehicles and machinery, the miner with a medical background saw to the team's health, and a spiritual leader emerged, who would go on to write a book about the experience, describing the transformation of the men from a rather motley crew of individuals to a cohesive unit:

> Among the thirty-three, there was a great diversity of personalities and experience. We did not start out as a cohesive group. After our first seventeen days together under those terrible living conditions, the thirty-three of us became well acquainted. The relationships between most of the men became much closer. Even though some of the miners said little, we spoke with one another about our lives in a deep way. We became more united and worked as a single team. We were becoming a society with a common goal and shared values. We were experiencing a unity of emotion . . . Down there, a different spirit had taken hold of each one of the men.[9]

Seventeen days in, the men decided to make a weak broth of what little tuna remained, with each man contributing his ration to the soup. Moving to an area away from the refuge with the best ventilation, they made a small fire, and shared what they called "the last supper." Not long after they had lain down to sleep, a sounding drill from the rescue team on the surface broke through the roof of the refuge.

The men knew instinctively what to do. After spraying the drill with orange paint and attaching a message to alert the rescue team that all were alive, the first step in the rescue phase was under way. It would be another fifty-two days before the last miner was pulled safely up to the surface in the slim rescue tube, with a record one billion people watching the televised event.

That last miner was indeed shift foreman Luis Urzúa.

TAKEAWAY

Much can be learned about the force multiplier ingredient of esprit de corps by looking at an involuntary and extreme form of pressure. First, it wasn't that the miners each wanted to survive, but that they all wanted to survive *together*. The ability of the shift foreman to keep the men together figured centrally in the unit's ability to do that. Given the very real possibility of failure and team breakdown under the harsh conditions, the outcome might have been completely different. We will never know for sure to what extent the will to survive may have necessitated unthinkable measures had the rescue team not broken through as food supplies ran out, but examples of similar crises—the 1972 plane crash of a Uruguayan rugby team in the Andes Mountains of Chile comes to mind—reinforce the idea that both individual and collective action are unified by pressure in the hands of a good leader.

Second, the fear of death and starvation resulted in an altogether different stance. When handed a big stretch goal as the force multiplier, most business teams naturally focus inward to figure out how they will achieve it. But the radical collaboration characteristic of esprit de corps comes from having an external focus as well. Extreme teams, such as those in the armed forces, law enforcement, firefighting, paramedical units, and space travel, balance the inward focus with an outward one, choosing to view their objective as not just chasing a goal, but of being on a mission to defeat a common enemy or opponent. Whether it's an elite surgical unit banding together to cheat death, firefighters referring to flames as "the beast," or a Formula 1 pit crew looking to crush the opposing team, it's the force-multiplying power of a shared external threat that enhances the chances of breakthrough performance.

Understanding both what you are fighting for and against is the sine qua non of winning.

Voice of the Operator

INTERVIEW WITH DAN PAGE[10]

Dan Page is Vice President, Sales Operations for Recorded Future, a data security and intelligence company. As an Army combat engineer during the Bosnian war in the mid-1990s, he designed, coordinated logistics, and led the construction of what was at the time the largest military fixed bridge built since World War II, for which he was awarded a U.S. Army Meritorious Service Medal.

Dan, I'm really interested in the practitioner's perspective on the principle of esprit de corps, especially how it figures into your leadership role today. Let's start with how you were introduced to the concept during your time in the military.
It's interesting. The term itself is not introduced right away. It's after you have felt it and start to live it. It's one of those things where you can't go into it and say, "Hey, I'm going to instill esprit de corps," and everyone is furiously taking notes. It doesn't work that way. They make you aware of it after the movement and the momentum have started to build. I was probably only in the military for about three weeks before I began to feel the dynamic of it, but it was not until three months later that the principle was formally introduced.

The way it's done, and the way I do it to this day with my team, is that it starts individually and then it builds collectively. In the military, leadership was taught to me as the process of influencing others to accomplish a mission by providing purpose, direction, and motivation. And that's done individually. You don't do that collectively. It's about understanding and working with each individual to provide that purpose, direction, and motivation. Only then does it move to the collective. It becomes embedded when you're working with those individuals, you start to build that sense of individual collectivism, if you will, so that you begin to understand that you're an individual who contributes to the greater good, you're an individual with unique skills who has a task and a place in this.

Experience it first, then begin to understand that feeling. So you learn the way, on the way, so to speak.
Right, and it starts with building the individual's mind around excellence and imparting the idea that you are someone who is going to make a difference. We had this book, you know, and part 22-100 was all about military leadership. They teach you about all these things—courage, candor, competence, commitment, purpose, direction—to work with people on an individual basis. Once they feel a sense of worth and start to see their own excellence build, then nature kicks in. I think it's human nature to want to be part of something. People want to inherently be part of something; we're tribal creatures. Now, that natural tendency for a human being to be tribal can be utilized for both good and bad. We see it play out in politics. People can be manipulated when they feel they're part of something, a fear of something, or pride in something. Glass half full, glass half empty. And esprit de corps is that glass half full part of it. We fear nothing. We are the positive force in this. You are part of something good. But again, it starts with building the individual . . . pride in self, then pride in unit. And that's the way it works.

And that translates well in the business environment?
Absolutely. In every position in every company I've ever worked, I begin with understanding the situation, but super-focused on the individuals first. Are things getting done, are people motivated, are they working as a unit or are things fragmented? Because I know that if they have started to fragment and people are demoralized, they begin to gravitate toward doing work for those that treat them well, which means they aren't acting as a team. They're acting like

buddies. But when you have a mission to hit aggressive targets and grow, that won't work.

The first thing I'll do in that situation is sit down with each person. I did it in my present role. I probably spent two weeks and talked one-on-one with over sixty people reporting to me. I got as good a perspective as I could on what was happening, with the most important piece being how the individuals were operating in that situation. I always, always tell people, there are only four types of problems in a business: strategic, tactical, personal, and political. Understanding the long term, understanding what's being done today, understanding the individual motivations within these various groups that are served or are serving them, and then what are the informal groups . . . how are things actually working, or not?

Once you have a decent understanding of it all, then it's person by person, because now I understand the environment that each individual works in, and I can relate better with what's going on with them and how they are interacting with the people requesting things from them. Then I can figure out the most important part, which is, what are the things that they're good at and how do I bring those to the surface and create that pride and a connection with them? If I understand them, and I understand what they're good at, and I help elevate and bring those to the surface, then I can start to make a connection with them. It always starts one-on-one.

That sounds very much like great coaching, versus what conventional wisdom says leaders do, which is focus on the larger group. It's people first.
It has to be. Once you figure out what motivates each person, you start to relate to people and they start to open up to you. It doesn't start with the whole team, it starts with you and me . . . you and I are going to set the cornerstone and the foundation to do something different. What are the things you would like to accomplish? What

would make you feel more accomplished in this job? How could we do it together? How do we make it easier? How do we make it more streamlined? How do we get you the recognition that you deserve, but more importantly, help you get better and stronger?

In the military it was, "I'm here to keep you alive and accomplish a mission." Mission first, people always. I'm going to accomplish the mission, but you're a human being. And when you realize that I'm not just telling you to do something, I'm in it with you and you truly feel that I am, it all starts there. Then we get to start to focus on the mission, pick it apart. Why are we, or aren't we, doing as well as we can? How do we make sure that your piece is the best? What can you control? How do you and I get as honed and sharp as we can at what we're doing? And it starts there, and you do that with every individual. You do it simultaneously. You do it in parallel. It doesn't take as long as some people think it does. But once there's that small degree of trust and that little aha moment when it's like, "This guy Dan . . . He really cares. I believe him. He knows what he's talking about, and when he doesn't, he willingly admits it."

Then we go on a journey together to figure it out.

That's when the magic of esprit de corps kicks in.
You know, I've thought about the military definition of leadership for probably thirty years, the one I shared earlier, that it's a process of influencing others to accomplish a mission by providing a purpose, direction, and motivation. Nowhere in there does it say you have to listen to me, nowhere in there does it say command and direct. It says influence. And I think that's the magic piece . . . that influencing is what builds the trust. I'm not telling you to do things or driving you to do things.

Once that trust is there, you feel it, and we start to get good, start to feel more confident. You start to trust yourself. Now it's *us*. It's *us* working in this environment. Then you introduce others into the *us*, because remember you've been doing this with other people, and they are all feeling that pride. And people are thirsty to win. Remember we're tribal creatures. When people have that hungry mindset, and you've got these percolating minds and these spirits that are starting to get hungry and feel good about themselves, you pull others in. You make these small groups, these little cohorts of individuals who intersect and start working together.

Business in general is one big Venn diagram. Everything is linked in these intersecting rings of the individual and collective, wrapped in the context of the mission, the force multiplier. None of it operates independently. You start connecting some of these little groups, getting people to work together. And then that group pulls in another. Now you've got a chain. Then you bring two more groups together. Now you're linking to the mission. And then they start to work independently. Now you can relax the individual attention and start to work on that collective direction.

But all the time you're reinforcing that we're building something great together, that we are a unit, a team. A winning team.

TRUST: AN INDIVIDUAL FACTOR

What is the most important exchange of value in business today?

When we ask this question of senior leaders of high-growth technology companies, the most frequently given answer centers on the tangible transfer of currency, a transaction, as one might reasonably expect, and is some version of "fee for service." It's the obvious and easy answer, and a good one, because it covers the various levels of service: to customers, to channel partners, to one's employer. Every once in a while, however, we get a deeper, more considered response: "trust."

Trust is the better answer, because although it concerns an intangible transfer of value, it is what enables the tangible transfer to exist. If a customer no longer trusts us, it won't be long before they leave, taking our fee with them. Out of trust comes value; no trust, no value.

The same holds true for any relationship that matters. In fact, our greatest professional capital isn't in our talent, skill, or competency, but rather in the cumulative value of our most important relationships. That portfolio isn't just a resource, it's an interpersonal asset for which the best measure of worth is trust. We would be nowhere without our trusted relationships. And, like any wealth-creating asset, to grow in value, trust requires continuous investment, constant protection, and a certain amount of leverage to accumulate more of it. In their 2021 Meta-Analysis of decades of data from over one hundred thousand teams and over 2.7 million employees to evaluate the connection between employee engagement and key business outcomes, the Gallup organization found that the best measure of workplace trust was having a best friend at work.[11]

The difficulty in offering an examination of trust as the key individual factor in creating esprit de corps is that in most business contexts, there is a tendency to speak in platitudes about trust. The term is thrown on the table as something valuable and necessary, but without defining it or even understanding how it actually works. Thanks to overuse in taglines everywhere, the word has all but lost its meaning as a differentiator. Trust is claimed by all, but owned by few.

UNPACKING TRUST

Underestimating the importance of trust is common in business. It's all too easy to assume that it comes from simply providing competent, reliable service. As we will discuss shortly, competency is necessary, but not sufficient. Building trust is considered by many to be a "soft skill." On the contrary; we believe that trust is critical at every level of interaction, and that it requires developing certain "muscles," along with constant exercise to maintain fitness.

Trust matters to the extent that distrust exists or has the potential to take root. Distrust is a non-lean condition, as it undermines every effort, prevents value-adding work from being performed, and renders commitments meaningless. What would happen if a Formula 1 driver didn't trust his pit crew, or a cardiac surgeon didn't trust his surgical team? Probably the same thing that would happen if a CEO didn't trust their executive team: someone would not be there much longer.

Anyone who has been exposed to organizational environments lacking trust understands just how powerful the restraining forces of drag, inertia, friction, and waste are. In those cultures, individuals tend to retreat from one another, afraid of any perceived vulnerability. Apathy, suspicion, and fear rule the day. Actions are seen as promoting a hidden agenda, and even the most sincere and helpful behavior becomes suspect. Cooperation occurs only under an edict, with teams and business units laboring under rigid policies and procedures and stifling governance. Enormous energy is wasted on compromise and enforcement, with a staggering loss in productivity.

Thankfully, most people have been fortunate enough to work in organizations with healthy levels of trust, where information is open, knowledge is abundant, and communication flows freely, honestly, accurately, and purposefully.

It's hard to find a good definition of "trust"; the term means different things to different people, becoming a catchall phrase for anything remotely related to belief. In the context of this discussion, trust is something short of pure faith, which is more of a blind belief existing largely beyond reason. Nothing can shake the conviction of the devoutly faithful.

Trust, on the other hand, is more fragile, more easily withdrawn. It's also something more than simple *confidence*, which is based purely on logic, experience, or fact. Trust lies somewhere between confidence and faith—part reason, part belief.

For our purposes, then, we can safely define trust as *the belief that those upon whom we rely will realistically fulfill our positive expectations of them.*

HOW TRUST WORKS

Ideally, trust is reciprocal and self-reinforcing. We place trust in those we believe will act in our best interest, and vice versa. As others place their trust in us, we behave in a manner consistent with becoming more worthy of that trust. As we trust others, they become more trustworthy. It sounds so simple.

Unfortunately, it doesn't always work that way. The need for trust is borne out of our belief that we are somehow at risk. Trust goes hand in hand with, and is entirely dependent on, our perceived vulnerability. Trust and risk give rise to one another. Without risk, trust isn't a concern; the higher the risk, the more important trust becomes.

Recall our treatment of Jobs Theory from our discussion of Accelerated Value. When people consider hiring any solution to help them complete their Jobs-to-Be-Done, they consider the value exchange through the lens of risk. Consumer behaviorist Ernest Dichter determined nearly seventy years ago that depending on what they are purchasing, most people perceive as many as five kinds of risk: *economic* ("Will this waste my money?"); *functional* ("Will this work reliably well?"); *social* ("What will people think of me?"); *physical* ("Will this somehow be painful?"), and *psychological* ("Will I think poorly of myself?").[12]

The same kinds of considerations happen in our relationships with others. We feel vulnerable when we place our trust in someone. We determine how much we are willing to risk. We may extend partial trust on a limited trial basis when we begin a new relationship, but as the relationship develops, the amount of exposure we are willing to accept grows to the extent our expectations continue to be met. If someone disappoints us, we may withdraw our trust, limit our exposure, and reduce our risk.

Here's the thing: when it comes to relationships, there is always going to be risk. Since we all depend and rely on others to some extent, it's unavoidable. And when we operate in a context in which the force multiplier is pressure, we simply *must* trust. We all want a guarantee of security, but individuals are as unique as their fingerprints, and we can no more guarantee the actions of someone else than we can foretell the future. Trust, then, will always be a defining individual factor in establishing esprit de corps.

Balancing trust and risk gets quite tricky in business settings. How do we gauge the degree of trust within a relationship if we haven't put it to the test? How do we determine whether we are right in trusting another unless we risk letdown? Likewise, how will others determine whether we can be trusted unless they risk placing their trust in us? In short, how do we determine whether trust is warranted?

There are no easy answers, no silver bullets. We all have a level of trust more easily lowered than raised. It is simply in our nature. This level is not unlike our differing pain thresholds, with varying degrees of tolerance for different kinds of distress and pain. When our discomfort reaches a point of zero tolerance, a threshold is established that we take care to avoid in the future. Trust, in concept, works much the same way: we each are willing to risk up to a certain level, and when it's breached, we withdraw that trust, sometimes permanently. The challenge is learning to manage our threshold, developing the level of trust others have in us, and enabling us to place our trust in others.

Imagine, for example, a continuum with distrust on one extreme and high trust on the other. The degree to which we trust someone floats along the scale, varying from situation to situation, relationship to relationship. The trust you place in a close advisor differs from the trust you place in your physician, your acquaintances, or your family, because the nature of dependence in each relationship varies.

Variance makes trust tricky. We can neither design trust nor demand it from others. In fact, we may make things worse if we even attempt to do so. "Trust me on this" always raises eyebrows.

BUILDING TRUST

We have observed that to be most effective when working with companies and teams that have high-trust environments is to do two things in tandem:

First, eliminate all reasons for distrust, by banning any behavior toxic to trust. We have documented twenty distinct interpersonal behaviors that are every bit as wasteful as the traditional seven process-related forms we learned about in the Lean Process discussion. In fact, we propose that distrustful behavior is the eighth waste. (See sidebar, "Top Twenty Trust Toxicities.")

Second, give demonstrable reasons to be trusted. In practical terms, this means simultaneously modeling trustworthiness while extending trust to others. This sounds easier than it is. What we often see instead of doing the hard work are pretty posters with "play nice" platitudes—honesty, transparency, integrity, et al.—none of which are actually practiced. Often just using such lofty words can convey the very opposite meaning, especially in the modern context of the alarming fall from grace of many once-respected leaders.

Grease and Glue leaders attempting to instill esprit de corps in their teams need to provide people with the latitude for action and give more specific guidance, accounting for the fact that no two relationships or situations are identical. They need a practical way to build trust, consistent with lean principles.

Enter the practice of *lean moves.*

TOP TWENTY TRUST TOXICITIES

The twenty characteristics below make the short list of wasteful, non-value-adding behaviors that may be considered "anti-trust." They have been collected, synthesized, and distilled from hundreds of performance reviews, 360 evaluations, Glassdoor.com reviews, and employee exit interviews.

Hypocrisy	Favoritism	Deception	Ego
Retaliation	Irrationality	Braggadocio	Misconduct
Secrecy	Ignorance	Gossip	Apathy
Cynicism	Segregation	Sarcasm	Selfishness
Envy	Defiance	Arrogance	Maneuvering

THREE LEAN MOVES

Demonstrating trust requires the careful weighing and balancing of three key lean moves: *consistency*, *competence*, and *caring*.

Trust requires *consistency* because we can't trust someone we can't count on. Trust requires *competence* because we can't trust someone who can't get the job done. Trust requires *caring* because we can't trust someone we believe doesn't care about us.

Let's take a closer look at all three.

Consistency

In its purest form, consistency is the clear and visible alignment of thought, word, and action. If we think one thing, say another, and act to belie either, no one will trust us. It's the constant demonstration of keeping our word over time and across many different situations that results in gaining and sustaining trust.

Consistency is a matter of consciously avoiding contradictory and, in the extreme, hypocritical behavior—conduct that can give the impression that one's selfish interest is the primary concern.

Inconsistency erodes trust, because it's not predictable, dependable, or reliable. Inconsistency creates doubt in our minds about someone's real motives, tells us they are either not truthful or not willing and able to meet their obligation to us.

For example, we become suspicious of someone who doesn't divulge the full extent of their knowledge of things that may have direct impact on or be of high importance to us. Such selective information sharing—whether outright lies, subtle manipulation, or obvious omission—is a form of deception. Further, we can't trust someone who gives the same message differently to different audiences in different settings. And, while one's beliefs and principles may evolve over time, any abrupt, dramatic shifts will destroy one's credibility.

Now, when inconsistency exists, we may seek to understand the cause. Remember, trust depends upon the situation and the relationship. For example, a close confidant's simple mistake that is easily explained and unlikely to happen in the future may not warrant distrust, because it's probably an outlier. However, with new affiliations, such early inconsistency is grounds for doubt.

Three practices can help strengthen consistency:

- **Honoring commitments.** This means holding ourselves accountable for following through on promises made, using everything in our control to deliver on the expectation.
- **Facing reality.** This means confronting difficult issues head-on with open communication, informing others of where we truly stand on an issue.
- **Revealing motive.** This means abandoning political posturing in favor of an agenda that supports the values and best interests of anyone connected to the situation.

Competence

Competence is the path to achieving the positive outcomes and results expected of us. If we don't have the capability to accomplish what is expected, no one will trust us to get the job done. It's a matter of making a commitment based on a realistic assessment and communication of our ability as it relates to the role or requirement. Incompetence—defined as long on promise and short on delivery—erodes trust. Competence is the most concrete aspect of trust, and perhaps the most unforgiving. Character aside, we trust only those we believe to possess the capacity—experience, effectiveness, and expertise—to produce the desired outcome. When we are untested and unknown, establishing our credibility will most likely begin with competency.

Three practices can help build competence:

- **Demonstrating confidence.** Demonstrating confidence in our own abilities instills confidence in others. This might take the form of sharing appropriate information on our successes as well as failures, providing an accurate picture of our ability to meet the demands of the situation.
- **Avoiding overstatement.** This means being forthright in communicating our limits to enable the other person to gauge the amount of risk they are willing to accept—when we are knowingly out of our depth, we must be willing to speak up.
- **Assessing oneself.** Accurate self-assessment demands constant feedback. Finding out how others see us is especially vital in our efforts to establish trustful relationships. When we encourage and receive honest feedback on our performance, it allows us to make timely corrections and improve our work—higher competency realized, higher trust enabled!

Caring

Caring is the softest side of trust, yet perhaps the most difficult. It is the most immediate gauge of one's trustworthiness. Consistency and competency require the test of time, but the caring behaviors demonstrated in a single interaction can signal future expectations, and thus set initial levels of trust.

Caring amounts to nothing more complex than exhibiting the kinds of behaviors that show we care: confidentiality, empathy, humility, sincerity, cooperation, objectivity, collaboration, self-disclosure, listening—the list goes on.

THE TRUST DILEMMA

If the three lean moves of consistency, competence, and caring are all required for building trust (and for regaining trust when we have lost it), how do we reconcile them when they are in conflict? It has been our experience that the facets of trust are often at odds with each other, because certain situations (or relationships) demand prioritizing one over the others. That itself is a dilemma, as it has the potential to erode trust.

For example, overemphasis on outcomes may signal a lack of concern for people. The need to achieve results and thus act competently may conflict with the need to demonstrate caring. A CEO who must reorganize or rethink an entire business model in order to keep the company viable may face workforce downsizing, an act that no matter how well managed or communicated destroys the caring component of trust. "They care more about money than people" is the common lament.

The competitive nature of today's business environment mandates quick shifts in direction and strategy, so sometimes commitments must be broken—thus damaging credibility and consistency—to ensure organizational survival. The ways in which an organization must be managed today often give the impression to employees that the leader is failing to follow through on promises. It's a double-edged sword: communicating every shift to keep everyone well-informed might be perceived as indecision, and not communicating at all in an effort to avoid setting short-lived expectations may imply dishonesty. "Program of the month" is the common lament here.

One practical way through the dilemma is to ensure that two of the three lean moves are especially strong. This has its limitations, however. For example, while we can sometimes overcome a perception of inconsistency by demonstrating real caring and delivering competent performance, over time the issue of consistency will become more apparent and important. Likewise, poor performance may be overlooked if we clearly keep our word on all matters and show concern for the welfare of others, but in the long run performance will be front and center.

The better strategy lands us on the third element of esprit de corps: the collective factor. If all individual actions are in full alignment with the collective, then all three elements of trust will align optimally.

PEOPLE/CULTURE FIT: A
COLLECTIVE FACTOR

When *The Wall Street Journal* columnist Sue Shellenbarger shared Netflix's "No Vacation Policy" over a decade ago[13], managers rushed to ditch their vacation policies, locking onto Netflix spokesperson Steve Swasey's quote: "Rules and policies and regulations and stipulations are innovation killers. People do their best work when they're unencumbered. If you're spending a lot of time accounting for the time you're spending, that's time you're not innovating." Like that of Zappos, the Netflix culture was the stuff of legend—unique, quirky, fun esprit de corps. Zappos had even started a culture training business from theirs, called Zappos Insights.

"If it's good enough for Netflix, it's good enough for us," the thinking went. We witnessed the snap decision to become a Results Only Work Environment (ROWE) firsthand in two different companies, along with the communication breakdown and mass confusion among employees that followed. No one bothered to acknowledge that it had taken Netflix years to work out the kinks in their system. No one bothered to peek under the hood to discover the "why" behind the "what." No one studied the unique core values that provided guidance for how the mostly remote Netflix employees worked: they didn't track time worked, so it made sense to not track time off.

When ROWE failed to live up to its promise, both companies that had tried it reverted to business as usual, unfortunately laying the foundation for the next big change to be met with cynicism. It was a hard lesson learned, not only about the willy-nilly adoption of a practice, but about the importance of *people/culture fit*.

People/culture fit is a parallel concept to product/market fit. Product/market fit is the degree to which a product satisfies a strong market demand. People/culture fit is the degree to which an employee syncs with the core values and collective behaviors of a company.

Allow us to parse the term, starting with the operative word, *fit*. Fit is all about context and the conditions for success. Just because you've built a better mousetrap doesn't mean that the whole world will want to buy one. The context needs to be right: we're overrun with mice, the existing mousetrap isn't working well, or, more likely, something else is going on that the current mousetrap maker didn't consider. Context provides meaning, which people crave. When context is properly set, people know how to behave without being knocked on the head. As noted urban designer Ben Hamilton-Baillie was fond of saying, "You don't need a sign in your living room that says 'no spitting on the floor.'"[14]

"Culture" is the umbrella term for the visible demonstration of underlying tenets, philosophies, values, beliefs, and norms. Culture includes the stories, traditions, and unique language that reflect the foundation on which a company was built. Of all the building blocks to culture, shared core values are perhaps the most important. Core values define how people should treat others. As one CEO told us, "Everyone understands where we want to go; now if I could just get them to understand how I expect them to behave along the way."

Good leaders know that strongly upheld values influence individual behaviors without the need to resort to formal control mechanisms. They provide a means of guiding the organization without having to resort to edict. This is what Steve Swasey was trying to explain about the Netflix policy, and it's what those who reflexively flipped their policy switch missed.

Once you understand that *people over process* is a founding philosophy upon which Netflix builds its culture, you can see how a "no policy" policy makes sense. The Netflix jobsite states that they "encourage independent decision making, share information openly, broadly, and deliberately, are extraordinarily candid with each other, keep only highly effective people, and avoid rules."[15] This puts every job seeker on the alert that unless they can thrive under those conditions, they are likely not a cultural fit. Further, Netflix makes it abundantly clear that the company's core values determine who is rewarded and who is let go, and that they are happy to pay a generous severance package to ill-fitting or merely adequately performing team members.

To find people/culture fit, focus on core, collective values. If that sounds like conventional wisdom to you, you're right. But it's not as easy as it sounds. It's not a simple matter of cherry-picking a few aspirational ideals. Indeed, most companies have some statement of guiding values on the wall or on a website visible to all. The concern isn't just about not *having* collective core values, it's about dynamically *applying* them to all company activities. The truth is, beyond the initial exercise of wordsmithing lofty platitudes and the occasional executive mention in company communiques, true values-based action is rare. Imagine if semper fi wasn't something every Marine lives and breathes!

Given that values can be one of the most powerful ways to elevate the work of both the individual and collective, the question simply becomes: *Why?*

Two reasons seem evident based on our work and research.

First, values are not well understood—we're told we need them, but we're not sure why or how they actually work to elevate us. Individuals do not spend enough time clarifying what matters most to them.

Second, we don't know how to align and leverage the power of values— beyond corporate values, little attention is spent on individual and team values.

Our experience has shown that overall employee commitment and engagement are highest when there is clarity around personal values, and those personal values are aligned with those of the team and broader organization. Clarity around company values alone sounds great, but in reality yields little.

Take the case of Toyota, with a monumental goal of becoming the most respected and successful car company in the world. Toyota's executive leadership knows that unless every employee comes to work ready to engage fully, that kind of marketplace primacy will remain elusive. They know that when individual values are in play, their employees have access to their best personal resources strengths, and abilities and can make choices based on principles, in turn elevating the status of their work. They also move beyond narrow self-interest to instead serve the collective good, and to establish a wide range of productive and meaningful relationships.

THE VALUES CHALLENGE

To tackle the values challenge, we need to understand how values work, how to create values-based alignment, and how to leverage the various levels of values. The concept of values isn't hard to grasp: they are qualities *intrinsically* important to the holder. They require no justification or rationalization. Whether at the individual, team, or organizational level, values are a source of strength. (The Latin root of "value" is "valor," meaning strength.) They not only give us power to take action, but they guide those actions—like an internal compass pointing to "true north."

Personal values provide the meaning we assign to the choices we make, and awareness of our values helps us understand why particular things are so important to us. Some of our personal values are inborn, some are acquired through experience or are influenced by others, and others are chosen. Whenever we make important decisions, we rely on our core values. It's not a matter of whether values will enter the equation—they do. They become a part of who we are, are generally non-negotiable, and we would rather fight or be punished before abandoning or compromising them. This holds true for both individual and organizational core values.

In general, values are dynamic and can change over time, but stay clustered around a few key themes. This is true because the environment in which we live and work is always changing and because we are always developing our values. But *core* values should remain stable over time, and as such are different from strategies, processes, and practices, which *should* change to reflect marketplace realities.

In a personal relationship, imposing our values on others generally leads to conflict. The same is true of collective values. If what matters most to the individual competes in any way with what is most important to the company, conflict is inevitable. The typical executive mandate related to values usually ends up backfiring—not for lack of good intentions but for the lack of savvy in properly executing a values-driven approach. This leads to people feeling that they do not "belong" in their company in some way, as though they are outsiders.

This lack of connection creates a mental distance—the proverbial "disconnect"—between the individual and the collective. The impact on the organization results in the individual investing only a part of their available discretionary energy in the work. The loss in productivity and performance can be staggering.

This brings us to the very real need to know how to build the right kinds of connections at every level.

Developing Values

The most common mistake we see is in the development of a statement of values. Executive teams huddling in offsite meetings designed to produce a document miss the power of values entirely. The goal is not a deliverable, and the objective is not to post a set of values; rather, the focus should be to discover what truly matters most. The secret is to work from the individual to the collective, because core values are best *discovered*, not designed. There are several ways to do this.

For example, when developing their core values, Zappos polled employees on what they thought the company's core values should be. By synthesizing the hundreds of responses that were submitted, over a dozen themes emerged, from which a final ten were finalized and launched internally, letting people know that the core values would remain the same no matter how the company grew and changed, including surviving the unicorn-creating acquisition by Amazon in 2009.[16]

When Toyota set out to codify "The Toyota Way," they spent months sifting through stories and speeches and significant events. The deeper they dug, the broader and more nebulous the critical success factors became. It went far beyond the Toyota Production System, far deeper than their widely studied lean methods. Finally, they arrived at two (yes, only two) core values: *continuous improvement* and *respect for people.* Every system, every product, every decision, every success the organization ever had could be traced to these two deep but vague principles. In Toyota's world, the more vague and deep, the better, because it enables all employees to interpret the meaning in their own way.

Toyota realized that the goal was not to induce adherence to a creed but to encourage a forum for dialogue, discussion, and discovery—the end result of which would be a profound connection to the mission. Small workshops were conducted at all levels of the organization, centered first on putting individuals in touch with their own values, then on showing how these values had contributed to Toyota's success, and finally how people's personal values aligned to the company's. These discussions concluded with uniquely personal commitments to furthering The Toyota Way. In effect, each individual became a keeper of the collective flame.

When we work with companies to create or reimagine their unique Tao, or way, we begin with core values, using an approach based on Toyota's. It is effective: first, because it allows individuals some focused time to get in touch with the personal values that they bring to work, and second, because it allows individual values to be the basis for the collective values. Both are critical requirements for people/culture fit.[17]

Step 1

First, we have as many people as the senior leadership team deems appropriate complete the following Values Finder exercise. The thirty-six universal values are those that have been shown to be the most stable over time and align to the four basic temperaments or intellects of humankind.[18]

TOOLKIT: VALUES FINDER

In this exercise you will see thirty-six of the most commonly held individual values, along with short descriptions. Most people spend about thirty to forty-five minutes on this activity.

Directions:

1. Read and categorize the thirty-six personal values appearing on the next page according to the column headings in the table below: "Always Me," Sometimes Me," or "Never Me." Sort the values into the columns (twelve per column) based on who you really are, *not* what you aspire to be. An easy test is to show your list to someone who knows you very well and ask whether the person agrees with your self-assessment.

2. Look at your twelve "Always Me" values, and select your top five, in order of descending importance, and insert them in the list on the next page.

ALWAYS ME	SOMETIMES ME	NEVER ME

TOP Five

1. _____
2. _____
3. _____
4. _____
5. _____

Ethics: Honoring and living the highest principles.
Authenticity: Being true to oneself.
Service: Making the world around us better.
Unity: Achieving the highest levels of teamwork and mutual support.
Diplomacy: Dealing with difficult people situations.
Advocacy: Passionately supporting an issue.
Growth: Committing to personal development.
Causes: Dedicating oneself to a meaningful goal.
Inspiration: Actively seeing and developing the potential of others.
Progress: Driving for ongoing improvement.
Vision: Creating compelling pictures of the future.
Excellence: Achieving the highest standards.
Competence: Demonstrating exceptional expertise and capability.
Challenge: Preferring difficult tasks that require skill and perseverance.
Ideas: Stimulating new thinking with concepts.
Influence: Having an impact on others.
Logic: Thinking based on sound reasoning.
Ingenuity: Creatively developing and applying ideas.
Results: Driving toward tangible and significant outcomes.

Adventure: Seeking excitement and challenge in experiences.
Action: Maintaining a bias toward "doing."
Variety: Seeking that which is unique.
Play: Engaging spontaneously without regard to outcome.
Exploration: Enjoying the freedom to explore.
Autonomy: Needing to act freely and without unnecessary restraint.
Achievement: Consistently accomplishing challenging goals.
Spontaneity: Responding quickly, with little planning.
Security: Enjoying freedom from doubt, anxiety, or fear.
Equity: Promoting fairness and the proper distribution of rewards.
Standards: Desiring clear standards and norms.
Order: Creating consistency and organization.
Authority: Relying on expert sources and positions in command.
Consistency: Remaining faithful to the same principles and practices.
Dependability: Demonstrating reliability and trustworthiness.
Tradition: Honoring customs and practices of historical significance.
Community: Belonging to and participating in groups.

Step 2

Second, we form what we call an *Advance Team*: no more than a handful of exemplary or evangelist operators tasked with establishing an entirely new office headquarters in an entirely different country with an entirely new workforce and embedding the best and most unique qualities of the company.

To help with the formation of the team, it can be useful to have a mix of the four basic value themes we call Peacekeeper, Thoughtstarter, Playmaker, and Taskmaster. A quick scan of the group members' top five personal values will usually reveal a dominant theme.

Individual Value Themes			
PEACEKEEPER	**THOUGHTSTARTER**	**PLAYMAKER**	**TASKMASTER**
Advocacy	Challenge	Achievement	Authority
Authenticity	Competence	Action	Community
Causes	Excellence	Adventure	Consistency
Diplomacy	Ideas	Autonomy	Dependability
Ethics	Influence	Exploration	Equity
Growth	Ingenuity	Play	Order
Inspiration	Logic	Results	Security
Service	Progress	Spontaneity	Standards
Unity	Vision	Variety	Tradition

Step 3

Third, the Advance Team draws on the twelve to fifteen values with the highest Top Three scores from the Values Finder input, and evaluates each against the five simple test criteria shown below.

YES	NO	TEST CRITERION
		Would you rather be let go than give up or compromise this value?
		If circumstances change tomorrow and we are penalized in some way for holding this core value, would you still keep it?

		A generation from now, will this core value be as valid as it is today?
		If this core value actually becomes a competitive disadvantage, would you still hold it as a core value?
		If you were to start a new team or organization tomorrow in a completely different line of work and industry, would you build this core value into the new organization?

Step 4

Fourth, the Advance Team narrows the values to those receiving 100 percent "yes" assessments. By now there should be three to five core values. Do not discard the values that don't make the cut, because they are obviously of some significance. Build strategies or operating practices around them. Remember, strategies and practices always change, but values seldom do.

Step 5

The final step is to decide what form the core values should take. We suggest drafting unique, declarative, and company-relevant statements about each to present to senior leadership for final wording and distribution. These can take the form of single phrases or short descriptions and bullet-point explanations.

Over time, defining values in this manner not only helps to create higher levels of employee commitment, engagement, and esprit de corps but also to counter the sometimes stressful forces of organizational life.

Aligning Values

The diversity of values within teams and organizations can be wide. To work better as a team and make decisions that lead to commitment and action, it's necessary to recognize the values that can influence decision-making. When personal values are aligned with those of the team and organization, individuals will feel that they are making a worthwhile contribution and that they "belong."

On a day-to-day basis, we often assume that values are at play at all levels. As we shared in our discussion of Strategic Speed, strategy designed is not automatically strategy deployed; it must cascade through the company. Just as business units, functions, and teams have strategies aligned to the higher-altitude company level, each of the various levels should consider having a set of values. If those values are no different from the company values, no further work is required. But specific units often have additional values unique to their operation, complementary to those of the company. The same development process described earlier may be used to find them.

Once company and team values are understood, the task is to align and practice values at the different levels. The simple matrix below shows the broader framework against which a values-centered approach can be applied.

	Understand	Align	Leverage
Company	What are our overarching values?	Are our overall values evolving in response to market realities?	Are these values part of the leadership agenda?
Team	What values are central to the work of the team?	Are our team values aligned to the company's?	Are these values reflected in the daily work of teams and business units?
Individual	What do I stand for? What matters most?	Are my values fully aligned to those of my team?	Do I feel empowered to act on my values?

In the end, values will always set the collective agenda. Understanding, aligning, and leveraging values—at the individual, team, and company levels—provides a clear pathway for higher performance.

ESPRIT DE CORPS RECAP

Realizing the synergistic power of the first four S.C.A.L.E. operating principles—Strategic Speed, Constant Experimentation, Accelerated Value, and Lean Process—requires the fifth principle, Esprit de Corps. French for "team spirit," esprit de corps leads to a leaner leadership approach called Grease and Glue. Grease and Glue leaders balance managing relationships and obtaining results and link individual motivation with the collective motivation in an effort to instill harmony and unity within the team. Creating esprit de corps requires three building blocks: an individual factor, a collective factor, and a force multiplier. Among the most powerful examples of each are *pressure* as the force multiplier, *trust* as the individual factor, and *people/culture fit* as the collective factor. The key to finding people/culture fit is in understanding, aligning, and leveraging core values at all levels.

CHECKPOINTS

☐ Does a feeling of esprit de corps characterize your culture?

☐ Do leaders at all levels balance relationships with results?

☐ Does positive pressure link individual motivations with collective goals?

☐ Do trustful relationships exist at all levels?

☐ Do you have a strong people/culture fit?

AFTERWORD

No place is more enchanted than where a unicorn has been born.
—Peter S. Beagle

f we have done our job right, you are now armed with a fistful of operating principles designed to help you remove the obstacles to efficient scale and sustainable growth. No seven habits, no ten steps, no forty-seven laws. Just five field-tested, actionable tenets that we know enable startups to more effectively transition to ScaleUps, and ScaleUps to more effectively transition to grownups.

This is the unicorn's journey, as entry into the class is in many respects about a future exit. Given that present-day valuation and sustainable long-term value are two different things, the question of how best to think about moving into an uncertain future looms large.

It has been over a century since Toyota founding father Sakichi Toyoda encouraged employees at the Toyoda Automatic Loomworks to improve their work continuously by advising them to "let the future be lit with the knowledge of the past." He chose his words wisely: knowledge of the past does not mean blindly repeating the past, which is what stops most enterprises from growing—they stick to processes and practices that generated their past success. Old methods left untouched often lead to rigidity and stagnation.

We hope that *What a Unicorn Knows* provides you with updated methods, as well as a new lens through which to view them and tools to keep them current. It may be tempting to ask, "What's the one thing I can take away from this book?" That mindset misses the point. It's not about implementing any one principle; it's about finding the right blend of them for your company that drives enduring growth. The challenge is not unlike that of a close-knit

Formula 1 race team searching for the perfect balance among the elements of performance, innovation, and control.

A better approach may be to ask, "Where do I begin?" It is best to answer this question with five others:

- Do you make decisive strategic moves swiftly?
- Is your product pipeline robust and continually refreshed?
- Is value to customers compelling enough to maintain revenue growth and retention?
- Are processes disciplined enough to enable control over productivity and profit?
- Is leadership of the ilk that can carry the company into the future?

Your answers should provide a good vector. Add your own unique prioritization for further focus. Use the resources we have provided here to begin your version of the unicorn's journey. It won't be easy.

On that note, we spent some time with Reshma Saujani, one of the most highly respected technology leaders in the world. Our great hope was that her voice would provide you with a last bit of inspiration and insight into the challenges of sustainable growth and reflect the principles we have shared. She did not disappoint.

Voice of the Operator

RESHMA SAUJANI[1]

Reshma Saujani is the founder and CEO of Girls Who Code and Marshall Plan for Moms. Her two books, Brave, Not Perfect *and* Pay Up *are bestsellers.*

I was a weird person to have started Girls Who Code, because I was not a coder. I'm a social entrepreneur. I hadn't even experienced what it was like to be a woman in tech. I was an activist. I had just come off a huge loss, running for Congress. I had something to prove. If you're not going to elect me and send me to Congress to change our educational system, then I'm going to build a massive nonprofit and teach more girls than any school district in the country. The problem I wanted to solve was why there were not more girls in tech. Could I somehow put tech tools in the arsenals of girls who are naturally inclined to do something to change the world? That was what drove me.

I did not intend to build a movement. It started as just a small experiment. Let me take twenty girls, borrow some conference room time from a friend, and try it. I'll never forget just watching those girls tackle a complex problem: how to help undocumented students. Just watching the wheels turn and watching all the different ways those girls were going to approach solving this problem by using coding just blew me away. I knew I needed to get every girl to learn how to code.

Sure, I had my billion-dollar slide. I was going to teach a million girls to code. Mind you, at that time, fewer than one in ten schools offered computer science. And I didn't even do the math, but putting that number, that big vision, out there, and not being afraid that someone might ask me to prove it, really inspired people to want to be a part of It. And that's what pushed me to want to scale it and grow. Every year I would come up with a new big number: "This year we're growing 300 percent." That kind of thing. Fast forward ten years, and we've taught half a million girls to code, and reached another half billion through our work. And I raised a hundred million dollars in ten years as somebody who wasn't really a nonprofit leader. It was just the drive to go big. If you're going to go tackle something, then let's really go tackle it.

Then came COVID. That upended everything for Girls Who Code. I had just had a baby via surrogate. I had a five-year-old in kindergarten, we had just run a Super Bowl ad, it was supposed to be the biggest year we had ever had, and I was going to take a minute as a mom. All of a sudden, I was back as a CEO with a newborn baby, homeschooling a five-year-old.

One of the biggest decisions that I had to make in 2020 was to make cuts to our programs. A lot of cuts. In that first six months of 2020, I saw *all* of my sister organizations close. Tech companies were closing offices, schools were closing, no afterschool programming allowed. Our summer immersion programs—about eighty—had to be shut down. We had ten thousand clubs at that point. Colleges—our pipeline to the tech workforce—all closed. A couple hundred thousand kids depended on our program and needed it even more because so many of them didn't have Wi-Fi at home, so they weren't getting *any* school.

But there was good news. A few years earlier we had tested a two-week program that we called Campus—essentially a two-week for-purchase product that never took off, for the simple reason that we had flooded the market with so many free products! We even threw a failure party and talked about lessons that we learned, but the point is we had this product on the shelf. The team said, Why not take that two-week program and turn it into a virtual program? So we did. We essentially just shifted all of our modeling to virtual. Almost overnight we had a code-at-home program for our girls.

That pivot—in the middle of a devastating pandemic—pushed us in a direction we might never have taken had we not been forced to. And I was not going to let go of scale; I was not going to go from teaching several hundred thousand girls a year to teaching nobody. That's just not on Resh's list of acceptable outcomes.

In the end, we were able to go back to our companies and sell the program to them, and it saved Girls Who Code. Yes, I made some really hard cuts at a time when it's the last thing you'd ever want to do. But we survived when others didn't, or couldn't.

My lesson from all of it is that it's really important to be disciplined about the thing you do best, but also to understand the forces at play. I would say no when, for example, a funder would come to us and offer millions of dollars if we built something to their specification. "That's not what we do." We changed the entire landscape in terms of who's graduating from computer science by being laser-focused on where we needed to play and what we needed to do to win. When COVID hit, it was a force majeure, and the ground beneath us shifted completely practically overnight. That meant we had to shift as well.

I always had a bias against virtual programs because data had shown that girls really didn't learn when they weren't in an immersive classroom where they had others who could help them. But we pivoted quickly to the new direction, a new space we had backed away from and said no to pre-pandemic. The sheer speed and scrappiness with which we came together as a team to take something to market that was really still in experimental form was crazy. It made a lot of people on the team nervous, honestly. But the alternative was even more scary.

That brings up a final lesson: Always operate from a sense of fear and deficit. It'll speed your decision-making, it'll preserve your scale, and in the end, you'll keep growing.

ACKNOWLEDGMENTS

A book about what unicorns know isn't possible without deep engagement with those in that class, so our heartfelt thanks goes first to the technology leaders who played integral roles in contributing to our narrative by lending their insight and wisdom: Nick Mehta at Gainsight, Michelle Collignon at OwnBackup, Alex Atzberger at Optimizely, Tony Ulwick at Strategyn, our colleague Samma Hafeez at Insight Partners, Dan Page at RecordedFuture, and Reshma Saujani at Girls Who Code and the Marshall Plan for Moms.

And to what must be the most author-centric publisher on the planet, we thank the entire team at BenBella Books, beginning with imprint owner and Editor-in-Chief Matt Holt, who leaned into our concept with great and immediate enthusiasm. To Brigid Pearson, thank you for an absolutely brilliant and head-turning cover design. To our development team, Katie Dickman and Jessika Rieck, thank you for helping shape and polish our words into something worthy of the cover. To Mallory Hyde and her team, thank you for helping cut through all the media noise and helping us grab a few moments in the spotlight.

Unicorns, while magical, don't magically appear. They are ushered into the world by consummate professionals with the ability to discover and develop business potential, which is as much art as it is science. No better example exists than the team at Insight Partners, to whom we extend our gratitude for indulging our desire to release these principles and practices into the wild. Special thanks to Jeff Horing and Hilary Gosher for standing behind the work, and to Nikki Parker for her promotional savvy.

To all those who suffered through early versions of our manuscript, your patience and support means the world to us.

Hook 'em Horns.

TOOLKIT RESOURCES

The following resources may be downloaded as high-resolution PDFs by navigating to the links below. All resources may be shared freely under a Creative Commons Attribution—Non Commercial—No Derivatives 4.0 International License. You may share this work freely as long as you: (a) provide appropriate credit to **Matthew E. May**; (b) do not use this work for commercial purposes of any kind; and (c) do not modify the work in any way.

The Playing-to-Win Strategy Canvas
https://bit.ly/PlayingToWinCanvas

Objectives & Key Results Canvas
https://bit.ly/OKRsCanvas

Customer Value Map Canvas
https://bit.ly/CustomerValueMapCanvas

Lean Kaizen Canvas
https://bit.ly/LeanKaizenCanvas

NOTES

Introduction

1 https://en.wikipedia.org/wiki/Scaleup_company

2 Marc Felgen et al., "Is It Time to Consider Co-CEOs?" *Harvard Business Review* (July–August 2022), https://hbr.org/2022/07/is-it-time-to-consider-co-ceos

3 *The Scale-up Revolution: A Force Multiplier of Economic Growth.* Wakefield Research, 2020.

4 Peter F. Drucker, "Managing for Business Effectiveness," *Harvard Business Review* (May 1963).

5 Forrester-commissioned study: The Total Economic Impact of Qualtrics CustomerXM (2019).

6 Matthew Lieberman, "Should Leaders Focus on Results, or on People?" *Harvard Business Review* (blog), December 27, 2013, https://hbr.org/2013/12/should-leaders-focus-on-results-or-on-people

7 https://jobs.netflix.com/culture

Principle 1: Strategic Speed

1 Dave Girouard, "Speed as a Habit." First Round Review, https://review.firstround.com/speed-as-a-habit

2 Peter Drucker, *Innovation and Entrepreneurship* (New York: Harper & Row, 1985).

3 Chet Richards, *Certain to Win: The Strategy of John Boyd, Applied to Business* (Xlibris, 2004).

4 Adrian McDermott, "479: Enterprise, SMB, and Everything In Between: How to Build a Business That Scales with Your Customers with ZenDesk's CTO," September 6, 2021, in *SaaStr*, podcast, https://saastr.libsyn.com/saastr-479

-enterprise-smb-and-everything-in-between-how-to-build-a-business-that-scales
-with-your-customers-with-zendesks-cto

5   A. G. Lafley and Roger L. Martin, *Playing to Win: How Strategy Really Works* (Boston: HBR Press, 2013).

6   A formalized version of the Catchball game is now one of the most popular sports in Israel played by female adult athletes. The game is similar to indoor volleyball except instead of hitting the ball, it is thrown.

7   *Talladega Nights: The Ballad of Ricky Bobby*, directed by Adam McKay (2006: Columbia Pictures).

8   Jim Collins, "Best New Year's Resolution? A Stop Doing List," *USA Today*, Dec. 30, 2003.

9   Marc Randolph, *That Will Never Work: The Birth of Netflix and the Amazing Life of an Idea* (New York: Little, Brown & Co., 2019).

10   Michelle Collignon, interview by Matthew May February 16, 2022.

11   A. G. Lafley and Roger L. Martin, *Playing to Win: How Strategy Really Works* (Boston: HBR Press, 2013).

12   "We don't do PowerPoint (or any other slide-oriented) presentations at Amazon. Instead, we write narratively structured six-page memos." 2018 Letter to Shareholders, Jeff Bezos, CEO, Amazon.

Principle 2: Constant Experimentation

1   2015 Jeff Bezos letter to shareholders, https://s2.q4cdn.com/299287126/files/doc _financials/annual/2015-Letter-to-Shareholders.PDF

2   2016 Pathfinder awards, https://www.geekwire.com/2016/jeff-bezos-pathfinder -drone-clock-space/

3   2016 Jeff Bezos letter to shareholders, https://www.aboutamazon.com/news /company-news/2016-letter-to-shareholders

4   Alex Astenberger, interview by Matthew May, October 2021.

5   "A Leader's Guide to After-Action Reviews," Department of the Army, Training Circular 25-20, September 1993.

6   Michael Schrage, *The Innovator's Hypothesis: How Cheap Experiments Are Worth More Than Good Ideas* (Cambridge, MA: MIT Press, 2014).

Principle 3: Accelerated Value

1   In the 2021 season, tire choice contributed greatly to the overall driver championship outcome.

2   NewVoiceMedia. "NewVoiceMedia Research Reveals Bad Customer Experiences Cost U.S. Businesses $75 Billion a Year." May 17, 2019. Business Wire. https://www.businesswire.com/news/home/20180517005043/en/NewVoiceMedia-Research-Reveals-Bad-Customer-Experiences-Cost-U.S.-Businesses-75-Billion-a-Year, accessed June 15, 2022.

3   To be fair, the "loss" is not a net figure, but rather customer churn; it's a zero-sum game: when you lose a customer, they don't stop consuming, it's just that a competitor gains them.

4   State of the Connected Customer 2019, Salesforce.com.

5   Forrester-commissioned study: "The Total Economic Impact of Qualtrics CustomerXM" (2019).

6   Toma Kulbyte, "Key Customer Experience Statistics You Need to Know," *SuperOffice* (blog), June 24, 2021, https://www.superoffice.com/blog/customer-experience-statistics/

7   "Forrester TEI Study: The Partner Opportunity for Building SaaS on Amazon Web Services," "https://amer.resources.awscloud.com/building-saas-on-aws/forrester-the-partner-opportunity-for-building-saas-on-aws

8   David C. Smith, "J.D. Power: The Man Behind Famous Awards," *WardsAuto*, March 27, 2012, https://www.wardsauto.com/industry/jd-power-man-behind-famous-awards

9   Amazon Re:Invent, 2019.

10 Reno Master Plumbers Association, "There is no Substitute!," *Reno Evening Gazette*, August 19, 1923, Page 8, Column 6.

11 Provident Mutual, Life Insurance Company of Philadelphia, Pennsylvania, *Somerset American*, December 12, 1942.

12 Percy H. Whiting, *The Five Great Rules of Selling* (New York: McGraw-Hill, 1947).

13 Clayton M. Christensen, Scott Cook, and Taddy Hall. "Marketing Malpractice: The Cause and the Cure," *Harvard Business Review*, December 2005, https://hbr.org/2005/12/marketing-malpractice-the-cause-and-the-cure

14 Ibid.

15 Jim Kalbach, *The Jobs to Be Done Playbook* (New York: Two Waves Books, 2020).

16   Tony Ulwick, interview by Matthew May, December 2021.

17   Gainsight's 10 New Laws of Customer Success. The entire e-book may be downloaded from https://info.gainsight.com/10-laws-of-customer-success -infographic.html

18   The original version of this article appeared on the Insight Partners blog: https:// www.insightpartners.com/blog/mind-the-value-gap-why-companies-fail-to-scale -customer-success

Principle 4: Lean Process

1   Taiichi Ohno, *Toyota Production System: Beyond Large Scale Production* (New York: Productivity Press, 1988).

2   Michael J. Saks and Stephan Landsman, "Use Systems Redesign and the Law to Prevent Medical Errors and Accidents," *STAT*, August 4, 2021, https://www .statnews.com/2021/08/04/medical-errors-accidents-ongoing-preventable-health -threat/

3   Bill Taylor, "Great People Are Overrated," *Harvard Business Review* (blog), June 20, 2011, https://hbr.org/2011/06/great-people-are-overrated

4   Donald Dinero, *Training Within Industry: The Foundation of Lean* (Boca Raton, FL: CRC Press, 2005).

5   Victor E. Sower, Jo Ann Duffy, and Gerald Kohers, "Great Ormond Street Hospital for Children: Ferrari's Formula 1 Handovers and Handovers from Surgery to Intensive Care," *ASQ Magazine*, August 2008.

6   Taiichi Ohno, *Toyota Production System: Beyond Large Scale Production* (New York: Productivity Press, 1988).

Principle 5: Esprit de Corps

1   Brian Muirhead was a frequent guest at Toyota during Matt's tenure from 1999 through 2006.

2   Henri Fayol, *General and Industrial Management*, trans. Constance Storrs (Sir Isaac Pitman & Sons, 1949).

3   Drue Schuler and Paula Weber, "Individual and Team Behaviors: Exploring the Role of Esprit de Corps," *Mountain Plains Journal of Business and Technology* 6 (October 2005).

4   *Department of the Airforce, Handbook 1, Airman* (2019).

5   Matthew D. Lieberman, *Social: Why Our Brains Are Wired to Connect* (New York: Crown, 2013).

6   Billie Jean King, *Pressure is a Privilege* (New York: LifeTime Media,Inc., 2008).

7   Ute Wilbert-Lampen, David Leistner, Sonja Greven et al., "Cardiovascular Events During World Cup Soccer," *The New England Journal of Medicine* 358 (January 2008): 475–83.

8   Alex Korb, "Sex, Dopamine, and the World Cup," *Psychology Today*, June 2014, https://www.psychologytoday.com/us/blog/prefrontal-nudity/201406/sex-dopamine-and-the-world-cup

9   José Henriquez, *Miracle in the Mine* (Grand Rapids, MI: Zondervan, 2011).

10   Interview with Dan Page by Matthew May, December 2021.

11   Gallup 2021 Q12 Meta-Analysis, https://www.gallup.com/workplace/321725/gallup-a12-meta-analysis-report.aspx

12   Ernest Dichter, "What are the Real Reasons People Buy," *Sales Management* 7 (February 1955): 36–89.

13   Sue Shellenbarger, "Unlimited Vacation: A Benefit or Burden," *Wall Street Journal*, July 20, 2011.

14   Matthew E. May, *In Pursuit of Elegance* (New York: Broadway Books, 2009).

15   "Netflix Culture—Seeking Excellence," Netflix, accessed June 16, 2022, https://jobs.netflix.com/culture

16   "Zappos 10 Core Values," Zappos Insights, accessed June 16, 2022, https://www.zapposinsights.com/about/core-values

17   Jim Collins and Jerry I. Porras, "Building Your Company's Vision," *Harvard Business Review*, September–October 1996, https://hbr.org/1996/09/building-your-companys-vision

18   Samuel H. Matthews, Thomas K. Keleman, and Mark C. Bolino, "How Follower Traits and Cultural Values Influence the Effects of Leadership," *The Leadership Quarterly* 32.1 (February 2021).

Afterword

1   Interview with Reshma Saujani by Matthew May and Pablo Dominguez, March 2022.

INDEX

ABOUT THE AUTHORS

Matthew May and Pablo Dominguez have been working together for over a decade to optimize performance of fast-growing technology companies. They lead, respectively, the Lean ScaleUp program and Sales & Customer Success Center of Excellence for the Onsite advisory unit of Insight Partners, a leading global venture capital and private equity firm investing in high-growth technology and software ScaleUp companies that are driving transformative change in their industries.

Matthew is the author of five previous books, including bestselling and award-winning titles *The Elegant Solution, In Pursuit of Elegance, The Laws of Subtraction*, and *Winning the Brain Game*. His background spans over thirty years of experience facilitating senior leadership teams through strategy, innovation, and lean initiatives. Matt's perspective is heavily influenced by spending nearly a decade with Toyota. His work has been published in high-profile publications such as the *New York Times, Harvard Business Review, Fast Company, Inc.,* and *The Rotman Management Magazine*. A graduate of The Wharton School and Johns Hopkins University, Matt is an avid cyclist and published songwriter, but considers winning *The New Yorker* cartoon caption contest one of his greatest creative achievements.

Pablo is Operating Partner at Insight, where he partners with a deep set of portfolios of companies to build and scale effective commercial teams through the application of proven and repeatable go-to-market and operational best practices. He brings over twenty-three years of global sales operations experience, including senior leadership roles at ADP, AppNexus, Avaya, and The Alexander Group. A graduate of NYU's Stern School of Business and the McCombs School of Business at The University of Texas, he enjoys skiing, mountain biking, chess, grilling/smoking BBQ, playing tennis with his wife, and watching movies with his kids. Above all else, Pablo is a die-hard Texas Longhorn fan. This is his first book.